FOUNDATIONS
OF
DEMOCRACY

Authority, Privacy, Responsibility, and Justice

Law in a Free Society Series

Student Text
High School Level

Center for Civic Education
5146 Douglas Fir Road ■ Calabasas, CA 91302 ■ (818) 591-9321

Cover:
Steel workers take a bow after the bronze statue Freedom was
placed back atop the Capitol dome Saturday, Oct. 23, 1993
(AP Photo/Marcy Nighswander)

© Copyright Center for Civic Education 1995

The first edition of this text was developed with the support of a grant from the National Endowment for the Humanities.

This new and revised edition has been prepared under Grant #85-JS-CX-0009 from the Office of Juvenile Justice and Delinquency Prevention, Office of Justice Programs, U.S. Department of Justice.

Points of view or opinions in this document are those of the author and do not necessarily represent the official position or policies of the U.S. Department of Justice.

ISBN 0-89818-152-6

EXECUTIVE DIRECTOR
Charles N. Quigley

Principal Writer Student Text
Joseph S. Jackson

Original Curriculum Developers
Charles N. Quigley
Mara Braverman
Marshall Croddy
Jerold A. Rosen

Contributing Writers
Kenneth Rodriguez
Jack N. Hoar

Staff Associates
Margaret S. Branson
Beth E. Farnbach

Production Director
Patricia Mathwig

Principal Writer Teacher's Guide
Kenneth Rodriguez

Editor
Theresa M. Richard

Assistant Editors
Michael J. Conroy
Michelle L. Forner

Art Director and Illustrator
Richard Stein

Desktop Publishing
Valerie Milianni

The Center for Civic Education thanks the following writers for their contributions to the first edition of these texts: Mara Braverman, Marshall Croddy, Edward Hirsch, and Jerold A. Rosen.

CONSULTANTS

William Landau
Associate Professor of English
Los Angeles Pierce College

Herbert Morris
Professor of Law and Philosophy
University of California, Los Angeles

Duane E. Smith
Professor Emeritus, Political Science
University of California, Los Angeles

Summary of Contents

Preface

Foundations of Democracy introduces you to four ideas which are basic to our constitutional form of government: **authority, privacy, responsibility,** and **justice**. These are not only ideas that need to be grasped in order to understand the foundations of our government, but they are crucial to evaluating the important differences between a constitutional democracy and a society that is not free.

There are costs or burdens that we must bear in order to preserve our freedom and the values on which our nation was founded. There are many situations in which hard choices need to be made between competing values and interests. In this course of study, you will be challenged to discuss and debate situations involving the use of authority and the protection of privacy. You will be asked to decide how responsibilities should be fulfilled and how justice could be achieved in a number of situations.

You will learn different approaches and ideas, which we call "intellectual tools," to evaluate these situations. Intellectual tools help you think clearly about issues of authority, privacy, responsibility, and justice. They help you develop your own positions, and support your positions with reasons.

The knowledge and skills you gain in this course of study will assist you not only in addressing issues of public policy, but also in everyday situations you face in your private life. By thinking for yourself, reaching your own conclusions, and defending your positions, you can be a more effective and active citizen in a free society.

AUTHORITY
Table of Contents

Introduction

What do Jefferson's words in the Declaration of Independence imply about the source of governmental authority?

"We hold these Truths to be self-evident.... Governments are instituted among Men, deriving their just Powers from the Consent of the Governed...."

This quotation from the Declaration of Independence contains one of our most basic ideas about government. We, the people, give our government the authority to rule us. We give the government the right, under certain conditions and limitations, to control our lives, liberty, and property.

We, as citizens, retain the ultimate right to control how our government uses the authority we have delegated to it. We exert this control by exercising our right to vote, by participating in the political process, and by having the government adhere to the limitations the Constitution imposes.

The rights of citizenship carry with them the responsibility to deal intelligently with issues of authority. To do this, we need to understand authority and make informed decisions about its use. We need to be able to answer such questions as "What is authority?" "Where does authority come from?" and "Why do we need authority?"

This text will help you gain a better understanding of the subject of authority and a greater ability to deal effectively with issues of authority as they arise in your daily life as a citizen in our free society.

Unit One: What Is Authority?

How do these photographs illustrate authority?

Purpose of Unit

- When does someone have the right to tell you what to do?

- When do you have the right to tell others what to do?

These are difficult questions. The answers have to do with authority—the rules and the people who govern our lives. We need to answer these questions to deal with issues of authority that confront us every day—at home, at school, in our jobs, and in our government.

In this unit you will begin to consider these questions. You will learn the difference between authority and power without authority—between those who have the right to use power and those who do not. You will examine different sources of authority and discuss the need for authority in society. This background will help you deal with difficult questions about people in authority and the rules that govern your life.

LESSON 1

What Is the Difference between Authority and Power Without Authority?

Purpose of Lesson

This lesson explains the definition of authority that we will use in this course of study. When you have completed this lesson, you should be able to explain the difference between authority and power without authority.

Terms to Know

authority
kangaroo court
power
paramilitary

Critical Thinking Exercise

DISTINGUISHING BETWEEN AUTHORITY AND POWER WITHOUT AUTHORITY

Read the news story below adapted from the July 6, 1993 edition of *The Wall Street Journal* and then answer the "What do you think"questions. Be prepared to share your answers with the class.

Vigilante Justice in Northern Ireland

By Tony Horwitz
Staff Reporter of THE WALL STREET JOURNAL

BELFAST, Northern Ireland – The kneecappers caught up with Eddie Kane outside a candy shop, in a Catholic/Protestant war zone known as "Murder Mile." Tossing a hood over his head, two masked men questioned Mr. Kane about an assault on one of their mates. Then they forced him to lie face down and pressed a gun to the back of his leg.

"Kneecapping" in Northern Ireland dates back to the beginnings of the civil strife—known here as "the Troubles"—in 1969. At first an IRA (Irish Republican Army) punishment for informers, kneecapping has come to cover a range of alleged crimes.

Do you think the government of Nazi Germany exercised authority or power without authority?

There is a circular argument used to justify kneecapping. It goes as follows: The Troubles have caused citizens, Catholics in particular, to consider the police as enemies. Indeed, because paramilitary groups often ambush police, law-enforcement groups do have trouble combating ordinary crime. So, if someone steals your car, don't call the police (and risk being branded an informer). Call the "Provos"—the IRA—or, if you are a Protestant, call loyalist groups such as the Ulster Freedom Fighters, who will take action.

"Kneecapping is brutal, but what are you supposed to do?" Asks Maureen Mcguire, a Catholic mother of two sons, aged seven and eight. Like many of her neighbors, she says "hoods" are running amok and police "won't or can't come get them."

Kneecapping has thus assumed the aura of a shadow legal system. People call it "rough justice," meted out by gunmen known as "circuit judges," who sometimes hold kangaroo courts. Defendants are found guilty of "antisocial behavior." Sentences are tailored to the misdeed. Minor miscreants—pot-smokers, say—will be warned. On second offense they will be beaten or shot through the calf or thigh. More serious offenders get a bullet through the knee. If they don't reform, they are shot again, through several limbs.

"Crimes" now deemed to merit kneecapping include failure to pay dues to paramilitary groups.

While police in Belfast are indeed hampered by public distrust, by their fear of booby traps, and by the need to patrol inside armor-plated jeeps, constables hardly overlook common crime. In recent months police have arrested a number of those kneecapped as lawbreakers. Many are now awaiting trial in the local courts.

The police have also begun a program to investigate the kneecappers themselves for taking matters of law enforcement in their own hands and for conducting kangaroo courts.

The police have made a number of arrests and several former vigilantes await their day in a court of law.

What do *you* think?

1. Who in the news article is using power?

2. What is the difference between the use of power by paramilitary groups to punish suspected criminals and the use of power by government to punish suspected criminals through the court system?

3. How does the "shadow legal system" of kneecapping differ from an established legal system of police and courts? How is it similar to an established legal system?

Power or Authority?

The exercise you have just completed raises questions of power and authority. The distinction between the two ideas is important. You may have been in situations where someone used power to force you to do something against your will. Sometimes that person may have had the **right** to do so; other times he or she may not have had the right. When does someone have the right to control your behavior?

■ Do your parents have the right to require you to be home at a certain time? Why or why not?

■ Do you have the right to make your younger brother or sister leave the TV set alone? Why or why not?

■ Does your principal have the right to require you not to leave the school campus during the school day? Why or why not?

■ Does your friend have the right to force you to do something you do not want to do? Why or why not?

■ Does the government have the right to require you to obey a law that you believe is wrong? Why or why not?

To answer these questions, we need to know the difference between power and authority. Although there may be more than one way to define these terms, for our purposes we will use the following definitions:

■ **Power** is the ability to control or direct something or someone. Sometimes people have the right to use power; sometimes they do not.

　　■ When a thief robs you at gunpoint, he has the power to do so. He does not have the right.

　　■ When the Supreme Court says a law is unconstitutional, it has both the power and the right to do so.

How do justices of the U.S. Supreme Court acquire both power and authority to declare laws unconstitutional?

■ **Authority** is power combined with the right to use that power. The right to use power usually comes from laws, customs, or principles of morality.

　　■ Police officers have the authority to arrest a person because the law gives them that right.

　　■ Congress has the authority to pass a law because the Constitution gives it that right.

Critical Thinking Exercise

DESCRIBING THE DIFFERENCE BETWEEN AUTHORITY AND POWER WITHOUT AUTHORITY

To help you understand the difference between authority and power without authority, read the sentences below and answer the questions that follow. Be prepared to explain your answers to the class.

1. Police officer Karen Weidman gives Allison Green a ticket for speeding.

2. Jerry Robinson tells Marty Karinsky to stay away from his girlfriend or Jerry will "take care of him."

3. Judge Alvarez places Maggie Jones on probation.

4. The government imprisons Juan Rodriguez for refusing to serve in the army during the Vietnam war because of his belief that it is morally wrong to kill.

Do you think the government should have had the authority to arrest those who burned their draft cards to protest the Vietnam war?

5. Arturo Lopez tells his daughter that she will have to stay home all week because she was out past her curfew on Saturday night.

6. Bob Jackson, who is bigger than most of his classmates, cuts in front of the cafeteria line.

7. Jane Doe, the owner of an illegal gambling house, tells a customer to pay his debt or prepare for trouble.

8. Two members of a gang shoot and cripple Eddie Kane for revenge.

9. Ali Darwish tells the two girls sitting next to him in the movie theater to move because they are making too much noise.

10. The manager tells Sally Hu that she is not allowed to smoke in the "no smoking" section of the restaurant.

What do *you* think?

1. Which situations illustrate the use of authority? Why?

2. Which situations illustrate the use of power without authority? Why?

3. Why is it important to know the difference between authority and power without authority?

Using the Lesson

1. While you are studying Authority, you should keep a journal. Begin by writing brief descriptions of four real or imaginary incidents that illustrate the use of authority and the use of power without authority. Make two of the descriptions examples of authority and the other two examples of power without authority. You may use incidents from your experiences or from newspapers, magazines, books, television, or movies.

2. Bring two newsclippings to class that illustrate the use of authority or power without authority and explain them.

LESSON 2

What Are Some Sources of Authority?

Purpose of Lesson

In this lesson you will learn where to find authority and some common arguments made to justify authority. When you have finished the lesson, you should be able to identify examples of authority and explain different arguments about its sources and justification.

Terms to Know

roles
institutions
supreme being
monarchies

divine right
consent
source of authority
aristocracies

What is the source of Congress's authority to enact laws?

Where can you find authority?

Where can you find authority? Every day we can see examples of people who have the authority to govern us and how we act. Parents, teachers, police officers, and government officials are just some of the people who have the authority to control our actions. Rules and laws also control or influence our behavior. Some of the most common places we can find authority include the following:

- **Rules and Laws.** Rules and laws control people's behavior. In this sense, they have authority. For example, when you obey a law requiring you to attend school, you are recognizing the authority of that law.

- **Customs.** Customs are ways of behavior that people have engaged in for a long time. When customs control people's behavior, they may be said to have authority. For example, when you follow the practice of "first come, first served," you are recognizing the authority of a well-established custom.

- **Roles.** Certain roles carry with them the right to control people, no matter who fills these roles. For example, anyone filling the role of a police officer has the authority to require people to obey traffic laws.

- **Institutions.** Groups of people working together in certain institutions also have the authority to control or influence others. For example, Congress as an institution, and not its individual members, has the authority to pass laws that people must obey.

- **Principles of Morality.** Fundamental ideas about right and wrong that come from religion, ethics, and individual conscience often govern our behavior. For example, the Bible has authority for many people.

Where does authority come from?

We have seen that authority may be found in a number of places, but where does it come from? How do certain roles, institutions, laws, customs, and moral principles get the authority, or right, to control our behavior? Where does the police officer get the right to tell us what to do? Why do some people believe that the Bible has the authority to govern their actions? Where does Congress get the right to pass laws we must obey? In short, what is the source of authority?

Sometimes the source of authority for a rule or a position may be traced back through a number of steps. For example: the authority of a teacher to maintain order in the class can be traced back to the principal in charge of the school, who hired the teacher, to the superintendent who appointed the principal, and to the board of education that appointed the superintendent. From here it can be traced back to the state board of education, and to the laws that gave it the authority to make regulations about how schools should be run. Finally, authority can be traced to the state legislature that made the laws, and to the state constitution that established the state legislature.

Eventually, however, we can ask, "What is the ultimate or final source of authority for government? For customs? For moral principles?" Depending on the answers, we may conclude that claims to authority are justified or unjustified. That is, examining the source of authority for a government, a custom, or a moral principle can help us decide whether we ought to obey it. For example: the ultimate authority of some customs may be simply that they have been followed for so long they are accepted without thought. If these customs are not supported by any good reason, you might decide not to follow them.

What arguments are made to justify the authority of rulers and governments?

Historically, rulers or governments have claimed their authority from one or more of the following sources:

- **Birth**. Some rulers have said that they inherited their authority from earlier rulers who received their right to govern from a Supreme Being. Hereditary monarchies and aristocracies have made such claims.

- **Knowledge.** Some people have claimed that those with superior knowledge should have the right to rule.

- **Consent of the Governed**. Many governments today claim that their authority comes from the **people** who are the ultimate **source of authority**. The people give their consent to the government and agree to be ruled by it.

- **A Supreme Being**. Rulers have often claimed that their authority comes from a Supreme Being or God. For example, kings and queens have often said they rule by **divine right**; that is, they get their authority from God.

How do the words in the Pledge of Allegiance reflect the idea of consent of the governed as a source of government authority? In what other ways do people exhibit their consent to be ruled by the government?

Why is it important to know the source of authority?

We need to know the source of people's authority to determine if they have the right to do what they are doing. If we know, for example, that the Constitution gives certain powers to Congress, we can look at the Constitution to judge whether or not a law passed by Congress is within the limits of its authority. We can also ask for the source of the Constitution's authority. In our democratic form of government, the authority of the Constitution comes from the consent of the people.

People have different ideas about what should be considered to be a source of authority. They also may differ on which sources of authority should be considered more important or higher than others. To discuss such questions, it is necessary to identify and evaluate different sources of authority.

Critical Thinking Exercise

IDENTIFYING SOURCES OF AUTHORITY

Each of the following selections deals with a different source of authority. Your teacher will divide your class into five groups to complete this exercise. Each group should read the selection assigned to it, discuss the questions that follow, and choose a spokesperson to report the group's answers to the class.

Group 1: The Law of Hospitality

This selection is adapted from *The Story of the Rheingold*, a folk tale from German and Scandinavian literature. It explains why the hero, Siegmund, could feel safe spending the night at the castle of his sworn enemy, Hunding.

There were three reasons why Siegmund had to spend the night in Hunding's castle. First, Siegmund was too brave a hero to fly from danger. Second, Siegmund did not want to leave the beautiful maiden alone with Hunding, the cruel and evil robber. Third, Hunding had said, "Custom makes you safe as a guest in my house." This meant that it would be unfair and wrong for Hunding to harm Siegmund while he was taking shelter under Hunding's roof. This was called the Law of Hospitality. Just as no host ever harmed a guest, no honorable guest ever took advantage of the law. If Siegmund had run away in the night with the maiden, after Hunding had so well observed the Law of Hospitality, he would have been dishonorable as well as cowardly. It was just as though Siegmund had given a promise to Hunding that he would not go away that night.

What do *you* think?

1. What is a custom?

2. How can a custom be a source of authority?

3. What are other examples of authority that have their source in custom or tradition?

4. What are some advantages and disadvantages of being bound by custom?

Group 2: *Tinker v. Des Moines Independent School District* (1969)

In December 1965, a small group of students and their parents in Des Moines, Iowa, decided to express their opposition to the Vietnam War by wearing black armbands. The principals of the public schools heard of the plan and adopted a policy specifically prohibiting students from wearing black armbands and place symbols in school. The Tinker children knew of the school policy and understood they would be suspended if they disobeyed the rule. On December 16 and 17, they wore black armbands to school. No disruptions of classroom activities, no demonstrations, and no threats of violence occurred.

What might the Tinker children claim as the source of their authority for wearing black armbands to school?

The principal of the school that the Tinkers attended called the students into his office and asked them to remove the armbands. They refused and were suspended until they agreed to attend school without the armbands. Mr. Tinker filed a complaint on behalf of his children claiming that the school had violated their right to free expression. He said that the children had not interfered with the rights of other students nor had they disrupted class routine. The school officials argued that they had made the ruling to avoid a disruption of school discipline. Schools, they claimed, were no place for political demonstrations.

The Supreme Court eventually heard the case and ruled in the students' favor. The Court claimed that the wearing of armbands was a form of expression that was protected under the First Amendment. In the majority opinion the Court stated, "It can hardly be argued that either students or teachers shed their constitutional rights to freedom of speech or expression at the schoolhouse gate."

What do *you* think?

1. What was the source of authority for the school's policy on wearing armbands?

2. What was the source of authority for the Supreme Court's decision?

3. What is the source of authority for the Constitution?

4. What are some advantages and disadvantages of being bound by the Constitution?

Group 3: "On the Duty of Civil Disobedience"

The selection below is adapted from an essay by the American essayist, Henry David Thoreau (1817–1862). Thoreau chose not to pay his poll tax as a form of protest against slavery and the war with Mexico. Authorities arrested him and he spent a night in jail. A few years later in 1849, he wrote the now classic defense of individual conscience, "On the Duty of Civil Disobedience."

What did Henry David Thoreau claim as the source of authority for his protest against the Mexican-American War of 1846?

Must the citizen ever give up his or her conscience to the legislator? Why does every person have a conscience then? I think we should be human beings first and subjects afterward. It is not desirable to cultivate a respect for the law so much as a respect for what is right. The only obligation I have is to do what is right. Law never made people act justly. In fact, many people who respect the law act unjustly because of it. A common and natural result of an undue respect for law is the following example: you have a line of soldiers—colonel, captain, corporal, privates—all marching in order over hill and dale to wars that are against their common sense and conscience. They have no doubt that the wars are wrong. They are all peacefully inclined. Now, what are they—people or small moveable forts and guns at the service of those in power?

What do *you* think?

1. What sources of authority does Thoreau write about?

2. How can individual conscience or a personal sense of morality be a source of authority?

3. Is there a higher law than that of the government? Why or why not?

4. When, if ever, should a person refuse to obey a law he or she thinks is unjust?

Group 4: The Mayflower Compact

The wind carried the Mayflower and its passengers to a place in the New World that was further north than they intended. Finding themselves outside the jurisdiction of their original charter from the Virginia Company, the Pilgrims decided to create their own government. In November 1620, they drew up an agreement that the forty-one men aboard the ship signed. By the terms of this agreement, known as the Mayflower Compact, the Pilgrims agreed to govern themselves.

In the Mayflower Compact, the Pilgrims decided, "there should be an agreement that we should combine together in one body, and submit to such government and governors as we should by common consent agree to make and choose." They agreed that it was best "to combine together into a civil body politic" that would create laws, constitutions, acts, and offices that were thought to be for the general good of the colony. The Pilgrims agreed to follow and obey this authority that they had created by their mutual consent.

What source of authority might the governor of Plymouth Colony claim under the Mayflower Compact?

The Mayflower Compact remained in force from 1620 until 1691, when the colony at Plymouth became part of the Massachusetts Bay Colony.

What do *you* think?

1. What was the source of the authority of the Mayflower Compact?

2. What was the belief underlying the Mayflower Compact about the source of a government's authority to make laws?

3. If some on board the ship had refused to sign, would they have been bound to obey it?

4. Since the men did not ask the women to sign the Compact, were they bound by its authority? Were children? Why or why not?

Group 5: The Constitution of the United States

The Constitution of the United States was drafted in Philadelphia in 1787. It did not become effective until the states ratified it. The following excerpts from the Constitution identify the source of the federal government's authority.

Preamble

We the People of the United States, in Order to form a more perfect Union, establish justice, insure domestic tranquillity, provide for the common defence, promote the general Welfare, and secure the Blessings of Liberty to ourselves and our Posterity, do ordain and establish this Constitution for the United States of America.

What source of authority might the Framers claim for the Constitution of the United States?

Article I

Section 1. All legislative Powers herein granted shall be vested in a Congress of the United States, which shall consist of a Senate and a House of Representatives.

Article II

Section 1. The executive Power shall be vested in a President of the United States of America.

Article III

Section 1. The judicial Power of the United States shall be vested in one supreme Court, and in such inferior Courts as the Congress may from time to time ordain and establish.

What do *you* think?

1. What is the source of authority for the Constitution?

2. What is the source of authority for the Congress? For the president? For the Supreme Court?

3. What beliefs about the source of authority of government underlie the Constitution? Do you think these beliefs are justified? Why or why not?

Using the Lesson

1. In your journal briefly describe three situations from your experience in which you exercised authority that came from different sources.

2. Consider the authority of a police officer who gives someone a ticket for speeding. Draw a chart or illustration that traces the authority of the officer back to its ultimate source. Be prepared to explain your chart to the class.

3. Write an editorial either opposing or defending the position of the Tinker children. Describe the source of authority for their actions.

LESSON 3

How Can We Use Authority?

Purpose of Lesson

In this lesson you will learn some uses of authority. You will examine two views on the need for governmental authority and evaluate a situation in which government authority helped to resolve a dispute about water pollution. When you have completed this lesson you should be able to explain how authority can be used to deal with problems.

Term to Know

state of nature

Why do we need authority?

Think of all the rules you follow every day. Then think about all the people in authority who sometimes tell you what to do. Are there too many rules? Are there too many people in authority?

Have you ever wondered what might happen if there were no rules and no people in authority? Imagine that you wake up one morning and all rules, laws, police, courts, school administrators, and governments have disappeared.

- What problems might arise?
- Would you have any rights?
- How would you protect your rights?

Critical Thinking Exercise

EVALUATING AND TAKING A POSITION ON THE NECESSITY OF GOVERNMENT

Read the two essays on the next page. Then with a study partner discuss the questions in the "What do you think?" section. Be prepared to share your answers with the class.

How do the 1992 Los Angeles riots illustrate the need for authority?

Adapted from "Two Treatises of Civil Government"
John Locke (1690)

Many people have thought about what life would be like without government, rules, and laws. John Locke (1632–1704), an English philosopher, wrote about life in a **state of nature**, an imaginary condition in which people lived together without government.

> People are free in the state of nature. Why do they give up this freedom and subject themselves to the authority of government? The answer to this question is obvious: in the state of nature the enjoyment of freedom is very uncertain. People are always open to attacks from others. Life is dangerous and full of fear. That is why people seek others who share their need for security and join with them. They do so in an effort to protect their lives, their liberty, and their property.
>
> In the state of nature there are many things missing to maintain a secure life. First, there is no established system of law that all people have agreed on and which all people know. And since there is no law, there is no standard of right and wrong that people can use to settle disagreements between them. Second, there is no judge with the authority to settle arguments. Third, there is no person or group of people who have the authority to enforce the law.
>
> So then, this is why people join together under the protection and authority of government. This is why they agree on the administration of punishment according to the system of rules that the community has agreed on. This agreement is the source of legislative, judicial, and executive governmental authority.

Adapted from "On the Duty of Civil Disobedience"
Henry David Thoreau (1849)

Henry David Thoreau, the American writer and essayist referred to in the last lesson, questioned whether government was needed at all.

> I heartily accept this motto: "That government is best which governs least." I also believe the following: "That government is best which governs not at all." When people are ready for such a state of affairs, government will not be necessary at all.
>
> There have been many good arguments made against having an army. These same arguments also can be made against having a government. After all, the army is only an arm of the government. Governmental authority may easily be abused before the people can do anything about it.
>
> A government does not have the energy or vitality of a single living person. The character of the American people has done all that has been accomplished in this country. Government never helped get anything done, except by getting out of people's way.

What do *you* think?

1. According to John Locke, what problems can arise when there is no government of authority?

2. What does Locke say is the source of governmental authority?

3. What was Thoreau's position about the need for governmental authority?

4. What changes in society would have to occur to make people ready to live without government?

What are the uses of authority?

You have been reading about problems that may occur without adequate authority. How can authority be used to solve some of these problems? Authority has a number of important purposes:

- **Authority** can be used to **protect important rights and freedoms**. For example, the Constitution protects our freedoms of expression and belief.

How is the authority of the Constitution used to protect freedom of religious beliefs?

- **Authority** can be used to **ensure that resources and burdens will be distributed fairly**. For example, our government sees that all children have an equal opportunity to receive a public education.
- **Authority** can be used to **manage conflict peacefully and fairly**. For example, our judicial system has the authority to provide a fair trial for a person accused of a crime.

How is the authority of the legal system used to manage conflict?

Critical Thinking Exercise

EVALUATING THE USE OF AUTHORITY

For several years, the Reserve Mining Company of Silver Bay, Minnesota, had been dumping 67,000 tons of taconite waste into Lake Superior every day. In Duluth, Minnesota, sixty miles south of Silver Bay, research by the Environmental Protection Agency (EPA) showed high concentrations of cancer-causing fibers in the drinking water. The source of the drinking water was Lake Superior. The EPA traced the contamination directly to the Reserve Mining Company's waste emptied into the lake.

To find a solution to this problem, the Reserve Mining Company and the EPA held discussions. When negotiations failed, the case went to court. The EPA asked the court to order the immediate shutdown of the plant until those responsible could eliminate the pollution of Lake Superior. The company argued that it would cost too much money to obey the pollution control regulations demanded by the EPA. Furthermore, the company said that it would have to lay off 3,000 employees if they shut down the plant.

A federal court of appeals eventually decided that the taconite waste might contribute to cancer. The court ruled, however, that the pollution was not an immediate danger. The court gave the Reserve Mining Company three and a half years to stop polluting Lake Superior.

What do *you* think?

1. How was authority used to deal with the water supply contamination problem?

2. What problems might have arisen if there had been no effective authority to deal with this situation?

3. In what other ways could authority have been used to deal with the problems in this situation?

Using the Lesson

1. Consider all your actions today from the moment you woke up until you started reading this assignment. How many of your actions were governed by a rule or law? What was the purpose of each of these rules or laws? Do you think they were necessary? Record your answers to these questions in your journal.

2. Read the newspaper for several days. From your reading, make a list of problems that occurred due to lack of effective authority. After you have finished the list, suggest ways authority could have helped deal with these problems

3. You have read what John Locke thought life would be like in a state of nature, that is, without government or laws. Do you agree or disagree with him? Write a story about what you think your life would be like in a state of nature.

Unit Two: How Can We Evaluate Candidates for Positions of Authority?

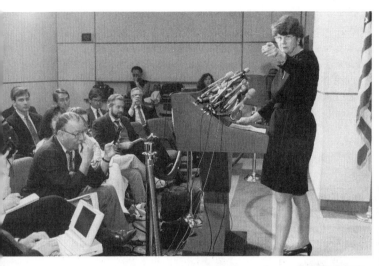

What qualifications should people have to fill different positions of authority?

Purpose of Unit

People who exercise authority often have the right to control or influence our lives. Members of Congress, state legislatures, and city councils make many important laws. Police officers see that people follow laws. Teachers, principals, and parents make rules that influence the lives of young people.

We must choose people in positions of authority with great care because they can have a great influence on our lives. People who are well qualified to exercise authority can make our lives easier and more pleasant. Unqualified people in positions of authority can make our lives difficult and unpleasant.

Different positions of authority call for different qualifications. Someone who is well qualified to be a police officer may not be qualified to be a judge. On the other hand, someone who makes a good judge might not make a good police officer. When selecting people to fill positions of authority, it is important to consider what qualifications they should have to be able to do their jobs well.

In this unit, you will learn some important steps to take when selecting people to fill positions of authority.

LESSON 4

How Should We Choose People for Positions of Authority?

Purpose of Lesson

This lesson introduces a set of intellectual tools that are useful in selecting people to fill positions of authority. These tools also are useful in evaluating the qualifications of persons who are in such positions.

When you have finished this lesson, you should be able to identify and explain the requirements of a position of authority. You also should be able to identify and explain the qualifications a person should possess to fill that position.

Terms to Know

position of authority   diligence
qualifications   abolitionist
woman suffrage   temperance

What qualities make a good leader?

Read the selection below then answer the "What do you think?" questions. These questions will help you begin thinking about the characteristics a person should possess to fill a position of authority.

Susan B. Anthony

Susan B. Anthony (1820–1906), abolitionist, temperance advocate, and most of all, champion of women's rights, held the strong conviction that women could never achieve their full rights until they first had won the right to vote. A skilled organizer, she played a key role in the passage of the Nineteenth Amendment giving women the right to vote. She was fearless in promoting the cause of women's rights and endured years of opposition and abuse as a result. The press slandered her, strangers jeered at her, and people often threw eggs and rotten fruit at her when she lectured.

Anthony grew up in a Quaker home and was a bright, independent child. She was well educated and spent a number of years teaching. Her interests, however, lay in other areas and she soon became deeply involved in the moral crusades that would absorb her time and energy for

years. At a time when people expected women to stay home, she used her intelligence, determination, and organizational skills to further the causes in which she believed. Discouraged by the limited role allowed to women in the temperance movement, she helped found the Woman's State Temperance Society of New York. She also served as an agent for the American Anti-Slavery Society. Her prime concern, however, was to further the rights of women. Anthony was one of the foremost leaders in the movement for **woman suffrage**, and in 1892 she was elected president of the National American Woman Suffrage Association.

What qualities should a person possess to be a successful leader or advocate for community change?

In November 1872, police arrested Anthony as she attempted to vote in the presidential election. A few months later, she compounded her crime by trying to vote in a city election. Although she was convicted, she refused to pay the fine. Neither public ridicule nor the fear of jail could deter her commitment to the cause in which she so fervently believed.

Anthony assisted in organizing international woman suffrage associations, helped compile and publish a history of the suffrage movement, and spoke tirelessly throughout the country on the subject of women's rights for more than half a century. She died in 1906, only a few years before her dream of woman suffrage became a reality.

What do *you* think?

1. What were the responsibilities of a position of authority in the woman suffrage movement?

2. What characteristics did Anthony have that helped make her a successful leader?

How should we choose someone for a position of authority?

In the preceding activity, you listed some responsibilities of a position of authority and the characteristics necessary to do the job well. You often will have the opportunity to select people for positions of authority. To make wise choices, you will need some intellectual tools. Just as there are tools with which to repair a car or bake a cake, there are tools of the mind with which to examine issues.

Intellectual tools include a variety of ideas, observations about society and our roles within it, and sets of questions that are useful in analyzing situations and reaching decisions. The following are some intellectual tools you can use when deciding if someone is qualified for a particular position:

1. **WHAT ARE THE DUTIES, POWERS, PRIVILEGES, AND LIMITATIONS OF THE POSITION?**
   Before you can decide how qualified a person is for a position, you must first consider what the job involves.

2. **WHAT CHARACTERISTICS SHOULD A PERSON HAVE TO BE SELECTED FOR THE POSITION?**
   The characteristics of the person for a particular job should enable that individual to fulfill the duties and powers of that position and to do the job well. Depending on the position, some characteristics that might be important include the following:

   - specialized knowledge or skills
   - physical capacity

   - impartiality
   - integrity
   - intelligence
   - diligence
   - reliability
   - courage
   - ability to work with other people
   - sensitivity to human needs and rights
   - views on job-related issues

3. **WHAT ARE THE STRENGTHS AND WEAKNESSES OF THE PERSONS BEING CONSIDERED FOR THE POSITION?**
   Each candidate's characteristics should be compared with the qualities needed for the job as well as with the characteristics of the other candidates.

4. **WHICH PERSON WOULD BEST FILL THE POSITION? WHY?**
   You should be able to explain the basis for your selection using the information gained from answering the first three questions in the procedure.

Critical Thinking Exercise
EVALUATING CHARACTERISTICS OF A WELL-QUALIFIED PRESIDENT

The following activity provides you with an opportunity to apply the intellectual tools you have just learned. Working in small groups, read the excerpt from Article II of the Constitution describing the position of president of the United States. Then work with your group to complete the chart on p. 19. Be prepared to share your answers with the class.

Article II

Section 1. ...Before he enter on the Execution of his Office, he shall take the following Oath or Affirmation: "I do solemnly swear (or affirm) that I will faithfully execute the Office of President of the United States, and will to the best of my Ability, preserve, protect and defend the Constitution of the United States."

How do the duties, powers, privileges, and limitations of a position of authority
help you decide what characteristics a person needs to have to fill it?

Section 2. The President shall be Commander in Chief of the Army and Navy of the United States, and of the Militia of the several States...and he shall have Power to grant Reprieves and Pardons for Offenses against the United States, except in Cases of Impeachment.

He shall have Power, by and with the Advice and Consent of the Senate, to make Treaties, provided two thirds of the Senators present concur; and he shall nominate, and by and with the Advice and Consent of the Senate, shall appoint Ambassadors, other public Ministers and Consuls, Judges of the Supreme Court, and all other Officers of the United States, whose Appointments are not herein otherwise provided for, and which shall be established by Law: but the Congress may by Law vest the Appointment of such inferior Officers, as they think proper, in the President alone, in the Courts of Law, or in the Heads of Departments.

The President shall have Power to fill up all Vacancies that may happen during the Recess of the Senate, by granting Commissions which shall expire at the End of their next Session.

Section 3. He shall from time to time give to the Congress Information of the State of the Union, and recommend to their Consideration such Measures as he shall judge necessary and expedient; he may, on extraordinary Occasions, convene both Houses, or either of them, and in Case of Disagreement between them, with Respect to the Time of Adjournment, he may adjourn them to such Time as he shall think proper; he shall receive Ambassadors and other public Ministers; he shall take Care that the Laws be faithfully executed, and shall Commission all the Officers of the United States.

What do *you* think?

1. What characteristics should a person have to be selected for the position of president?

2. Think about the characteristics you identified for Susan B. Anthony that qualified her to lead the woman suffrage movement. What similarities do you see between those characteristics and the ones you have identified for the presidency? What characteristics are different?

Using the Lesson

1. Choose a television program that shows someone in a position of authority. Write the duties, powers, privileges, and limitations of the position. Then describe the characteristics of the person in that job that qualify him or her for the position. Explain whether or not you would select this person for the position.

2. Think of a position of authority you might like to serve in some day. In your journal, write a short description of the position, the characteristics someone should possess to do it well, and explain why you might qualify for the job.

Duties, Powers, Privileges, and Limitations of the Position of President	Characteristics a President Should Have
Questions	**Answers**
Duties and Power. The president has the duty and power to	To perform these duties and exercise these powers, the president should be
■ give Congress periodic information on the state of the Union	
■ make sure that the laws of the land are faithfully executed	
■ command the armed forces	
■ appoint judges to the Supreme Court	
■ appoint the heads of the executive departments	
■ preserve, protect, and defend the Constitution of the United States	
Privileges. The president has the following privileges:	To be trusted with these privileges, the president should be
■ receives a substantial salary and expense allowance	
■ uses special air and ground transportation	
■ lives in the White House and has the use of Camp David	
■ receives protection by the Secret Service	
■ receives the assistance of the Cabinet and other members of the executive department	
■ receives free medical care	
Limitations. The president may not do the following:	To comply with these limitations, the president should be
■ serve more than two terms of office	
■ engage in treason, bribery, or other high crimes and misdemeanors	
■ violate the Constitution of the United States	

LESSON 5

Who Would You Select for This Position of Authority?

Purpose of Lesson

This lesson gives you an opportunity to use the intellectual tools you have just studied to decide which candidate is most qualified for a position of authority. When you have completed the lesson, you should be able to explain what considerations you used to justify the choices you made.

Terms to Know

levying
pollution
welfare program

Critical Thinking Exercise

TAKING A POSITION ON A CANDIDATE FOR PUBLIC OFFICE

In this exercise you will select a person to serve in your state legislature. Your class will conduct Editorial Board Endorsement Interviews in which reporters and editors of the city's daily newspaper question four candidates for the position. To prepare for this exercise, read the description of Central City and the "Memorandum to the People of Central City." Then follow the "Instructions for Conducting the Editorial Board Endorsement Interviews" that follow the memorandum.

Central City

Central City is a large city located in the midwest region of the United States. The city is largely industrialized with a variety of manufacturing plants located throughout the town. These manufacturing plants provide jobs for many people who live in Central City.

The central part of the city has many problems. The crime rate is high; housing and school facilities are sub-standard, and there is a large amount of unemployment, drug use, violence, and pollution.

Central City has thirty-three elementary schools, twenty junior high schools, and seventeen high schools. Students attend these schools from the entire county. The county government just built a new hospital with some help from the state.

The city contains two major parks and there is a state park just a few miles away. In the winter, the parks are good places for sledding and ice skating; in summer, people use them for picnics, swimming, and baseball.

A system of highways that was built with state and federal taxes connects Central City to other communities.

Central City has a municipal government. Every four years the people elect a mayor and a city council to provide local government for the city. The voters in the city also have the right to elect a representative to the state

What qualifications should a person have to govern a large municipality?

legislature every two years. The state legislature has the authority to perform certain duties, including the following:

- **Levying taxes.** The legislature has the authority to tax personal incomes and place a sales tax on some items that people buy.

- **Deciding how to spend tax money.** The legislature has the authority to decide how to spend the state's tax money. In the past, they used tax money for such things as schools, state highways, state parks, wildlife preserves, dams, and water systems. They also used it to aid farmers and people who were poor or disabled.

- **Passing new legislation.** The legislature has the authority to make or change the laws of the state. For example, members of the state legislature pass laws that do the following:

  - define what actions will be considered crimes
  - govern the owning, licensing, and driving of automobiles
  - regulate the qualifications necessary for certain professions
  - affect school curricula

- **Deciding on minimum wage levels and employee benefits.** The legislature has the authority to decide the minimum hourly wage rate and any allowable exceptions. It also can decide the kinds of benefits employers must provide for their workers. These benefits include paid sick leave, maternity leave, and payment for injuries that happen on the job.

Memorandum to the People of Central City

FROM: THE LEAGUE OF VOTERS   **SUBJECT: NEXT WEEK'S ELECTION**

Since we believe that next week's election is important, we have prepared the following information for your consideration. We hope that you will find it helpful when choosing among the candidates.

Our legislator has the duty and power to do the following:

- work for the good of all people of Central City
- attend meetings of the state legislature
- serve on committees
- conduct and participate in hearings
- propose new laws
- vote on proposed new laws
- give fair consideration to the needs and interests of other communities in the state

To fulfill these duties and powers, our legislator should do the following:

- know the interests of all the people and be willing to work for the good of everyone
- be reliable, attend as many meetings as possible, and be at meetings on time
- work well with others and be able to compromise, bargain, and persuade

- be well prepared, open-minded, a good listener, and a good questioner
- be skilled in creating and writing new laws
- consider the welfare of all the people of Central City and the rest of the state
- be fair when the interests of Central City conflict with the interests of other communities

As privileges of office, our legislator is entitled to the following:

- an income of $45,000 per year
- exemption from libel or slander lawsuits for anything said while on the floor of the legislature

To receive these privileges, our legislator should do the following:

- be diligent and devote the time necessary to earn the salary for the position
- speak with good taste and discretion

As limitations of office, our legislator cannot do the following:

- hold or be paid for other jobs while serving as a legislator
- vote on bills in which there is any conflict of interest
- work to pass laws that are prohibited by the Constitution of the United States or the constitution of our state

To fulfill these limitations, our legislator should do the following:

- be honest and trustworthy and refuse money for outside work
- avoid voting on bills in which he or she has any personal interest
- know and support the basic principles of both the U.S. and our state constitutions

How can televised debates and news media interviews help us evaluate candidates for positions of authority?

Instructions for Conducting the Editorial Board Endorsement Interviews

Your teacher will divide your class into five groups. One group will represent the members of the *Central City Daily Journal* editorial board. Each of the other groups will represent one of the four candidates for the office of state legislator. Each group should follow the directions below to prepare for the Editorial Board Endorsement Interviews.

Students should follow a "meet the press" format in which the editorial board interviews the four candidates. After each candidate has made an opening statement, members of the editorial board may ask questions. Other members of each candidate group may assist their candidate in responding to questions.

Group 1: Editorial Board Group

You represent the editorial board of the *Central City Daily Journal*, the largest newspaper in Central City. Your board will endorse one of the candidates for state representative and your endorsement will give a substantial boost to the campaign of the candidate you select.

Your group should read and discuss the candidate profiles that follow. List the strengths and weaknesses of each candidate. To help you with this task, refer to the description of Central City. You also should look at the memorandum that outlines the responsibilities of a state legislator and the characteristics that a person should have to fill that position.

Prepare a list of questions to ask each candidate. You will have about five minutes to question each candidate after he or she has presented an opening statement of three to four minutes. Your questions should probe the candidates about their ability to fulfill the responsibilities of the position.

Select a chairperson to conduct the interviews. The chairperson will explain the procedure to the candidates. The chairperson also will moderate the discussion period after each candidate's opening statement. Note that other members of each candidate group can assist their candidate in responding to questions.

Group 2: Candidate Groups

Your group should read and discuss the profile of your candidate. List your candidate's strengths and weaknesses. To help you with this task, refer to the description of Central City and the "Memorandum to the People of Central City."

Your group should then choose one member to play the candidate. Help that person get ready for the editorial board interview; prepare a short opening statement in which your candidate will try to convince the editorial board that he or she has the characteristics required to perform the job well. The group also should help the candidate rehearse answers to possible questions from the editorial board. Remember to stress why he or she is the best candidate for the position. Other group members will be allowed to help the candidate in the question-and-answer period.

Candidate Profiles

Raul Garcia

Background: Raul was born and raised in Central City. He is married and has three grown children. Raul's wife, Sue, works in the General Clothing Store on Elm Street.

Employment: Raul has worked in a manufacturing plant since he was seventeen and has advanced to the position of foreman. Raul was one of the first workers at the plant to join. Some say he is largely responsible for union workers getting higher pay and more benefits.

Position on the issues: Raul believes the minimum wage for workers is too low and that they need more benefits such as a better medical plan. He also thinks that the state should pass a law requiring that employers pay for more of these benefits.

Jennifer Brown

Background: Jennifer was born in Central City, but when she was young, her family moved to a nearby town. She received her law degree at the state university and returned to Central City to practice law.

Employment: Jennifer is a partner in one of the largest law firms in Central City. She handles all kinds of cases. When workers were first organizing a union, Jennifer worked to protect their rights. Later, when the union made demands for higher wages and greater benefits, the industry hired her to argue their side of the issue. Jennifer is a member of the State Bar Association and the Chamber of Commerce.

Position on the issues: Jennifer is interested in problems on both the local and state levels. She believes that her experience in practicing law will help her be an effective legislator. She also thinks that laws controlling industrial pollution are neither fair to industry nor effective in protecting the environment. She wants to improve these laws.

Patricia Chang

Background: Pat was born and raised in Central City. She is married, has one child, and has been active in the PTA and in women's groups.

Employment: Pat has taught American history and American government at Central City High School for eleven years. She has been head of the social studies department for the past four years. Students like her and other teachers respect her. Pat is a member of the Social Studies Teachers Association.

Position on the issues: Pat believes that public education needs more state support. She thinks that increasing teachers' salaries and reducing the number of students in each class would be beneficial. She is concerned about environmental pollution, especially from the local cement plant. Pat thinks there should be strict state laws to control pollution. She also believes that the legislature should spend more money on welfare programs.

William "Bill" Meyers

Background: Bill is married and has three children who are still in school. He and his wife were born on farms in a nearby county. Bill and his family love the parks and lakes around Central City.

Employment: When he graduated from high school, Bill began working in the Cement Block and Pipe Company. He has been manager of that company for ten years. People consider Bill to be a good and efficient manager. Bill is past-president of the Chamber of Commerce and the Central City Fish and Game Club.

Position on the issues: Bill thinks that employers and employees should agree on workers' salaries and benefits without regulation from the state. He does not favor increased spending for welfare; he believes local charities should take care of such needs. He believes that the state should spend more money on wildlife preserves and state parks.

Which candidate will you endorse?

After the editorial board has completed the interviews, it should select a candidate to endorse for the position of state legislator. When making its selection, the editorial board should consider the following questions:

- What are the strengths and weaknesses of each candidate running for the office?

- Which candidate do you think is best qualified to be a state legislator?

The chairperson of the editorial board should announce the boards' decision to the class, and explain the reasons for the board's endorsement of the candidate it chose. The class as a whole may then conduct a mock election for the position of state representative.

Using the Lesson

1. Pick a candidate for state legislature other than the one the editorial board selected. Write a letter to the editor of the *Central City Daily Journal* defending your choice of candidate for the legislature.

2. Compare the candidates from the last presidential election using the criteria you have learned in this unit. Write a script for a thirty-second-long television commercial for the candidate of your choice.

Unit Three: How Can We Evaluate Rules and Laws?

How can you evaluate whether a rule or law is good?

Purpose of Unit

You have learned that sometimes it is helpful to give certain people the right to exercise authority. Most positions of authority involve rules. Some people in positions of authority make rules. Others enforce them. Still others settle arguments about the meaning of rules and decide what to do with people who have disobeyed them.

In our democratic system, people we elect to public office have a right to make rules or laws. They make many laws to protect people's rights. They make other laws that are supposed to ensure that all citizens receive their fair share of community resources.

Some people think that just because a rule exists, it must be a good rule. This is not always so. Rules can have many things wrong with them. It is not always easy to make a good rule. In this unit you will learn how to evaluate whether a rule is good or not. You also will learn how to improve rules and how to develop good rules.

LESSON 6

What Should You Consider When Evaluating Rules?

Purpose of Lesson

This lesson introduces you to some intellectual tools useful in making and evaluating rules and laws. When you have completed the lesson, you should be able to use these tools to evaluate rules and to suggest ways to improve them.

Terms to Know

characteristics
criteria
hypothetical

What makes a rule well designed?

Think about how important rules and laws are in your life. Since they are so important, we need to make sure that the rules we follow are well designed.

■ What might happen if a rule is not well designed?

■ What criteria would you use to evaluate a rule?

Critical Thinking Exercise

IDENTIFYING WHAT IS WRONG WITH THESE RULES

Each of the following hypothetical rules has a problem or weakness. Thinking about how to correct these weaknesses will help you identify some criteria or standards for evaluating rules. As you read each example, write what you think is wrong with the rule. After completing all six examples, make a list of the characteristics or qualities you think a rule should have by completing the sentence, "A good rule should be...". Be prepared to share your answers with the class.

1. To qualify to vote, a citizen must own at least ten acres or $10,000 worth of property.

2. No person shall, may, or will, unnecessarily, or without cause, fustigate another person's cranial orb or any other segment of his corporeal being, whatsoever.

3. To promote health and fitness, a new federal law allows only those citizens weighing 145 pounds or less to vote in presidential elections.

4. Anyone who uses too much water will have to pay a fine.

5. Police and other government officials may search a person's home whenever they feel like it.

6. All students must eat twenty-eight hamburgers for lunch every day.

How can you evaluate a rule?

As a citizen in a democracy, you will have many opportunities to vote for rules and laws either directly or through your elected representatives. In the previous activity, you were asked to evaluate some rules and think about how to improve them. In doing so, you made a list of characteristics or features a good rule should have. Your list may have included some of the following characteristics.

A good rule should be

■ fair

■ easy to understand

■ well designed to achieve its purpose

■ clear as to what is expected

- designed so that it doesn't interfere unnecessarily with other values such as privacy or freedom

- possible to follow

When you evaluate a rule or law it is useful to consider whether it has these characteristics. That is, asking whether a rule or a law has these characteristics is one of the intellectual tools you can use to evaluate the rule or the law. Other intellectual tools you can use to evaluate rules and laws are printed in the chart on page 29.

Critical Thinking Exercise

EVALUATING A LAW

You have learned some important tools for evaluating rules and laws. The following activity gives you an opportunity to use these tools. Working in small groups, read the story and answer the questions in the Intellectual Tool Chart on the next page. Be prepared to share your answers with the class.

The Amplified Car Stereo Law

As technology has advanced, companies have developed super-amplified car stereo systems that can blast music at ear-splitting levels. Frequently drivers with these stereo systems play them at full volume and the noise often distracts other drivers. To combat this problem, the governor signed a law that makes it illegal to operate a sound system in a vehicle if the sound can be heard more than fifty feet away. Offenders are subject to a $50 fine for the first violation and higher fines for later offenses.

Reaction to the new law has varied. Police and sheriff's departments support the measure, claiming that issuing a citation and a fine will deter the high-volume sound abuse. Manufacturers of the high-powered stereo systems oppose the law, arguing that education would be a better deterrent.

Using the Lesson

1. Think of a problem at your school. Develop a rule with a group of your classmates to help deal with that problem. Present the problem and your rule to the rest of the class. Discuss your rule using the procedure for evaluating rules you just learned.

2. Look at newspaper or magazine articles and find one about a rule that interests you. It can be in government, business, sports, or another area. Evaluate this rule using the intellectual tools you have learned and write an editorial supporting your position.

How can you evaluate whether a law regulating the use of a car stereo is well designed?

Intellectual Tool Chart for Evaluating Rules and Laws

Questions	Answers
1. What is the rule to be evaluated?	
2. What is the purpose of the rule?	
3. Is a rule necessary or are there better ways to accomplish the same purpose?	
4. What might be the effects of the rule?	
5. What are the strengths and weaknesses of the rule? Is the rule ■ fair ■ easy to understand ■ well designed to achieve its purpose ■ clear as to what is expected ■ designed so that it doesn't interfere unnecessarily with other values such as privacy or freedom ■ possible to follow	
6. What do you think? Should the rule be kept as it is, changed, or eliminated? Why?	

LESSON 7

How Would You Create a Law?

Purpose of Lesson

In this lesson you take part in a simulated debate in the United States Senate. You consider a problem that is before the Senate, help develop a bill to solve this problem, and try to convince other senators that your bill is the best solution. When you have completed this lesson you should be able to explain and defend the position you have taken.

Terms to Know

extinct
endangered species
wildlife preservation

Critical Thinking Exercise

CREATING AND DEFENDING A LAW

Imagine that you are a member of the United States Senate. You learn that various species of fish, wildlife, and plants have become extinct in the United States. In addition, the populations of certain other species have become so diminished that it is likely they also will become extinct if action is not taken quickly.

This situation has occurred for several reasons. First, there have not been adequate laws to protect the endangered species. Second, urban industrial growth has taken place without adequate protection of plants, fish, and wildlife. Third, the use of dangerous pesticides in agriculture has destroyed certain plants and animals.

You and the other members of Congress have the duty and power to make new laws. A colleague has introduced a bill that might help protect endangered species. This bill, called the Federal Endangered Species Act, provides a program for the conservation of endangered species of fish, wildlife, and plants in the particular locations where they live and grow.

How can you decide whether a law protecting endangered species such as the spotted owl is a good law?

With regard to the animals specified in this bill, it would become a federal crime to do the following:

- import any such species into, or export any such species out of, the United States

- own, deliver, carry, transport, or ship by any means any such species

- sell or offer for sale any such species

The bill would impose a $10,000 fine on any person who knowingly violates its provisions.

Evaluating the Endangered Species Law

Read the questions below and share your answers with the rest of the class.

1. What proposed law is to be evaluated?

2. What is the purpose of the proposed law?

3. Is a law necessary or are there better ways to achieve the purpose?

4. What do you think would be some effects of the proposed law?

5. What are the strengths and weaknesses of the proposed law?

6. Do you think the proposed law should be kept as it is, changed, or eliminated? Why?

Positions of Senatorial Groups

The bill has been referred to the Senate Committee on Environment and Public Works. Your teacher will divide your class into the following three groups of senators on the committee. Each group will take a different position on how to solve the endangered species problem.

Group 1: Senators who believe the national government has a major responsibility

You believe that the federal government should take a major role in helping to solve the problem of endangered species. You think the national government should set general policies and provide funds, and local governments should have to help with the federal programs. You also think that educational institutions should teach methods of saving our wildlife. You are willing to reduce other parts of the budget to pay for the endangered species program.

Group 2: Senators who believe the national government has a limited responsibility

You think that the federal government should not take the main responsibility for dealing with the problem of endangered species. You believe that each state should maintain its own ecological balance and that we should spend tax money on more urgently needed programs than wildlife conservation. You also recognize that hunting and fishing bring considerable income to certain states. You believe that federal government policies concerning wildlife preservation hurt those states that depend on income from hunting and fishing.

What arguments should members of Congress consider in deciding whether to support a proposed law?

Group 3: Senators who favor a compromise

You agree with parts of the other two groups' positions. You think the states should protect their wildlife. On the other hand, you believe that the federal government should play a more active role. For example, you believe that we need federal laws to prevent the sale of wild animal products (such as fur coats) that require the death of the animal. You also think that both the federal and state governments should share the responsibility and the cost of protecting wildlife.

Developing a Bill

Each group should begin by selecting a spokesperson and a recorder. Then each group should develop an alternative bill that represents its position on how to solve the problem of endangered species. You should evaluate the alternative you proposed by answering the following questions:

- What is the purpose of your alternative bill?

- Do you think there are better ways than making a law to achieve the purpose? Explain.

- What effects would your bill have if it became law?

- What are the strengths and weaknesses of your bill?

- Why should the senators pass your bill?

Directions for a Senate Debate

1. The class should select a person to serve as chairman of the Senate Committee on Environment and Public Works who will chair the proceedings.

2. Each group will have three minutes to present its bill to the committee. After each presentation, other senators may question or criticize the bill presented. Members of the group creating the bill may respond to these criticisms.

3. Each group may amend its bill if necessary to win votes or they may develop and present a compromise bill.

4. After completing the debate, the committee should vote on the bills before it. When voting, consider the following questions:

- What is the purpose of each bill?

- What would be the effects of each bill if it were passed?

- What are the strengths and weaknesses of each bill?

Using the Lesson

1. Did you agree with the class decision? Why or why not? Write a short essay in your journal describing your reaction to the Senate committee debate and vote. Discuss your views on what type of law would best deal with the problem of endangered species.

2. Choose a bill that is before your state legislature or Congress. Evaluate the proposed legislation using the criteria in this lesson. Write a letter to your representative urging him or her to support your position on the bill.

Unit Four: What Are the Benefits and Costs of Authority?

What might be some consequences of a government decision to exercise authority by sending troops to maintain peace in another part of the world? Which of these consequences would be benefits, which would be costs?

Purpose of Unit

Every use of authority has certain results. For example, when U.S. troops are sent overseas as part of a United Nations force, the results may include restoring peace or assisting refugees in a troubled part of the world. Other results, however, might include the death of some civilians and military service members, the destruction of public facilities, and financial costs to U.S. taxpayers. We need to decide whether the benefits (advantages) of a particular use of authority outweigh the costs (disadvantages) for us as individuals and for society.

In this unit you will learn some of the common benefits and costs of authority. You also will learn some intellectual tools to use in evaluating positions and institutions which have authority. These tools will help you decide whether the duties, powers, privileges, and limitations of a position or an institution have been well planned, or if they need to be changed. You also will have the opportunity to use these tools to design a position of authority.

LESSON 8

What Are Some Consequences of Authority?

Purpose of Lesson

In this lesson you will identify consequences of the use of authority. You will classify these consequences as benefits or costs. When you have completed the lesson, you should be able to explain some common benefits and costs of authority. You also should be able to use these ideas in evaluating and taking positions on issues of authority.

Terms to Know

efficiency	inaccessibility
accountability	economic costs
vigilance	incompetence

What are the benefits and costs of authority?

To begin thinking about the consequences of authority, we will look at a hypothetical situation. Suppose that the number of automobile accidents among teenage drivers has increased sharply. To reduce the number of such accidents, the state legislature passed a law stating that no one under the age of twenty-one could get a driver's license.

- What might be some consequences of such a law?

- Which of these consequences would be benefits? Which would be costs?

- How do you think the various people affected by this law—teenagers, their parents, the police, the state legislators—would feel about the benefits and costs involved?

Critical Thinking Exercise

DECIDING WHETHER A CONSEQUENCE IS A BENEFIT OR COST

In this activity you will work with a study partner to discuss some benefits and costs of using authority. Read the following situations and answer the "What do *you*

think?" questions. Be prepared to share your answers with the rest of the class.

- To combat an increase in juvenile crime, the city council passed a law imposing a 10:30 p.m. curfew on people under the age of eighteen.

- To control pollution, Congress passed a law that set high standards for waste disposal from industrial plants. Any factory that did not follow these standards within six months would receive heavy fines.

- To reduce violence, the state legislature passed a law that made it a crime to print or sell books or magazines that showed or described acts of violence.

What do *you* think?

1. What might be some consequences of authority in each situation?

2. Which of these consequences would be benefits?

3. Which of these consequences would be costs?

What are some common benefits and costs of authority?

When making decisions about issues of authority, it is important to identify the possible benefits and costs involved.

Benefits might include the following:

- **Security.** The use of authority may make people feel more secure by providing a predictable order and by protecting the rights of individuals and groups. For example, laws against murder, assault, drunk driving, and other offenses are uses of authority that provide security.

- **Fairness**. People can use authority to promote the fair distribution of resources and the fair management of conflicts. For example, laws protect people's rights to a hearing in court.

- **Freedom.** Laws such as the Bill of Rights may protect the individual's right to freedom of religion and expression.

- **Efficiency**. The clear assignment of responsibilities to various authorities may promote greater efficiency in making and carrying out decisions. For example, a principal might assign administrative tasks to several teachers to ensure the smooth operation of the school.

- **Quality of life**. Laws and the people who enforce them may protect and improve the quality of life. For example, laws may forbid the dumping of poisonous substances near water supplies.

What might be some benefits of using authority to protect the environment?

- **Accountability**. When we place people in positions of authority, we can hold them accountable for fulfilling the responsibilities of their jobs. For example, voters can hold the president accountable for performing the duties of his or her office as listed in the Constitution.

- **Provision of essential services**. We can provide some services we need by passing laws and appointing people to positions of authority to perform these services. For example, laws may allow hiring teachers, police officers, welfare workers, and health and safety inspectors.

Costs might include the following:

- **Misuse of power**. People filling positions of authority might misuse their positions and the power allocated

to them. For example, in the Soviet Union Josef Stalin (1879–1953) abused his power by causing many of his political opponents to be murdered.

- **Need for vigilance**. We must make sure that people in positions of authority perform their responsibilities within acceptable limits. For example, citizen "watchdog" groups monitor the activities of government agencies and elected representatives.

What might be some costs of Governor George Wallace exercising authority to block integration at the University of Alabama in 1963?

- **Inflexibility and resistance to change.** In some instances, positions of authority can promote an unwillingness to change among those who hold these positions. This rigidity may make adjusting to new and different situations difficult. For example, many local government officials opposed the Supreme Court's school desegregation rulings.

- **Inaccessibility.** Due to the complexity and size of many large institutions, gaining access to people in specific positions of authority may be difficult. For example, a family needing affordable housing might need to visit several different government agencies to get help.

- **Limitations on freedom.** Every exercise of authority involves by definition a limitation on freedom. For example, parents' authority to set curfews for their children limits the children's freedom.

- **Economic costs.** It costs money to support people and institutions in positions of authority. For example, we pay taxes to the federal government to pay the salaries of bureaucrats, elected officials, judges, law enforcement officers, and members of the armed services.

What do *you* think?

1. What examples can you give from your own experience of the benefits of authority?

2. What examples can you give from your own experience of the costs of authority?

Which benefits and costs are most important?

Identifying the benefits and costs of a law is important in deciding whether to support it. However, we also must decide which benefits and costs are most important to us as individuals. For example, recall the earlier discussion of a 10:30 p.m. curfew for teenagers. Both adults and juveniles would agree that this curfew would have the cost of limiting teenagers' freedom but might also have the benefit of decreasing juvenile crime. Some might think that the benefit of decreased crime is more important than the cost of limiting the freedom of juveniles. Others might not agree. We should consider different points of view when examining the benefits and costs of authority in any given situation.

Critical Thinking Exercise
TAKING A POSITION

Assume that your state legislature is considering a bill to ban the sale and possession of assault-type automatic weapons. Your teacher will divide your class into five groups to develop positions on the bill. Each group should represent one of the organizations listed below.

Each organization should make a presentation about which benefits and costs are most important from its point of view.

- Committee for a Safe Community
- Main Town Gun Owners Association
- Police Department
- Eagle Arms Weapons Factory
- Association of Principled Pacifists

What do *you* think?

1. What benefits and costs did each group consider most important?

2. What interests affected how each group saw the importance of the various benefits and costs?

Using the Lesson

1. What are some rules you have at school? Pick two or three of these rules and describe the benefits and costs of each.

2. Think about a television program or a movie you have seen that showed an exercise of authority. In your journal, make a list of the consequences of that exercise of authority. For each consequence, decide if it is a benefit or a cost.

LESSON 9

How Can You Evaluate the Benefits and Costs of Authority?

Purpose of Lesson

In this lesson you will consider the benefits and costs of authority in a courtroom situation. After studying the situation, everyone in the class will participate in a hearing and judge the issues involved. When you have completed the lesson, you should be able to explain the usefulness of considering benefits and costs in making decisions about authority.

Terms to Know

public defender
bailiff

Critical Thinking Exercise

EVALUATING THE BENEFITS AND COSTS OF AUTHORITY

Your teacher will divide your class into three groups. One group will act as lawyers for Mr. Allen, one group will act as lawyers for the government, and one group will act as judges considering the case on appeal. To prepare for the hearing, each group should read the background of the case, consider the facts involved, and answer the three questions on benefits and costs on p. 38.

Illinois v. Allen

On August 12, 1956, William Allen walked into a tavern and took $200 from the bartender at gunpoint. Later that day, police arrested Allen. The bartender identified him as the robber.

Since he could not afford to hire his own attorney, the court offered Allen a choice between the public defender or an attorney from the Bar Association Defense Committee. Allen refused both. He asked to represent himself. The judge told Allen, "I'll let you be your own lawyer, but I'll ask Mr. Kelly (a court-appointed lawyer) to sit in and protect your rights."

The trial began on September 9, 1957. Allen questioned the first potential juror at great length. Finally, the trial judge interrupted. He told Allen to ask questions only about the person's qualifications. At that point Allen began to argue with the judge in a very disrespectful way.

Then the judge asked Kelly to continue examining the jurors. Allen continued to talk, saying that Kelly was not going to act as his lawyer. He said to the judge, "When I go for lunch, you're going to be a corpse here." Then Allen tore up his attorney's files and threw the papers on the floor.

The trial judge said, "One more outbreak of that sort and I'll remove you from the courtroom." Allen ignored the warning.

What might be some consequences when a judge orders an unruly defendant removed from the courtroom? Which consequences would be benefits, which would be costs?

"There's not going to be no trial," Allen said. "You can bring your shackles and straitjacket and put them on me and tape my mouth, but it will do no good because there's not going to be no trial."

The judge ordered the court officers to remove Allen from the courtroom. The jury was selected without Allen present. Later, when the jury was not present, the judge brought Allen into the courtroom. Allen said that he wanted to be in the courtroom during his trial. The judge said that he would permit Allen to remain if he did not interfere with the presentation of the case.

The jury came in and sat down. Allen stood up and said, "There is going to be no proceeding. I'm going to start talking and I'm going to keep on talking all through the trial." The trial judge again ordered the bailiff to remove Allen from the courtroom.

After this second removal, Allen remained out of the courtroom except when they brought him in for witnesses to identify. During one of these appearances, Allen used obscene language to the judge. After the prosecution presented its case, the judge again told Allen that he could return to the courtroom whenever he agreed to conduct himself properly. Allen promised that he would conduct himself properly, but due to the way he had behaved, the court officers bound and gagged him during the presentation of his defense.

What are the benefits and costs of a judge's order to bind and gag an unruly defendant in the case?

The jury found Allen guilty of armed robbery. He was sentenced to ten to thirty years in prison.

Allen appealed his conviction, and his case eventually reached the Supreme Court of the United States. Allen claimed that the trial judge had conducted the trial unfairly and had deprived him of rights guaranteed by the Sixth Amendment of the Constitution. Specifically, Allen claimed that the Constitution gave him the right to be present at his own trial and to act as his own lawyer. He also argued that his trial was fundamentally unfair because he was bound and gagged during the presentation of his defense.

What do *you* think?

1. What might be the consequences of the trial judge's exercise of authority in this case? Consider the judge's decisions

    ■ to require Allen to be represented by an attorney

    ■ to remove Allen from the courtroom

    ■ to require Allen to be bound and gagged during the presentation of his defense

2. Which consequences are costs?

3. Which consequences are benefits?

Preparation for the Hearings

Consider the following question: In view of the benefits and costs involved, was the trial judge justified in requiring an attorney to represent Allen; in ordering Allen's removal from the courtroom; in ordering Allen to be bound and gagged during the presentation of his defense?

Group 1: You represent lawyers for the government.

Group 2: You represent lawyers for Mr. Allen.

Group 3: You represent judges hearing the case on appeal.

Each group should discuss the issues from their assigned point of view and prepare arguments to present before the judges. Judges should review the case and prepare questions to ask each side.

Procedures for the Appeal Hearings

1. After the preparation period, the class will be divided into "triads"—or small groups of three students. Each triad will consist of a judge, a lawyer for Mr. Allen, and a lawyer for the government.

2. The judge will call the hearing to order. Each side will have six minutes to present its arguments. The lawyer for Mr. Allen should go first. During the arguments, the judge may interrupt to ask questions. After each side has presented its arguments and been questioned by the judge, a two-minute rebuttal may be presented by each side. Again, the lawyer for Mr. Allen should go first. Finally, the judge should make his or her decision and explain the reasoning that supports it.

3. The class as a whole should then discuss the case. Begin the discussion by having judges report their decisions to the class as a whole. Did all the judges reach the same conclusion? Which arguments were perceived to be the strongest? Finally, the class should discuss the process that was used in the triads, which is similar to the process actually used in an appellate court. Is it fair? Why or why not? What changes would you suggest to make it better?

Using the Lesson

1. Write a letter to the editor supporting or opposing the position taken by the judges. Defend your position in terms of the benefits and costs involved in the case.

2. Interview someone who is in a position of authority (school principal, police officer, city official, etc.). Ask this person to describe some of the benefits and costs of his or her exercise of authority. Then interview someone who this person's authority affects (student, citizen, or resident of the city). Ask this person to describe some of the benefits and costs of the exercise of authority. Compare your two lists of benefits and costs. Write a report describing the similarities and differences.

Unit Five: What Should Be the Scope and Limits of Authority?

What might be the proper scope and limits of authority of a president, such as Harry Truman, and a commander in the field, such as General Douglas MacArthur during World War II?

Purpose of Unit

Some of the most important issues we face as citizens involve questions about the scope (extent) and limits of authority. Is a particular position of authority well designed? Does it give enough power to the person in charge while establishing effective limits to prevent abuse of that power?

In this unit you will learn some ways to evaluate positions of authority. You will decide if the duties, powers, privileges, and limitations of a position of authority have been well planned or if they should be changed. Finally you will put into practice what you have been studying. You will design a position of authority.

LESSON 10

What Makes a Well-Designed Position of Authority?

Purpose of Lesson

This lesson introduces you to a set of intellectual tools useful in evaluating both positions of authority and institutions that have authority. When you have completed the lesson, you should be able to use these tools in evaluating and suggesting improvements for positions of authority.

Terms to Know

scope
limits
humane

What makes a position of authority well designed?

By now you must have realized that people in positions of authority affect you in important ways every day. Parents, teachers, and school officials make decisions and take actions that can influence your life. Our local, state, and federal governments are run largely by people in positions of authority. These include such diverse positions as crossing guard, police officer, judge, member of Congress, and president. We, the people of the United States, have given great responsibilities and powers to many of these people. We hope that these powers will make them able to provide us with the services we want and need.

Some of the most important issues we face as citizens involve questions about the positions of authority in our system.

People have different opinions about whether some positions of authority are well designed. People have different opinions about whether certain positions have too much or too little authority.

One thing is certain. Because people in positions of authority affect our lives so much, it is important to plan and evaluate what their duties, powers, privileges, and limitations should be. If we fail to consider how positions of authority are designed, it can lead to consequences that could threaten the basic freedoms on which our nation was founded.

■ What historical or contemporary examples can you give of positions of authority that were poorly designed? What were the flaws in these positions of authority? What were the consequences of these flaws?

■ Why might it be important to evaluate positions of authority?

Critical Thinking Exercise
EVALUATING ERRORS IN DESIGNING A POSITION OF AUTHORITY

The list below describes several positions of authority. Each position has something wrong with it. Read the list and answer the questions that follow.

1. The constitution of the state of Confusion said that the governor had to make all the laws, deliver the mail, sweep the streets, patrol for stray animals, preside over all criminal trials, and run the television station.

Do you think the governor of the State of Confusion has too much or too little authority?

2. In the state of Perpetua, all members of the legislature were appointed for life. They could not be removed from office no matter what they did.

3. When Leroy Hawkins was appointed Boot City High's monitor by the principal, she gave him complete authority over students in the halls. She said he could make them do anything he wanted.

4. The newly elected mayor of Agoraphobia City would not allow any citizen to speak to him or write him letters. While he was mayor, he locked himself in his office and took the phone off the hook.

5. The city council hired six traffic control officers to enforce the speeding laws. It did not give the officers any police cars, motorcycles, or whistles.

6. The Grand Inquisitor was like a judge. His job was to determine guilt or innocence. He often tortured those accused of crimes to force confessions out of them. Innocent people confessed just to escape the pains of torture.

What do *you* think?

1. What is wrong with each position of authority described above?

2. Look at each weakness you identified. What do these weaknesses suggest about what to include in a well-designed position of authority?

How should we determine the scope and limits of authority?

The preceding activity should give you some insight into what can go wrong if a position of authority is designed badly. How can we prevent such problems? Below are eight questions—intellectual tools—you can use to evaluate the scope and limits of a particular position of authority. Work with a study partner or in small groups to review the intellectual tools and to answer the what do you think questions. Be prepared to share your answers with the class.

1. What is the position to be evaluated?

2. What is the purpose or purposes of the position?

3. Is the position necessary to accomplish these purposes?

4. What are the duties, powers, privileges, and limitations of the position?

5. What are some of the probable effects of the position as it is now designed?

6. What are the strengths and weaknesses of the position?

   - Is it well designed to achieve its purposes?
   - Does it have enough power—adequate but not excessive?
   - Are there ways to hold people in the position accountable for what they do?
   - Is the position overburdened with duties?
   - Are sufficient resources available to accomplish the duties of the position?
   - Is there a reasonable degree of public access and input?
   - Must the position use fair and humane procedures in the exercise of its powers?
   - Is the position designed to protect such rights as freedom and privacy?
   - Is the position designed so that people are likely to help with the exercise of its powers?

7. How could you change the position to correct any weaknesses you have identified?

8. Should the position be kept as it is, changed, or eliminated? Explain your decision about the position in terms of the strengths and weaknesses involved.

What do *you* think?

1. How might this set of intellectual tools be useful in evaluating positions of authority?

2. Why is it important to be able to evaluate positions of authority?

Using the Lesson

1. Select a position of authority that you have seen on television or read about in a newspaper, magazine, or book. Use the intellectual tools you have just learned in this lesson to evaluate the position.

2. Write a short story describing what might happen in a country where the position of president has not been planned well.

LESSON 11

How Would You Evaluate This Position of Authority?

Purpose of Lesson

In this lesson you role-play a naval review board hearing that has been convened to consider the authority of a ship's captain. You evaluate this position of authority using the intellectual tools you studied in the last lesson.

When you have completed the lesson, you should be able to explain and defend the position you have taken on the authority of a ship's captain.

Terms to Know

flogging

Critical Thinking Exercise
EVALUATING A POSITION OF AUTHORITY

The following selection has been adapted from Richard Henry Dana's book, *Two Years Before the Mast* (1840). It tells of a young sailor's adventures at sea. The problem described by the sailor in "A Flogging at Sea" was probably not an isolated incident. Therefore, the Naval Review Board wanted to evaluate the authority held by ship's captains.

Your teacher will divide your class into groups and assign each group one of the following roles:

- Narrator
- Captain
- Sam, a sailor
- John, a sailor
- Naval Review Board

First, each group will read the "Background," the "Job Description," "A Flogging at Sea," and the "Postscript" and then complete the intellectual tool chart on p. 46. Next, the groups representing characters in the story will develop testimony to present to the Naval Review Board, and will select a spokesperson to present the group's testimony. All group members should be prepared to answer questions from the Naval Review Board, however. Meanwhile, the group playing the Naval

How much authority should a ship's captain be given?

Review Board will develop questions to ask each group and will select a chairperson to conduct the hearing. After all groups have presented their testimony, the Naval Review Board should discuss the scope and limits of the authority of a ship's captain, and decide whether to make any changes in the position, keep it as it is, or eliminate it. The Board should explain its decision to the class.

The Background

The year is 1840. The Naval Review Board has decided to examine problems that occur on sailing ships and decide what should be done about them. Recently, a new problem has come to the board's attention because of a story written by a sailor. The story raises questions about the limits of authority of a ship's captain.

The Naval Review Board will conduct a hearing to evaluate the position of the ship's captain and gather suggestions for ways to improve the position. To help you do this, you will have the following:

- a ship's captain's job description

- the sailor's story, "A Flogging at Sea"

- an intellectual tool chart that will help you evaluate the position and make suggestions for improvement

If you served on a Naval Review Board, what information would you need before suggesting changes in the authority of a ship's captain?

Ship's Captain: A Job Description

Duties and Powers. A ship's captain has the duty and the power to do the following:

- supervise the running of the ship

- decide the course of the ship

- assign people to different jobs on board ship

- settle disagreements among sailors

- punish sailors who break rules

- decide who will receive special privileges (such as shore leave)

- write reports to the ship's owners

- keep a daily log of the ship's progress

- represent the ship's owners whenever the ship reaches a foreign port

Privileges. A ship's captain is entitled to receive the following:

- a salary from the ship's owners and a percentage of the profits from the voyage

- a special uniform

- a private cabin

- specially prepared food

Limitations. A ship's captain may not do the following:

- risk the success of the voyage

- break the law of the land in a foreign port

- punish by death sailors who have broken rules

A Flogging at Sea

The captain of our ship had been losing his temper about a lot of little things. He threatened to flog the cook for throwing wood on deck. He became furious when the first mate bragged that he could tie knots better than the captain. He directed most of his anger to a large man called Sam. Sam could not speak very well and he was a little slow. Yet he was a pretty good sailor and tried his best. The captain just didn't like him.

One Saturday morning, I heard him shouting at someone. Then I heard noises that sounded like a fight.

"You may well keep still, for I have you," said the captain. "Will you ever talk back to me again?"

"I never did, sir," said Sam.

"That's not what I asked you. Will you ever talk back to me again?"

"I never did, sir," Sam repeated.

"Answer my question or I'll make a spread eagle of you! I'll flog you!" The captain was almost beside himself with anger.

"I'm no slave," said Sam.

"Then I'll make you one," said the captain. He sprang to the deck and called to the first mate, "Tie that man up! Make a spread eagle of him! I'll teach you all who is the master of this ship!" The mate took Sam to the deck. Sam did not struggle.

"What are you going to flog that man for, sir?" said John, a sailor to the captain. The captain turned and ordered other sailors to put him in irons.

By this time the first mate had tied Sam, taken off his jacket, and bared his back. The captain stood a few feet away so he could have a good swing at him. In his hand he held a thick, strong rope.

Watching this made me feel sick. I wanted to stop it, but there were only a few others who felt as I did. The captain and his officers outnumbered us. If we started a fight, we would lose. Then they would accuse us of mutiny. Even if we could win, they would brand us as pirates for life. If they ever caught us, they would severely punish us. A sailor has no rights. He has to do whatever the captain orders, or he becomes a mutineer or pirate.

Swinging as hard as he could, the captain lashed into poor Sam's back. Six times he struck Sam with the rope.

"Will you ever talk back to me again?" shouted the captain.

Sam said nothing. Three more times the captain flogged him. Finally he cut Sam down and sent him to the front of the ship.

"Now you," said the captain, walking to John and taking off the irons. The first mate tied John and the captain prepared to flog him.

"Why are you flogging me, sir?" asked John. "Have I ever refused my duty? Have I ever been lazy or talked back?"

"No," answered the captain, "I'm flogging you because you ask questions."

"Aren't I allowed to ask questions?" asked John.

"No!" shouted the captain. "I will not allow anyone to do anything unless I tell them to." He started flogging John. He reached way back to hit harder and harder. The more he flogged, the wilder he became. I was horrified. I couldn't watch anymore. At last the captain stopped and the first mate cut John down. The captain turned to the rest of us.

"Now you see how things are! Now you know who I am! I'm the slave driver and you are my slaves! I'll make you all do as I say or I'll flog the lot of you!"

Postscript

Those who have followed me in my narrative will remember that I was witness to an act of great cruelty inflicted upon my own shipmates; and indeed the simple mention of the word flogging brings up in me feelings which I can hardly control. Yet, when the proposition is made to abolish it entirely and at once; to prohibit the captain from ever, under any circumstances, inflicting corporal punishment, I am obliged to pause.

I should not wish to take the command of a ship tomorrow and know, and have my crew know, that I could not, under any circumstances, inflict even moderate chastisement. I should trust that I might never have to resort to it; and, indeed, I scarcely know what risk I would not run, and to what inconvenience I would not subject myself, rather than do so. Yet not to have the power of holding it up as a threat and indeed of protecting myself, and all under my charge, by it, if some extreme case should arise, would be a situation I should not wish to be placed in myself, or to take the responsibility of placing another in.

Using the Lesson

1. Can you think of any circumstances that might require someone to have absolute authority? If so, what are they? Why do they require unchecked power to be used at the sole discretion of the person in authority?

2. As a class project, arrange to have a person in a position of authority (police officer, judge, district attorney, public defender, or mayor) visit your classroom. Ask that person to describe and evaluate the duties, powers, privileges, and limitations of the authority of his or her position.

Intellectual Tool Chart for Evaluating Positions of Authority

Questions	Answers
1. What position of authority is to be evaluated?	
2. What is the purpose of the position?	
3. Is the position necessary? Why or why not?	
4. What are the duties, powers, privileges, and limitations of the position?	
5. What might be the consequences of this position as it is designed?	
6. What are the weaknesses (if any) in the way the position is designed? Consider: ■ number of duties ■ resources provided ■ grant and limitation ■ accountability ■ controls to prevent misuse of authority ■ requirement of fair procedures and respect for important values	
7. What changes would you suggest to improve the position? What would be the benefits and costs of these changes?	
8. Do you think the position should be eliminated, left as it is, or changed? Explain your reasoning.	

LESSON 12

What Should Be the Scope and Limits of Authority During Wartime?

Purpose of Lesson

In this lesson you consider two examples of the use of authority during wartime. The first concerns President Lincoln's exercise of authority at the beginning of the Civil War. The second concerns the government's treatment of Japanese Americans during World War II. Then you participate in a debate on the issue of what the limits of authority should be during wartime.

When you have completed the lesson, you should be able to explain and defend the positions you have taken on the use of authority during wartime.

Terms to Know

dilemma	espionage
secede	sabotage
proclamation	internment camp
blockade	writ of habeas corpus

Critical Thinking Exercise

EXAMINING THE SCOPE AND LIMITS OF AUTHORITY DURING WARTIME

As you read these selections, think about the following question: Under what circumstances, if any, should a person in authority go beyond the normal limits of his or her authority? Work in small groups to answer the "What do you think?" questions that follow each selection.

Lincoln's Dilemma

Abraham Lincoln stood alone in his White House office one April night in 1861. He was facing a terrible dilemma. Hostility between the northern and southern states had been increasing, especially over the issue of slavery. Seven southern states had those officially withdrawn, from the United States. Southern troops had occupied federal forts and navy yards in the states. War seemed inevitable.

What might be the proper limits to presidential authority during wartime?

Then it happened. On April 12, 1861, Confederate troops fired on Fort Sumter at Charleston, South Carolina. Northern troops returned the fire. The Civil War had begun. Lincoln hoped that he could end the war in a short time and save the Union. He knew that to end the war quickly, he would have to act fast and perhaps take some actions unauthorized by the Constitution.

This was Lincoln's dilemma: He had sworn "an oath registered in Heaven" to uphold and defend the Constitution. He also had promised his fellow citizens to save the Union. He believed that without the Union, the Constitution would be little more than a scrap of paper. He believed that this threat to the nation's existence called for the exercise of the government's powers of self-preservation.

On April 15, 1861, Lincoln issued a proclamation calling 75,000 members of the state militias to fight the Southern rebellion. In that same proclamation, Lincoln called for

Congress to convene on July 4, almost three months later. Lincoln was determined to bring an end to the war without interference from Congress or anyone else.

On April 19, Lincoln ordered a blockade on the seaports of all seceded states. On April 20, he ordered an additional nineteen vessels for the naval fleets. He extended the blockade to the ports of North Carolina and Virginia.

On May 3, he issued a nationwide call for 42,000 volunteers and enlarged the regular army by 24,000 and the navy by 18,000. This proclamation was contrary to Article I of the Constitution that gives Congress the power to "raise and support armies" and "to provide and maintain a navy."

On April 20, he directed the Secretary of the Treasury to pay $2 million to three private individuals in New York to provide supplies for the military, even though the Constitution provides, "no money shall be drawn from the Treasury but in consequence of appropriations made by law." Lincoln said that this move was necessary because there were so many disloyal persons in the government.

Lincoln also took steps to maintain public order in the North and to prevent interference with the war effort. He authorized the suspension of the writ of habeas corpus in certain areas; this meant that people could be arrested and held without any opportunity to go before a judge. He forbade the post office to process "treasonable correspondence."

When Congress met on July 4, Lincoln greeted them with a special message asking for approval of his actions. In his paper he argued that every constitutional government must have the power of self-preservation and that in the American government the president exercised this power. In this message, he wrote about his actions since April 12:

> These measures, whether strictly legal or not, were ventured upon under what appeared to be a popular demand and a public necessity....

What do *you* think?

1. How did President Lincoln's exercise of authority exceed the scope and limits of the constitutional authority of his position?

2. What arguments can you make to justify President Lincoln's actions? What values and interests underlie these arguments?

3. What arguments can you make to oppose President Lincoln's actions? What values and interests underlie these arguments?

4. Why might it be important to limit the authority of government officials? If we allow exceptions to these limits, why might it be important to clearly define the circumstances under which we permit the exceptions?

The Internment of Japanese Americans

Following the Japanese attack on Pearl Harbor in December 1941, the United States entered World War II by declaring war against Japan, Germany, and Italy. Never in the history of the nation had the American people faced such a difficult military challenge. The United States had to fight major wars in two faraway parts of the globe: Europe and the Far East. Conducting a war on two fronts simultaneously was extremely difficult, but most Americans believed that they were fighting for their country's freedom and security. They believed that the future of the nation was in their hands.

What were the consequences when the government used its authority to relocate citizens of Japanese ancestry to internment camps during World War II?

At the time of the Pearl Harbor attack, more than 125,000 Japanese Americans lived in the United States, mostly on

the West Coast. More than two-thirds of these people were United States citizens. Although there never had been a case of espionage or sabotage by an American of Japanese descent, many people feared that it could happen. Japanese Americans had long suffered from racial discrimination and prejudice in the United States. The situation worsened with the attack on Pearl Harbor. Shocked by the early Japanese victories in the South Pacific, many Americans feared that the Japanese might invade the West Coast.

On February 19, 1942, President Roosevelt responded to this fear by issuing an executive order. This order allowed American military commanders to relocate people of Japanese ancestry from the West Coast to camps further inland. The relocation program made no distinction between citizens and aliens.

The presidential executive order also gave military commanders the authority to declare certain places "military areas." The military commander could, at his discretion, exclude anyone from these military areas to prevent spying or sabotage. On March 2, 1942, Congress passed a law stating that anyone in a military area who disobeyed the orders of the military commander of that area could be sent to prison, fined, or both.

On May 3, 1942, General De Witt, the commander of the San Leandro, California, military area, issued Civilian Exclusion Order No. 34. This order stated that after May 9, 1942, all persons of Japanese ancestry would be excluded from San Leandro. The order said that the reason for this exclusion was the possibility of the "presence of. . . disloyal [to the United States] members of the group." Before the end of 1942, the entire West Coast had been declared a "military area," and persons of Japanese descent had been ordered to internment camps by similar exclusion orders.

During the war, the military forcibly moved approximately 120,000 Japanese Americans from their homes to internment camps further inland. No charges were filed against these individuals; no claim of actual espionage or sabotage, or of any other crime, was asserted to justify their relocation and internment. Most were required to remain in the internment camps for the duration of the war—essentially imprisoned for three years. Businesses had to be abandoned; homes and other property were similarly lost.

What do *you* think?

1. What were some consequences of the following three exercises of authority? Which consequences were benefits, and which were costs?

   - President Roosevelt's Executive Order of February 19, 1942

   - The law passed by Congress on March 2, 1942

   - Civilian Exclusion Order No. 34 issued by General De Witt on May 9, 1942

2. What might have been the consequences if President Roosevelt had lacked the authority to issue the Executive Order of February 19, 1942? If Congress had lacked the authority to pass the March 2, 1942 law? If General De Witt had lacked the authority to issue Civilian Exclusion Order No. 34?

3. Do you think the internment of Japanese Americans during World War II illustrates the need to relax constitutional limitations during wartime, or the need to maintain constitutional limitations even when the country is at war? Explain your position.

Preparing for a Class Debate

Now that you have considered the selections on pp. 47–49, your class will debate the following issue:

RESOLVED: That the president should be allowed to exceed the constitutional limits on his or her authority during wartime.

To prepare for the debate, your class will be divided into four groups, two on each side of the issue. One group on each side will present initial arguments supporting or opposing the resolution. The other group on each side will present rebuttal arguments, responding to and challenging the initial arguments the group anticipates the other side will make. Each group will have five minutes to make its presentation, and should select two or three spokespersons to present the group's arguments. The remainder of each group, after participating in the preparation of the group's presentation, will form the audience for the debate.

Conducting the Debate

One student from the audience should be selected to serve as the moderator of the debate, and another should serve as timekeeper. The moderator will briefly introduce the topic, and state the resolution to be debated. The group presenting initial arguments in favor of the resolution will make their presentation first, followed by the group presenting initial arguments against the resolution. The order is reversed for rebuttal arguments, with the group presenting arguments against the resolution going first,

followed by the group presenting arguments in favor of the resolution. At the conclusion of the debate, the audience may vote on the resolution. The class as a whole should discuss how the debate affected their views on the issue, which arguments were persuasive, which were not, and why.

Using the Lesson

1. Issues regarding the internment of Japanese Americans during World War II reached the United States Supreme Court in the cases of *Hirabayashi v. United States*, 320 U.S. 81 (1943), *Korematsu v. United States*, 323 U.S. 214 (1944), and *Ex parte Endo*, 323 U.S. 283 (1944). Find out what happened in these cases, and report what you learn to the class. In your report, be sure to explain your views about how the Supreme Court dealt with the cases.

2. What might be the dangers of allowing limitations on authority to be superseded in emergencies? Before World War II, the German Constitution contained "emergency" provisions (Articles 25 and 48) which were instrumental in Hitler's assumption of dictatorial powers. Do research to find out what these emergency provisions authorized, what safeguards and limitations existed to prevent abuse of these emergency provisions, and evaluate why these safeguards and limitations proved ineffective.

3. Work with several classmates to prepare a simulated television interview with a Japanese American citizen who the government forced to live in an internment camp. In preparation for the interview, you may do additional research on the camps. Your teacher can suggest books for you to read.

LESSON 13

How Would You Design a Position of Authority?

Purpose of Lesson

In this lesson you use the knowledge and skills you have acquired to decide the scope and limits of authority of a particular position. When you have completed this lesson you should be able to design the duties, powers, privileges, and limitations of a position of authority.

Term to Know

hypothetical

Critical Thinking Exercise

DESIGNING A POSITION OF AUTHORITY

Your class will be dealing with a problem in a hypothetical school known as Taft High. Read the story below and divide into small groups of about three to five students. Each group will act as one of the student government committees assigned to develop a new position of authority at Taft High. Members of each group should read the "Directions for the Committees" and answer the questions. After each group has made its presentation, the class should discuss what would be the best solution to the problem at Taft High.

A Problem at Taft High School

There had been a student government at Taft High School for several years. Each semester students elected a student body president and representatives from each homeroom. The student government had the right to make some school rules and to plan special events such as sports activities and dances. Most of the students, teachers, and school administrators thought the student government did a good job.

During the past two years, trouble had been developing at the school. More students were breaking school rules, the number of fights had increased, and a feeling of

tension replaced the previous easy-going atmosphere. In some cases, the principal accused students of breaking into lockers and stealing. There were rumors of certain students carrying weapons. The student restrooms were becoming dangerous places.

How would you design a position of authority to deal with violence and rule-breaking at school?

For many years, teachers and administrators had the responsibility of dealing with students accused of breaking rules. The law required them to take this responsibility. The increase in fighting and rule-breaking was creating a difficult situation for teachers. Many believed that they were spending more time disciplining students than teaching them. They thought that this was unfair to the students who wanted to learn.

How teachers dealt with discipline problems sometimes upset students. They believed that some teachers did not give a fair hearing to those accused of breaking rules. Most students agreed that teachers were too busy to take the time necessary to hear all sides of a dispute.

What might be the proper scope and limits of a position of authority to deal with violence and rule-breaking at school?

Many students believed that something should be done to improve the situation. At a student government meeting they discussed the problem of how to give suspected rule-breakers a fair hearing. Members of the student government, a number of teachers, and members of the school administration also attended the meeting. After a long discussion of the problems facing the school, the principal, Ms. Willis, spoke.

"We have a pretty good idea of the problem facing us," she said. "I want to turn its solution over to you, the student government. If your recommendations are reasonable, I'll go with them. Remember that under state law I must maintain order at this school. So whatever you decide must agree with the law."

Everyone agreed that Ms. Willis's suggestion was fair. After the administrators and teachers left, one student suggested they needed a position of authority. The others agreed, and the student representatives broke into committees to work on the task of designing a position of authority for Taft High.

Directions for the Committees

Each group should act as one of the student government committees assigned the job of developing a new position of authority at Taft High School. Select a chairperson to lead your discussion and a recorder to take notes. Use the chart on p. 53 to assist you in designing a position of authority. Read, discuss, and answer each question in the chart carefully.

When you have completed the chart, prepare a description of a new position at Taft High. Have the chairperson of your committee present your plan to the rest of the class. The presentation should include the following:

- a statement of the purpose of the position

- a description of the position listing its duties, powers, privileges, and limitations

- a statement of the probable consequences (costs and benefits) of creating the position

The class should discuss the strengths and weaknesses of each proposed position and attempt to reach a consensus on the design of a new position of authority for Taft High.

Using the Lesson

1. Did you agree with your class decision on designing a position of authority for Taft High? Write a letter to the editor of the Taft High newspaper either supporting or opposing the new position for the school.

2. Think about a problem in your neighborhood or town that creating a position of authority might help. Use what you have learned in this unit to design a position of authority to help solve this problem.

Intellectual Tool Chart for Designing Positions of Authority

Questions	Answers
1. What problem or problems are you trying to solve?	
2. Would establishing a position of authority help, or are there better ways to deal with the problem? Explain your views.	
3. What type of position of authority is your group suggesting: ■ one position or more than one? ■ individual or committee? ■ elected or appointed? Explain the reasons for your choices.	
4. What duties, powers, privileges, and limitations should the position of authority have? Consider: ■ number of duties ■ resources provided ■ grant and limitation of power ■ accountability ■ controls to prevent misuse of authority ■ requirement of fair procedures and respect for important values	
5. What would be the consequences of having such a position of authority? Consider the benefits and costs of the position as you have designed it.	

LESSON 14

What Should Be the Limits on Challenging Authority?

Purpose of Lesson

This final lesson on authority provides an opportunity to evaluate the limits on challenging authority. You examine an act of civil disobedience adapted from the ancient Greek tragedy *Antigone*, written by Sophocles. The class debates the propriety of disobeying a law in order to follow the dictates of one's conscience.

When you have completed the lesson, you should be able to evaluate, take, and defend positions on what the limits should be on challenging authority.

Terms to Know

civil disobedience
higher law

What is the American tradition of civil disobedience?

In Unit Five you learned how to determine the scope and limits of a position of authority. You have seen what can happen when a position of authority is designed badly or when a person holding such a position misuses or abuses authority. The framers of our Constitution understood the importance of limiting authority. That is why they created the system of shared powers and checks and balances in our Constitution. They designed the Bill of Rights to further protect individual liberties against possible abuse by those in authority.

Our constitutional system of government is based on majority rule, but it also protects individual rights and the rights of minorities. It allows those who do not agree with the decisions of the government to protest those decisions and try to change them. The following are some of the ways people can express their opinions:

- voting

- writing letters to the media or to a public official

- signing petitions

- joining a protest group or political organization

Which forms of protest are acceptable, and which forms of protest are not?

- marching in demonstrations

- participating in boycotts

What happens when such forms of protest are not enough? What if you believe that it is against your moral or religious principles to support a law and all your legal efforts to change that law have failed? What choices do you have? How far should a person go in challenging authority?

These are very difficult questions. For centuries philosophers and scholars have been trying to find the answers. Throughout history, people have refused to obey laws they believed were unjust or morally wrong and have chosen to suffer the consequences of their actions, no matter how severe. Some people have chosen to engage in rebellion or revolution; others have looked to less violent forms of protest.

Civil disobedience is a form of nonviolent protest. It is an act done in defiance of a law or policy of the government to bring about change. Civil disobedience involves a willingness to accept the consequences involved. When we talk about civil disobedience, we are not simply talking about breaking the law. We are talking about a deliberate protest of a law or policy believed to be unjust. Such protest can take many forms. It may be a decision to do the following:

- not pay taxes

- burn a draft card

- help fugitive slaves
- chain oneself to a nuclear power plant

Civil disobedience is deeply rooted in the history of the United States and has, in some instances, led to profound changes in the Constitution. The abolitionists refused to recognize laws that supported slavery and preferred jail to a system they believed was immoral. They preferred to follow the "higher law" of their own religious and moral principles rather than the authority of the government.

Leaders of the woman suffrage, civil rights, and antiwar movements also chose to disobey laws and go to jail rather than support laws they believed were wrong. Rev. Martin Luther King, Jr., who was greatly influenced by the teachings of Mohandas Gandhi, wrote in his *Letter from Birmingham City Jail,* "I submit that an individual who breaks a law that his conscience tells him is unjust, and willingly accepts the penalty by staying in jail to arouse the conscience of the community over its injustice, is in reality expressing the very highest respect for the law."

What questions did Mohandas Gandhi have to consider in choosing to use civil disobedience to challenge the authority of India's government during the 1940s?

Civil disobedience is an extreme choice made only when there seems to be no other alternative. When is it an appropriate choice? In this lesson you will consider the limits on challenging authority. You may never engage in an act of civil disobedience, but you may very well confront laws that you believe are against your moral or religious principles. The following activity will help you

think about some questions you should consider in such a situation. It will give you some tools to deal with a very difficult subject.

Critical Thinking Exercise
TAKING A POSITION ON THE CIVIL DISOBEDIENCE IN ANTIGONE

Read the story below, then follow the instructions for a class debate. The story is adapted from the Greek tragedy *Antigone,* written by Sophocles in 442 B.C. It tells of a young woman, Antigone, who violates a law to follow the dictates of her conscience and suffers the consequences.

The Tragedy of *Antigone*

When Antigone was about eighteen years old, her uncle Creon became ruler of Thebes, an important city in ancient Greece. Both Antigone and Creon were strong-willed; both believed deeply in what they thought was right. Because neither would give in to the other, they brought great tragedy on both themselves and their city.

When is it right to disobey political authority? Antigone answered that question to her own satisfaction and died for it. Creon had a different answer and lost everything he loved.

Creon's Decree

Before Creon became king of Thebes, his brother Oedipus ruled the land. The former king had two daughters, Antigone and Ismene, and two sons, Eteocles and Polyneices. Tragedy drove Oedipus from the land, and Thebes was left without a ruler. The citizens of Thebes held an election and chose Eteocles to be king.

Polyneices believed that since he was the older brother it was his right to rule the land. The two brothers quarreled and Eteocles banished Polyneices, who pledged revenge. Polyneices left Thebes and gathered a large army to fight for the throne.

Polyneices and his army returned to Thebes and waged a fierce attack against the city. It was a long and bitter civil war, with brother fighting against brother. During the course of the war, many died and much property was destroyed. Finally, Polyneices and Eteocles fought and killed each other.

Once again, the people of Thebes were without a ruler. So they elected Creon king. Creon spoke to the people and reminded them about what happened when authority was ignored. He told them that for the good of their land, they must learn from this sad time. As an example, he decreed that Eteocles was to receive a hero's funeral, while Polyneices, who fought against Thebes, was to rot on the field of battle. No person could erect a gravestone in Polyneices' memory; no person could mourn for him. Any person who disobeyed this decree and buried Polyneices's body would be put to death.

The people of Thebes debated the wisdom of Creon's decree. On one side, many believed it was a sacred duty to bury the dead. According to their beliefs, unburied souls were doomed to wander alone throughout eternity. Others believed that Creon's decree was justified because the city had suffered from rebels and lawbreakers. Polyneices's fate would serve as an example to those who did not respect the authority of the state.

A Higher Law

Antigone, Polyneices's sister, passionately believed that the laws of the gods were higher and more important than the laws of the state. She intended to follow the laws of the gods and bury her brother. Antigone attempted to convince Ismene to join her.

"Do you mean to bury our brother's body, Antigone, when it is forbidden by law?" Ismene asked her sister.

"If you will not join me, I will do your share too," Antigone replied. "I will never be false to my brother!"

"Are you not going too far, exceeding the limits," Ismene asked, "when you do what Creon, who is the king, has forbidden?"

"He has no right to keep me from observing sacred custom." Antigone spoke with great firmness.

"If we do as you wish and defy the law," Ismene continued, "we will find ourselves alone against the powers of the king and we will perish! Since we are forced to obey this law, we can ask the gods' forgiveness."

"Obey the law if you must, Ismene," said Antigone. "I will not urge you further to join me. But I will bury Polyneices without your help. If I am killed because of it, then so be it. My 'crime' will be no sin, for I owe a greater allegiance to the laws made by the gods than I do to those made by man. If you do not join me in my action, you will be guilty of dishonoring the gods' laws."

"I have no wish to dishonor the gods' laws, Antigone," Ismene replied, "but I have no strength to defy the state."

"Then I will act alone to honor the brother I love," Antigone said.

Punishment

As Antigone went to bury her brother, Creon entered the garden with two attendants. He was deeply worried about the decision he had just made.

"It is our loyalty to the state that is the highest good. Those who look on their friends or family as of greater worth than their city are wrong. They forget that it is the ship of state that carries us safely through life's stormy voyage and only while she prospers can we make true friends or live decently at all. Worse are those like my nephew Polyneices who turn against their own land and make war against it. No honor shall be given to them.

"These are my rules! That is why my edict honors all those who died in battle fighting for our city but forbids touching Polyneices, who made war against his own land. He tried to taste the blood of his own kin and make slaves of all the others; his body shall be left untouched, unmourned, and unburied as a mark of shame and dishonor. Only by these rules can our city be safe and prosper. Only by obedience to them can this city avoid civil war and ruin."

Suddenly, a guard burst into the garden and brought news that Polyneices had been buried. Creon angrily gave orders to find the guilty person. The guard returned with Antigone in custody.

"I caught this woman in the act of burying the body of Polyneices."

Creon turned to his niece Antigone and asked if she denied trying to bury Polyneices's body. She did not deny it.

Creon now said to Antigone, "Tell me, did you not know that there is a law forbidding what you did; and if you did know, why did you disobey it? You are my niece and are soon to marry my son, Haemon. How can this be?"

"I knew the law," Antigone answered. "It was public knowledge. As for why I did it, hear this: It was not Zeus, king of the gods, who published that edict. Your law is not part of eternal justice, and I do not believe that your laws always compel me to obey. The unwritten laws of eternal justice are a higher law and in their name I disobeyed your lesser law.

"Antigone, it is my belief that a single unburied corpse is a fair payment for restoring peace and order to Thebes, but you refuse to accept that. So be it. You leave me no choice. Guards, take this woman from my sight and lock her away! She must not escape from her appointment with death!"

Haemon's Appeal

When Haemon, Antigone's fiance, heard what had happened, he went to his father Creon to beg for a pardon. Creon refused.

"Of all citizens of Thebes, I have found Antigone and Antigone alone disobedient to my law," Creon explained to Haemon. "If I do not kill her, I will look like a liar to my own people. The citizens of Thebes will think me weak. The public order, the state itself will be in jeopardy. I cannot have two rules, one for my kin and another for everyone else.

"My son, if this city is to survive, authority must be obeyed in small as well as great matters, even in unjust as well as just things. Disobedience is the worst of evils. It ruins cities. It makes wastelands out of homes."

After hearing his father speak, Haemon answered, "Father, hear me out. Far be it from me to say you are not right. Yet others—even I—may also have useful thoughts. I am your eyes and ears, and I can tell you what citizens fear to tell you to your face. Father, they are talking. I hear people murmuring in the dark; they are moaning for Antigone. They say she deserves reward not punishment for what she has done. Such is the dark rumor that spreads in secret.

"Those who are truly wise must know that there is a time to bend and not insist on their will. Don't you see, father, when the wind blows fiercely, the trees that yield to it save every twig, while the stiff and unbending perish root and branch? Spare Antigone, for if you kill her the people will turn against you."

"Is it your wish that I honor lawlessness?" asked Creon, "For that is what Antigone represents. Should I show respect for evil doers?" Said Haemon, "The people of Thebes with one voice deny that Antigone is evil. You have no authority, father, to disobey the gods' requirements. The gods have their own laws, superior to yours."

"Don't talk to me about laws, Haemon. The laws of this world hold together our city, our civilization. Civil war has torn apart our city. Our wounds are fresh and still unhealed. If Antigone has her way, it will mean that anyone can disobey whatever laws they decide are

"Your law is the law of today," she continued, "but the laws of heaven are for eternity, for all times and all places. No one even knows when they were first put forth. Eternal law commands that I bury my brother, Polyneices. I will die for doing so, but I would die someday in any case. Being put to death by you is of no importance to me. If I had allowed my brother to lie untouched, unburied, and uncared for, that would have disturbed me deeply. I am therefore not sorry for what I did."

"This brother of yours was attacking his own state!" Creon retorted. "There is no glory in aiding those who make treasonous attack on your own country, which ought to hold your highest loyalty and allegiance. What of your other brother, who died defending the state?"

"Nevertheless, the gods require what I have done," said Antigone. "In honoring the dead I follow a higher law than the law of the state. What is more, my fellow Thebeans agree with me, only fear seals their lips."

"The gods require no loyalty to such evil doers," said Creon.

"You cannot speak for the gods. Who can say that they don't agree with me?" replied Antigone.

"It is my duty to produce order and peace in this war-torn land," Creon went on. "Our city is still in danger, divided between the supporters of both your dead brothers. The fate of the rebel Polyneices must serve as a warning to all those who would disobey the laws and overthrow the state.

"You have thrown away your future happiness to bury one rebellious brother, Antigone. In disobeying the law on which the safety and well-being of the whole city depends, you make it impossible for me to avoid putting you to death."

wrong. If those who break the law go unpunished, our fragile civic order will be reduced to chaos. Even the innocent will suffer! We will be a lawless city, no different from barbarians."

Tragic Consequences

Creon ordered Antigone taken to a cave and abandoned. On the road to the cave that would be both prison and tomb, Antigone spoke to the crowd who had gathered to see her.

What might be the consequences of allowing Antigone to go unpunished for disobeying the laws of the state?

"See me, people of Thebes, citizens of my homeland," she called out. "See me setting out on my last journey, looking at sunlight for the last time. I will die unwed, unmourned, and friendless. What a miserable creature I am! As night follows the day, the fate I cannot escape has overtaken me. Why am I to die?"

Creon entered from the palace and said, "Citizens of Thebes, hear what I have to say. It is a sad command that I give, but one that I must. Antigone has knowingly defied the law of the state by attempting to bury Polyneices.

"If we allow people to defy the law," he continued, "our city will not survive. It is my duty, my solemn obligation as ruler, not to allow our city to be threatened by such a rebellious act. Antigone will therefore be taken to the mountain and imprisoned in a cave. Food will be left for her, but only enough to protect the reputation of Thebes against an accusation of excessive cruelty."

He turned to the woman before him and said, "Do you, Antigone, have any final words? "

"Only this, Creon. I am being sent to my death because I have chosen to obey the laws of heaven rather than those of earth. I know my reverence for the gods has offended you, but in my own mind and heart I feel I have not sinned; I have committed no crime. I have done no more than my duty. I will trust myself to the gods I have served, knowing that I have disobeyed no laws of theirs."

After the guards took Antigone away, a blind prophet warned Creon against putting Antigone to death. "The sun's chariot will race scarcely once across the sky before you pay for Antigone's fate with a corpse of your own flesh. Soon your house will be filled with wailing. You shall not escape my prophecy!"

If you were Creon, what questions might you ask in deciding whether to punish Antigone?

Finally, with great reluctance, Creon agreed to reverse his decision. It was too late. As he approached the prison cave, he heard his son Haemon's voice grieving for his beloved Antigone, who had hanged herself.

Looking in the cave, Creon saw his son weeping with his arms around his would-be bride. Creon begged his son to come away. But Haemon screamed curses at him and stabbed himself to death, clinging to Antigone in his last dying moments.

Not many hours later, a messenger arrived to tell Creon that the dimensions of the tragedy were even greater than he knew. When his wife heard of Haemon's death, she too took her life. Creon's life was in ruins. All that he loved was gone. He became a broken man longing for nothing more than the release of death.

Preparing for a Class Debate

Your teacher will divide your class into five groups:

- Group 1 will develop and present initial arguments for Creon's position.

- Group 2 will develop and present rebuttal arguments responding to the arguments made for Antigone's position.

- Group 3 will develop and present initial arguments for Antigone's position.

- Group 4 will develop and present rebuttal arguments responding to the arguments made for Creon's position.

- Group 5 will represent the citizens of Thebes, who will listen to the presentations of both sides, ask questions, and decide which groups have presented the better arguments.

Each group should follow the instructions below in preparing for the debate.

Group 1: Creon

Your group will defend Creon's position. Prepare your arguments and select spokespersons to present your arguments to the class.

Group 2: Creon's rebuttal

Your group will respond to the arguments made for Antigone's position. Anticipate what those arguments will be, prepare your rebuttal arguments, and select spokespersons to present your rebuttal argument to the class.

Group 3: Antigone

Your group will defend Antigone's position. Prepare your arguments and select spokespersons to present your arguments to the class.

Group 4: Antigone's rebuttal

Your group will respond to the arguments made for Creon's position. Anticipate what those arguments will be, prepare your rebuttal arguments and select spokespersons to present your rebuttal arguments to the class.

Group 5: Citizens of Thebes

Your group will represent the citizens of Thebes. You will question all the above groups to decide whose position you prefer.

Select a chairperson for your group. Develop a list of questions to evaluate the positions of the other groups and to challenge their arguments.

Conducting the Class Debate

1. After all groups have had time to prepare, the chairperson of the citizens' group should call the debate to order.

2. Each group will have five minutes to make its presentations, the order will be Group 1, Group 3, Group 4, Group 2. After each presentation, citizens of Thebes may ask questions.

3. Members of the group making the presentation may consult with each other before answering questions. Any member of the group may answer a question.

4. After each group has presented its arguments and answered questions, the citizens' group should meet to decide who made the most persuasive arguments. The chairperson should explain the group's decision to the class. The class should then discuss the decision of the citizens' group and answer the What do you think? questions on the next page.

What do *you* think?

1. What were the strengths and weaknesses of Creon's position? Of Antigone's?

2. Were there other effective ways for Antigone to protest Creon's law? If so, what were they?

3. What factors should be considered in deciding to disobey a law?

4. What if people of different religious or moral values disagree about the meaning of the higher law?

5. Do you think civil disobedience is ever justified? Explain your position.

Using the Lesson

1. Many states, including Michigan, have laws which prohibit assisting in suicide attempts. Dr. Jack Kevorkian openly violated Michigan's law, claiming that a higher law—the Constitution—gave people the right to end their own lives, and to have the assistance of a doctor in order to do so. Do research to find out what happened to Dr. Kevorkian, and report to the class what you learn.

2. During World War II, many people risked their lives by disobeying Nazi laws that required Jews to surrender themselves for deportation. For example, in Chambon-sur-Lignon, a village in the south of France, the entire town provided hiding places for Jewish refugees. In Denmark, leaders such as King Christian X and the Lutheran Bishop of Copenhagen publicly opposed the Nazi deportation laws, and with the crucial assistance of non-Jewish Danes more than nine-tenths of the Jewish population managed to escape to Sweden. Working with a group of classmates, do library research to learn more about these or other efforts to resist unjust Nazi laws, and prepare a skit to dramatize what happened. Perform your skit for the class, and then discuss the issues of authority that are involved.

PRIVACY
Table of Contents

Introduction

How have the Constitution and the Supreme Court protected the right to privacy?

"The right of the people to be secure in their persons, houses, papers, and effects, against unreasonable searches and seizures, shall not be violated ...."

The Fourth Amendment to the United States Constitution, quoted above, requires the government to respect our **right to privacy.** Today, the right to privacy includes much more than the protection of our homes and persons against unreasonable searches and seizures. The Supreme Court has recognized that privacy also involves being able to decide for ourselves what personal information we will share with others and how we will resolve certain issues that fundamentally affect our lives, such as whether we will marry or have children.

Although the Bill of Rights does not specifically refer to a right to privacy, the Supreme Court has found protections of privacy in the Fourth Amendment, in the Fifth Amendment's privilege against self-incrimination, in the Third Amendment's prohibition against housing soldiers in private homes, and in the First Amendment's protection of assembly and expression. Most impor-

tantly, the court has determined that the right to privacy is a fundamental part of the "liberty" guaranteed by the Fourteenth Amendment.

The right to privacy is an essential protection of human freedom and dignity. Privacy is valuable not only for itself, but also for the enjoyment of our rights to property and to freedom of thought, expression, religion, and conscience. Without the right to privacy, these other important rights would not mean very much at all.

But the right to privacy is not absolute; there are times when an individual's right to privacy must be limited to protect society's need for order and information. As Americans, we need to be able to think and decide for ourselves when it is reasonable to limit our right to privacy to protect other important interests of our society.

This study of privacy should help you gain a greater understanding of its importance. It should also help you deal more effectively with issues of privacy as they arise in your daily life as an individual in a free society.

Unit One: What Is the Importance of Privacy?

How do these photographs illustrate the importance of privacy?

Purpose of Unit

This unit will help you develop a greater understanding of the meaning and importance of privacy. You will learn to identify and describe examples of privacy in a variety of situations and to discriminate between situations in which privacy does and does not exist.

You also will learn some common ways people behave to protect their privacy, and you will examine the privacy needs of individuals and institutions.

LESSON 1

What Is Privacy?

What information about yourself are you willing to share with your classmates or a close friend? What information are you not willing to share at all?

Purpose of Lesson

This lesson introduces you to the importance of privacy and defines privacy as it is used in this textbook. When you have completed this lesson, you should be able to distinguish between situations in which privacy does and does not exist. You also should be able to describe common objects of privacy and the reasons people may wish to have privacy in specific situations.

Terms to Know

privacy
solitude
objects of privacy

Critical Thinking Exercise
EXAMINING DEGREES OF PRIVACY

Most people will share some information about themselves with just about anyone, but keep other information to themselves or only share it with close friends or family. Similarly, people do not mind doing some things in public, while they will do other things only in private or with people they know and trust.

In this exercise, create separate lists of the kinds of information and activities that you think people would

- be willing to share with strangers, such as newspaper or TV reporters, librarians, or government census workers

- be willing to share with classmates, neighbors, and other acquaintances

- be willing to share only with certain close friends or relatives

- not be willing to share with anyone

Each list should include four or five items. Work with a study partner or in small groups to create the lists. After

everyone has finished, each pair or group of students should share their lists with the class. As a class, discuss the following questions:

1. What are the similarities among the lists?

2. What are the common characteristics of the information and activities people keep most private?

3. How would you feel if the information and activities you keep most private were broadcast on the TV news?

4. How would you feel if you could not share private information with your closest friends or relatives? How would it affect your relationships with them?

What is privacy?

As you have seen, privacy involves the ability to control or decide the extent to which information will be shared with others. But privacy also involves other things. For our purposes, **privacy** can be defined as the **right to be** left alone. This right can be threatened or invaded in different ways. We say "leave me alone" when someone asks us questions we do not want to answer; we also say "leave me alone" when we want someone to go away, or when someone is bothering us or interfering with something we are doing. Thus, the right to privacy may include:

- the right to decide whether information will be shared with others

- the right to solitude—that is, to be alone, away from other people

- the right to be free from the interference of others

The things we want to keep others from finding out about, observing, or interfering with are called **objects of privacy**. Objects of privacy may include:

- **facts** such as your birthplace, who your parents are, and your age or weight

- **actions** such as where you go or who you see

- **places and possessions** such as your room or the contents of a box or closet

- **thoughts and feelings** such as who you like and dislike, what you are afraid of, and what your religious or political beliefs are

- **communications** such as your letters or telephone conversations

Critical Thinking Exercise

EXAMINING SITUATIONS THAT INVOLVE PRIVACY

Read the following situations. List the numbers that are examples of privacy. Then answer the "What do *you* think?" questions. Be prepared to share your answers with the class.

1. Tomas went into his room to talk with his friend Roberto because he did not want his mother to hear them.

2. Sometimes Farid went to the park to draw pictures so his family would not tease him about his drawings.

3. Misha walked up to Steven and said, "The basketball tournament starts today."

4. Jessie and Loretta were best friends. They had a place in the mall where they met on Saturdays, but they agreed not to let anyone else know where it was.

5. Tonya went for a walk in the forest and suddenly realized she was lost. Tonya yelled for help, but no one could hear her. Now she was really alone.

6. When Alita got her report card, she kept it secret from her friends.

7. Although Theo supported the proposal to send troops overseas to restore order, he did not speak about it to his friends at work because they were opposed to the idea.

What do *you* think?

Answer the following questions for each situation that is an example of privacy.

1. **Why** is this situation an example of privacy?

2. **Who** wants to keep something private?

3. What is the **object of privacy**?

4. From **whom** is something to be kept private?

5. Why do you suppose the person wanted privacy?

Using the Lesson

1. Write several rules that you would like people to obey to protect your privacy at school. Be prepared to explain your rules to the class.

2. Bring a news clipping to class or report on a TV news program that illustrates an issue involving privacy. Be prepared to explain the issue to your class.

3. While you are studying privacy, keep a privacy notebook or journal. Over the next twenty-four hours, note at least five situations involving privacy, and answer the following questions about the situations:

    - Who wishes to keep something private?

    - What is the object of privacy?

    - From whom does the person want to keep the object private?

    Then explain why the person might have wanted to keep the object private.

LESSON 2

How Do People Maintain Their Privacy?

Purpose of Lesson

This lesson describes different ways people behave to maintain their privacy. When you have finished this lesson, you should be able to explain some common ways people behave to keep others from observing or finding out about objects of privacy.

Terms to Know

isolation
secrecy
confidentiality
exclusion

How do people behave to keep things private?

The following are some of the most common ways that people behave to protect their privacy:

1. **Isolation**. People may **isolate** themselves, that is, they may keep away from other people. For example, they may stay in a room or a house or go to some far-away place to live.

2. **Secrecy**. People may keep objects of privacy **secret**, that is, they may purposely not tell others about them. For example, you and your friends may keep your plans for a weekend a secret, or agree not to tell anyone about something you have seen or done. People may keep facts about their income or their debts a secret.

3. **Confidentiality**. When people share private information with someone who is expected and trusted not to tell anyone else, this is called **confidentiality**. For example, you may tell a secret to a friend, relative, or guidance counselor and expect him or her not to repeat the information. What people say in private to their doctors, lawyers, and religious counselors is confidential.

4. **Exclusion**. People may keep things private or secret by **excluding** others. For example, you may keep something private by not allowing others to look into your wallet, locker, room, or home. Some

government agencies try to maintain secrecy by not allowing unauthorized people to go into certain buildings or on the grounds of military bases.

Critical Thinking Exercise
IDENTIFYING HOW PEOPLE MAINTAIN PRIVACY

As you read the following selection adapted from the book, *Assignment: Rescue* by Varian Fry, identify the different ways people behave to keep things private. Then answer the "What do you think?" questions. Be prepared to discuss your answers with the class.

Excerpt from *Assignment: Rescue*

Hitler's rise to power in Germany in the late 1930s began a time of terror for millions of Jews and others on the Nazi's hit list. Many fled Germany's borders to the unoccupied zone of southern France. But when France fell to Hitler in June of 1940, these refugees were in danger of being turned over to the Gestapo, who imprisoned, tortured, and executed them in concentration camps.

A group of New Yorkers shocked by the Third Reich's actions formed the Emergency Rescue Committee. Their goal was to get artists, writers, musicians, scientists, professors, and political figures out of France before the Gestapo seized them. They had to find the right person to be their agent, someone who would be allowed into France and be willing to risk the dangers of a secret mission. Thus, Varian Fry—a man with no secret agent experience but who had an excellent cover through the International Y.M.C.A.—managed to smuggle more than a thousand refugees out of Marseilles in thirteen months through his efficient underground organization.

With my three helpers—Beamish the outside man, Franzi the interviewer, and Lena the secretary—we interviewed those who came to seek our help all day long. We wrote their names down on white file cards, but we never listed their addresses. In case of a sudden raid by the police, we did not want a lot of cards lying around with addresses where people could be picked up and arrested.

In the evening, when all the refugees had finally gone, Beamish, Franzi, Lena, and I would hold a staff meeting.

We would go over all the cards for that day and try to decide what action to take on each case. Since we were always afraid the police might plant a hidden microphone in the room, we discussed all secret subjects in the bathroom, where we turned all the water faucets on full. We figured the noise of the water would make a recording sound like one long thunderstorm and not a word of what we said could be understood.

Secret subjects included false passports, false identity cards, false residence permits, and false safe-conduct passes. They also included secret escape routes over the Pyrenees Mountains into Spain and the names of those refugees who were in the greatest immediate danger from the Gestapo.

How might wars or other conflicts require people to alter their privacy behavior?

We couldn't cable these names to New York. We couldn't even mention them in a letter, because all letters were opened and read by a censor. So Lena typed out our secret messages on narrow sheets of thin paper. Then Beamish, Franzi, and I pasted the ends of the papers together and when the paste was dry, we made the long

strips into tight rolls. We put each roll into a rubber finger and tied the end with a thin thread. Then we opened the bottom of a partly used tube of toothpaste or shaving cream. We pushed the rubber-covered packages well up into the tube. After we closed the end of the tube, we rolled it up a little way, so it would look as if it were in daily use. Whenever a refugee we trusted was leaving France, we sent the tube with him and asked him to mail the roll to New York when he reached Lisbon. All our secret messages got safely through to New York, and the police never caught on to our toothpaste trick.

What do *you* think?

1. Who in the story wished to keep something private or secret?

2. What did they wish to keep secret?

3. From whom did they wish to keep something secret?

4. How did they behave to maintain privacy or keep secrets?

5. What examples in the story are there of the following:

    ■ isolation

    ■ secrecy

    ■ confidentiality

    ■ exclusion

Using the Lesson

1. Draw a picture or make a collage to illustrate each of the four means described in this lesson that people use to maintain privacy: isolation, secrecy, confidentiality, and exclusion.

2. Why might it be important to protect from disclosure confidential communications, such as those with a doctor or lawyer? Are there any circumstances when such confidential communications should be disclosed? Explain your answer.

LESSON 3

Why Is Privacy Important to Individuals and to Institutions?

Purpose of Lesson

This lesson asks you to consider the importance of privacy for individuals and for institutions. You will have the opportunity to role-play a congressional hearing on the issue of press censorship during war time. When you have finished this lesson, you should be able to explain why individuals and institutions may wish to keep things secret.

Term to Know

institution

Critical Thinking Exercise

EXAMINING THE IMPORTANCE OF PRIVACY TO INDIVIDUALS

Poems, song lyrics, essays and other writings can make us think in new ways, or make us more aware of our own thoughts and feelings. As you read the following selections, think about the author's point of view. What is the author trying to tell us about privacy? Be prepared to share your thoughts with your class, then answer the "What do *you* think?" questions after discussing them with a study partner.

1. From *Something So Right*
   by Paul Simon (American songwriter, 1942–)

   They got a wall in China!
   It's a thousand miles long.
   To keep out the foreigners they made it strong.
   And I got a wall around me
   That you can't even see.
   It took a little time to get next to me.
   Copyright 1973 Paul Simon. Used by permission of the publisher.

2. From *Mending Wall*
   by Robert Frost (American poet, 1874–1963)

   Before I built a wall I'd ask to know
   What I was walling in or walling out,

And to whom I was like to give offense.
Something there is that doesn't love a wall,
That wants it down.

3. From *Childe Harold's Pilgrimage*
   by Lord Byron (English poet, 1788–1824)

   There is a pleasure in the pathless woods,
   There is a rapture on the lonely shore,
   There is society where none intrudes,
   By the deep Sea, and music in its roar:
   I love not Man the less, but Nature more,
   From these our interviews, in which I steal
   From all I may be or have been before,
   To mingle with the Universe, and feel
   What I can ne'er express, yet cannot all conceal.

Why is it important for people to have places to go where they can find privacy?

4. From *Walden*
   by Henry David Thoreau (American essayist, 1817–1862)

   My nearest neighbor is a mile distant, and no house is visible from any place but the hilltops within half a mile of my own. I have my horizon bounded by woods all to myself; a distant view of the railroad where it touches the pond on the one hand, and of the fence which skirts the woodland road on the other. But for the most part it is as solitary where I live as on the prairies. I have, as it were, my own sun and moon and stars, and a little world all to myself.

Men frequently say to me, I should think you feel lonesome down there, and want to be nearer to folks, rainy and snowy days and nights especially. [But] I find it wholesome to be alone the greater part of the time. To be in company, even with the best, is soon wearisome and dissipating. I love to be alone. I never found the companion that was so companionable as solitude.

Society is commonly too cheap. We meet at very short intervals, not having had time to acquire any new value for each other. We meet at the post-office, and at the sociable, and about the fireside every night; we live thick and are in each other's way, and stumble over one another, and I think that we thus lose some respect for one another.

What do *you* think?

1. What does Paul Simon think about the invisible walls around people? What purpose do they serve? What problems or disadvantages do they cause?

2. What does Robert Frost think the disadvantages are of building walls? What do you think the disadvantages are? What are the benefits?

3. What does Lord Byron think are the advantages of being alone? What does Henry Thoreau think? What do you think the advantages are? What are the disadvantages?

4. Do you ever try to keep a wall around you? When? What do you gain? What do you lose? Do you think you should try to keep a wall around you more often? Less often? Why?

5. Do you ever want to be alone? When? How do you feel when you want to be alone, but you can't?

6. Can you feel lonely even when you are around other people? What is the difference between being alone and being lonely?

Why is privacy important for institutions?

Just like privacy is important for individuals it also is important for some institutions. Institutions are established organizations, such as

■ schools and universities

■ business corporations

■ museums

■ hospitals

■ federal, state, and local governments

Some institutions have a need to keep certain things private. For example, hospitals keep medical records confidential; schools and universities keep student records confidential. Museums may want to keep their plans for buying new works of art private, and business corporations usually want to keep plans for new products and strategies for distributing and advertising them secret. Many governments have hidden weapons or secret military plans; they may have spies whose names are secret, and they often have letters and other documents that they want to keep top secret. In a democracy the government must be open to the people, but in the interest of national security some things must be kept private.

EVALUATING INSTITUTIONAL SECRECY

In this exercise the class is divided into groups to engage in a simulated congressional hearing on press censorship during wartime. First, read the following selection to find out what the military wanted to keep secret and why. Work in small groups to answer the "What do *you* think?" questions. Then follow the instructions in the next section to prepare for the hearing.

Congress Investigates Wartime Censorship

The Committee on Government Affairs of the United States Senate has decided to hold a hearing to investigate the extent to which the military should be able to censor the press during wartime. Witnesses from the Department of Defense and the news media have been asked to testify.

What is the reason for the hearing? During the 1991 war in the Persian Gulf, a number of reporters complained that the Department of Defense was placing too many restrictions on the news media. In the battlefield area, reporters were assigned to small groups or pools that military officers had to escort at all times. They could only go where the military guides took them. Reporters had to submit their battlefield stories to military officers for review before publication. If the military officers found information they thought might aid the enemy, they cut it out of the stories. Some of the military escorts may have been overly strict in supervising the reporters.

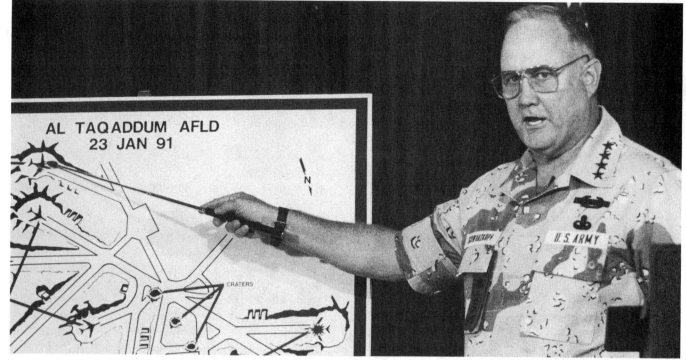

What information about events during the Persian Gulf War (1991) should have been shared by General Norman Schwartzkopf with members of the press? What information should have been withheld?

Military censorship procedures had been different in the past. For example, during World War II, reporters had been free to travel anywhere and see anything. Then they wrote their stories and submitted them to the military censor. The censor took out any information that might be helpful to the enemy; the rest was published.

During the Persian Gulf War reporters were not free to travel wherever and whenever they wanted. Reporters were told what they **could not see** instead of what they **could not report**. Arguably, this system did not allow reporters to gather information and report it properly. Limitations on access to information was a far more serious form of censorship which made it more difficult for the American public to decide whether the news reports were accurate and trustworthy.

On the other hand, from a military standpoint the press had sent too many reporters to the region to be handled effectively. Moreover, reporters often asked questions during televised briefings that the military could not answer without endangering the troops. Additionally, live satellite transmissions and other modern technologies involved in newsgathering during the Persian Gulf War made it impossible to allow reporters the freedom they enjoyed in the pre-television days of World War II.

What do *you* think?

1. What did the military want to keep secret?

2. From whom did the military wish to keep the information secret?

3. How did the military plan to keep the information secret?

4. Why did the military want to keep the information secret?

Preparing for the Hearing

To prepare for the hearing, the class should be divided into five groups, with each group assigned to play one of the following roles:

- **Department of Defense:** You will seek to justify the restrictions placed on the press by the military.

- **Coalition of Radio and Television Broadcasters:** You will seek the broadest possible freedom to observe and report the news as it happens.

- **Associated Press (AP):** Your members are news-paper and magazine reporters who seek complete freedom of access to information on the condition that they submit their stories to a military censor before publication.

- **Center for National Defense Policy Studies:** Your group generally uses arguments based on practical necessity to support the military's point of view.

- **Senate Committee on Government Affairs:** As elected representatives of the people of the United States, you seek to make the best decision possible for the good of the country. You will listen carefully to all sides and attempt to resolve this privacy issue wisely, keeping in mind both the need for national security and the people's right to know.

The first four groups should prepare a three-minute presentation explaining and justifying their position on what role the military should have in censoring the press during wartime. Each group should select one or two spokespersons to present its position to the committee, but all group members should be prepared to assist in answering the committee's questions.

While the first four groups are preparing their presentations, the Senate Committee on Government Affairs should prepare questions to ask each group, and should select a chairperson to conduct the hearing.

Conducting the Hearing

The chairperson of the Senate Committee on Government Affairs should call the hearing to order. Each group should be given three minutes to present its arguments, followed by three minutes of questioning by members of the committee. After all four groups have completed their testimony, members of the committee should discuss the arguments presented and attempt to reach a consensus on how to deal with this privacy issue. The committee's deliberations should be conducted in front of the class, and the committee should propose a formal resolution that sets forth their decision on the extent to which the military should be allowed to censor the press during wartime.

Using the Lesson

1. What other institutions might have information about people that they want to keep secret? What kind of information might they want to keep secret? Why?

2. What information might you want that an institution could refuse to give to you because it is secret? Should it be kept secret? Why?

3. Do you think there are some kinds of information that our government should be allowed to keep secret? What are some reasons the government might want to keep a secret? Do you think there are some kinds of information that the government should not be allowed to keep secret, even if it wants to? Explain your position.

Unit Two: What Factors Explain Differences in Privacy Behavior?

How do you explain differences in the privacy behavior of different people?

Purpose of Unit

This unit will introduce you to the factors that explain differences in the privacy behavior of individuals. You will learn that although privacy exists in all societies and cultures, there are often differences in the privacy behavior of individuals within a society and between different societies. You will examine some areas in which differences are common as well as the reasons for these differences.

LESSON 4

Why Might People's Privacy Behavior Differ?

Purpose of Lesson

This lesson examines some of the common reasons for the differences in privacy behavior among people. When you have finished this lesson, you should be able to describe and explain similarities and differences in privacy behavior.

Terms to Know

factor
occupation
role
values

Critical Thinking Exercise

EXAMINING PRIVACY BEHAVIOR

As you read the following excerpt from "A Journey," a short story by the American writer Edith Wharton (1862–1937), identify examples of the main character's privacy behavior. Then work with a study partner to answer the "What do *you* think?" questions. Be prepared to share your answers with the class.

A Journey

The sleeping car had sunk into its night silence. Through the wet windowpane she watched the sudden lights, the long stretches of hurrying blackness. Now and then she turned her head and looked through the opening in the hangings at her husband's curtains across the aisle. She wondered restlessly if he wanted anything and if she could hear him if he called. His voice had grown very weak within the last months and it irritated him when she did not hear.... She crept to the dressing room. When she had washed her face and adjusted her dress she felt more hopeful.... In ten hours they would be at home!

She stepped to her husband's berth. She leaned over him and drew up the shade. As she did so she touched one of his hands. It felt cold.... She bent closer, laying her hand on his arm and calling him by name. He did not move.

She gently shook his shoulder. He lay motionless. She caught hold of his hand again: it slipped from her limply, like a dead thing. A dead thing?

She leaned forward, and shrinkingly, with a sickening reluctance, laid her hands on his shoulders and turned him over. His head fell back; his face looked small and smooth; he gazed at her with steady eyes.

She remained motionless for a long time, holding him. Suddenly she shrank back: the longing to scream, to call out, to fly from him, had almost overpowered her. But a strong hand arrested her. Good God! If it were known that he was dead they would be put off the train at the next station.

In a terrifying flash of remembrance there arose before her a scene she had once witnessed in traveling, when a husband and wife, whose child had died on the train, had

What reasons might the woman in this story have to conceal her husband's unexpected death in their private berth aboard this passenger train?

been thrust out at some chance station. She saw them standing on the platform with the child's body between them. And this was what would happen to her. Within the next hour she might find herself on the platform of some strange station, alone with her husband's body.... It was too horrible.

She felt the train moving more slowly. They were approaching a station! With a violent gesture she drew down the shade to hide her husband's face.

Feeling dizzy, she sank down on the edge of the berth, keeping away from his outstretched body, and pulling the curtains close, so that he and she were shut into a kind of sepulchral twilight.... She tried to think. At all costs she must conceal the fact that he was dead. But how?

She heard the porter making up her bed; people were beginning to move about the car. With a supreme effort she rose to her feet, stepping into the aisle of the car and drawing the curtains tight behind her. She noticed that they still parted slightly with the motion of the car, and finding a pin in her dress she fastened them together. Now she was safe....

The porter, moving to and fro under his burden of sheets and pillows, glanced at her as he passed.

At length he said: "Ain't he going to get up? We're ordered to make up the berths as early as we can."

She turned cold with fear. They were just entering the station. "Oh, not yet," she stammered. "Not till he's had his milk. Won't you get it, please?"

"All right. Soon as we start again."

When the train moved on he reappeared with the milk. She took it from him and sat vaguely looking at it. At length she became aware that the porter still hovered expectantly.

"Will I give it to him?" he suggested. "Oh, no," she cried, rising. "He, he's asleep yet, I think."

She waited until the porter had passed on; then she unpinned the curtains and slipped behind them. In the semi-obscurity her husband's face stared up at her like a marble mask with agate eyes. She put out her hand and drew down the lids. Then she remembered the glass of milk: what was she to do with it? She thought of throwing it out the window; but to do so she would have to lean across his body and bring her face close to his. She decided to drink the milk.

After a while the porter came back. "When'll I fold up his bed?" he asked. "Oh, not yet; he's ill, he's very ill. Can't you let him stay as he is?" He took the empty milk glass and walked away....

Suddenly she found herself picturing what would happen when the train reached New York. She shuddered as it occurred to her that he would be quite cold and that someone might perceive he had been dead since morning.

She thought, "If they see I am not surprised they will suspect something. They will ask questions, and if I tell them the truth they won't believe me, no one would believe me! It will be terrible. I must pretend I don't know. When they open the curtains I must go up to him quite naturally, and then I must scream!" She had an idea that the scream would be very hard to do.

What do *you* think?

1. What does the main character try to keep private?

2. How does the main character behave—what does she do—to maintain privacy?

How does the character in this story behave to maintain the secret of her husband's death aboard the passenger train?

3. Are these behaviors examples of isolation, secrecy, confidentiality, or exclusion?

4. How do you explain the main character's privacy behavior? Why does she attempt to maintain privacy as she does?

What factors influence privacy behavior?

People often differ in the objects they wish to keep private and in the ways they behave to keep these objects secret. How can we explain these differences? Various **factors**, or elements, in people's lives explain differences in their privacy behavior. The following are some factors that typically influence a person's privacy behavior:

1. **Family**. A person's family environment may influence his or her privacy behavior. For example:

   ■ In LaToya's family, no one ever talks about Uncle Hubert, especially in front of Grandma, because he became severely depressed and committed suicide several years ago.

   ■ Oksana and her seven bothers and sisters live with their grandparents in a tiny apartment. It is very crowded and no one has a private space to call their own. Oksana dreams of having her own room where she can be alone.

2. **Occupation or role**. A person's job or role may require him or her to maintain privacy. For example:

   ■ Michael is a famous professional athlete. To avoid being harassed by reporters and mobbed by fans, Michael keeps his home address and telephone number confidential.

   ■ Sonya works in product development for a large corporation. She is sworn to secrecy and cannot discuss her work with her friends.

3. **Individual experiences**. Past experiences may influence how a person wants to live to maintain privacy. For example:

   ■ A friend Frank trusted embarrassed him several years ago when he revealed to the whole class something Frank had whispered in confidence. Since then, Frank has not trusted anyone to keep a secret, and he keeps his private thoughts to himself.

   ■ Martina's family always discussed their problems openly. When Martina became an adult, there were very few things she would not discuss with her friends.

4. **Opportunities for privacy**. People's behavior may be influenced by the opportunities for privacy that exist in their environment. For example:

   ■ In his book *1984*, George Orwell described a society in which there was a special television screen (telescreen) in every home. This telescreen allowed the government to watch and listen to everything people did. The main character, Winston Smith, found a tiny room above a shop that did not have a telescreen. Even though it was small and run-down, it was like paradise for Winston.

   ■ Many people who live in large cities find privacy in the anonymous crowds of people.

5. **Value placed on privacy**. People's behavior may differ depending on the value they, their family, or their culture place on privacy. For example:

   ■ Some people who grow up in small towns have neighbors that share everything that happens in their lives.

6. **Competing values**. Although people may value privacy highly, sometimes other things may be more important to them in specific situations. For example:

   ■ In *The Adventures of Tom Sawyer* by Mark Twain, Tom and Huck swore to each other that they would never tell anyone about the murder they witnessed. But after searching his conscience, Tom decided to testify to save a man wrongly accused of the crime.

7. **Individual differences** sometimes lead people to make **different choices** with regard to privacy. For example:

   ■ Jamal and Eli are students at Central High. They each have many friends and enjoy talking with them. Jamal does not mind telling his friends just about anything. On the other hand, Eli keeps some things to himself.

Critical Thinking Exercise

IDENTIFYING THE FACTORS THAT INFLUENCE PRIVACY BEHAVIOR

Work with a study partner to answer the following questions. You may use the examples of privacy behavior you have just read, or examples from your experience or imagination, to explain your answers. Be prepared to discuss your answers with the class.

1. How might a person's family environment and past experiences influence his or her privacy behavior?

2. How might a person's occupation or role require him or her to maintain privacy?

3. How might differences in people's values explain differences in their privacy behavior?

4. How might differences in the opportunities for privacy explain differences in privacy behavior?

What factors explain the privacy behavior of celebrities?

Critical Thinking Exercise

EVALUATING HOW DIFFERENT OCCUPATIONS INFLUENCE PRIVACY BEHAVIOR

In this exercise your class will role-play two TV talk show discussions. The subject is the influence of different occupations on privacy behavior. Half the class—Group A—will examine how certain occupations influence a person's privacy needs, and half the class—Group B—will examine how certain other occupations require a person to intrude on—or to protect—the privacy of others. One or two students from each group should be assigned the role of interviewer, to lead and moderate the discussion and to ask questions of the other group members.

Group A–Members of this group should be assigned to play the role of one of the following occupations, and should be prepared to describe how their occupation influences their need for privacy:

■ magician

■ movie actor/actress

■ inventor

■ politician

■ writer

■ lawyer

Group B–Members of this group should be assigned to play the role of one of the following occupations, and should be prepared to explain how their occupation requires them to intrude on, and to protect, the privacy of others:

■ newspaper reporter

■ talk show host

■ police officer

■ doctor

■ private investigator

■ psychiatrist

Group B should play the role of studio audience during the presentation by Group A and vice versa.

Using the Lesson

1. How does your privacy behavior compare with the privacy behavior described in the examples in this? What factors explain the similarities and differences?

2. What factors explain the differences between your privacy behavior and that of your friends? What factors explain the similarities?

3. Should people in certain jobs—top athletes or public officials, for example—be allowed less privacy than the rest of us? Why or why not?

LESSON 5

How Do Different Societies Deal with Privacy?

Purpose of Lesson

This lesson provides an opportunity to examine some ways that different societies, and different generations in the same society, deal with privacy. When you have finished this lesson, you should be able to explain societal similarities and differences in privacy behavior.

What differences exist among societies in the way they maintain privacy?

Privacy is found in all societies. People of different societies, however, may differ in the objects they choose to keep private and the means they use to maintain privacy. Even within one society, people of different generations may have very different privacy behavior. For example, some people think their age should be kept private. Others may reveal their age, but not feel comfortable revealing their religious or political beliefs. In some cultures, people always eat in private; it is considered indecent to eat in public.

People also may differ in the ways they maintain privacy. For example, the people in some societies build homes with soundproof walls to promote privacy. In other societies, walls may be thin and sound can easily travel through them. In such societies, people maintain a sense of privacy by purposely not listening or by pretending not to overhear one another.

Societies can be complicated. In some cases, people of one society might be uncomfortable if they are more than one foot away from others while talking to them. On the other hand, people from another society might be uncomfortable if others are less than one foot from them. What do you think might happen when people from these different societies talk to each other?

In the following exercises you will examine similarities and differences in the privacy behavior of people from different generations and different societies.

Critical Thinking Exercise

EXAMINING PRIVACY IN ANOTHER CULTURE

Read the following selection carefully. As you do, try to identify the privacy behavior of the Zuni and think about what might account for this behavior. Answer the "What do *you* think?" questions. Be prepared to discuss your answers with the class.

Privacy and the Zuni

The Zuni are a tribe of American Indians who live in the southwestern United States. Generally, the Zuni live in large houses. Each house is for an extended family. When the daughters of a family are married they bring their husbands to live in the family home. A typical eight-room house for twenty or so people has four rooms for common use—a living room, a kitchen, a storeroom, and a workroom. Each of the married daughters has a bedroom/workroom for herself and her family. The rooms are linked by connecting doors and interior windows. The approach area to each house is watched by family members. This is done so that whenever someone comes to visit, the family can be prepared. In this way the activities of the family can be kept private.

What factors help explain the different ways in which the Zuni people maintain their privacy behavior?

The most private areas of a Zuni household are the storeroom and the storage areas within each bedroom where sacred religious objects are kept. These objects are considered to be very powerful. Members of the tribe who are not authorized to use sacred objects are afraid even to handle them. Even the rooms in which they are kept are taboo to visitors.

When these objects are used in religious rituals, the greatest secrecy is in effect. All unauthorized Zuni and foreigners are forbidden to be in the area. This is essential so that religious activities can be conducted without interference and so that information about them will not be revealed.

There are many methods for maintaining the secrecy of these religious objects and rituals. Looking in through the windows of houses, especially at night, is not permitted. In 1890, two people who looked in through the windows at night were considered to be witches and were tried and beaten. Even today, most Zuni houses have outdoor lights for night surveillance and guard dogs to warn of intruders. When rituals are in progress, security is maintained by people standing guard inside and outside the room. It is also maintained by solid walls. In addition, customary respect for the taboos and ordinary good manners help preserve privacy and secrecy in the Zuni village.

What do *you* think?

1. What are the objects of privacy or secrecy for the Zuni?

2. From whom are these objects of privacy kept private or secret?

3. How do the Zuni behave to keep these objects of privacy secret, that is, to maintain privacy with regard to these things?

4. Why do you suppose the Zuni seek privacy with regard to these things?

Critical Thinking Exercise

IDENTIFYING DIFFERENCES IN PRIVACY BEHAVIOR

Read the following selection carefully. As you do, identify the differences in privacy behavior the author describes among people of different societies and different generations. Then answer the "What do *you* think?" questions. Be prepared to discuss your answers with the class.

The Right to Privacy Is a Myth

by Bruno Bettelheim
from **The Saturday Evening Post**, July 7, 1968

Everywhere one turns these days it seems that the right to privacy is constantly under assault. If one is not being assailed by gratuitous noise and information, then some company or government agency is asking indiscreet questions, probing for innermost feelings. Is nothing private any more, nothing sacred to the individual? Can't people live their own lives, be left alone to be themselves in this country? Don't we all resent these intrusions? Then why do we permit such disregard for our privacy?

I was pondering these questions one night recently, in solitude, behind the closed doors of my room. As I began to write these thoughts down, my eyes strayed to the picture I had hung on the wall over my desk, and I had to laugh at myself. There I had put a copy of a Breughel painting, teeming with people and life. The figures in the painting were going about their business, and doing it, apparently, with all the more gusto because they were in the presence of others. They didn't seem to want or need privacy. Why was this? Is our passion for privacy just a recent, temporary phenomenon, destined soon to die away?

When I studied as a youngster, the door to my room had to be closed, and everything had to be quiet. Only then could I concentrate on myself and my work to the exclusion of everything else. But my own children study best with the door open and the record player going full blast, and in this radically different setting they learn as much and as well as I did. Why, then, do I still need privacy, and why do they not seem to need it?

Maybe the answer is that we all function best when in closest communion with what seems (to us) to symbolize our highest values. I, growing up before the age of mass culture, had to create for myself a setting that emphasized personal uniqueness and individual development before I could concentrate on a learning task designed (whether I knew it or not) to achieve a high degree of individuality. My children, for the same reason, need to emphasize communality as they work. The music of the Beatles reassures them, just as my studying in privacy reassured me. It gives them the feeling that even when alone at their studies they are still in touch with what counts most in their lives: a sense of connection with their age group. How fast the attitude toward privacy can change, I thought....

My Victorian parents, when they went out to dinner, preferred a spacious restaurant with their table set off by ample distance from the next one. Nowadays young people prefer to crowd together in small discotheques, and the hippies think nothing of sleeping many to a room....

Historically, privacy has always been a luxury few could afford. One need not go far back to a time when whole families lived together in one room. Nobody had privacy then. One could not hide skeletons in the closet, because there were no closets. In colonial days, even among the affluent, a family had to be quite well off to afford separate bedrooms, one for the parents and one for all the children....

Lewis Mumford writes that the first radical change, which was to alter the form of the medieval house, was the development of a sense of privacy. This meant, in effect, withdrawal at will from the common life and the common interest of one's fellows. Privacy in sleep, privacy in eating, privacy in religious and social rituals, finally privacy in thought.... In the castles of the 13th Century, one notes the existence of a private bedroom for the noble owners.... Privacy in bed came first in Italy among the upper classes only....

This wish for privacy is closely connected with the increased value placed on private property. My home is my castle, where I am protected from anyone's intruding on my privacy. It was the lord of the castle

who first claimed privacy for himself. Whoever owns no place of his own, owns no privacy either.

The more class-structured a society becomes, the more privacy do its privileged members demand. How understandable, then, that a society which tries to do away with class structure should also try to do away with privacy, and demand that ever-larger areas of life should be public.

What is harder to realize is that as long as everyone knows everything about everyone else, there is no need for informers, for elaborate spy systems, for bugging, in order to know what people do, say and think. Witness the absence of crime, delinquency and other antisocial behavior in the Israeli agricultural communal settlements, the kibbutzim. They have no police because there is no need for policing. This is because everyone there lives much more collectively and openly than we do here. Personally, I felt suffocated by the lack of privacy when I visited a kibbutz. But I could not blind myself to the incredibly successful control of antisocial behavior in this society.

Among the unresolved problems of modern city life is the prevalence of fear in our streets. Perhaps here the solution has nothing to do with reconstructing our cities, or an endless enlarging of the police forces within them. What we need, in my opinion, is a return to much smaller, more self-contained communities

In what way might ideas of privacy be related to an absence of crime and other antisocial behavior on this Israeli kibbutz?

where a great deal of what is now private can become public; where we would share more and know much more about each other.

Where does all this leave me? Despite all of my realizations, I do not cherish privacy less, and I still resent deeply any intrusion upon it....

Neither a medieval absence of privacy nor a Big Brother's spying that leaves nothing unpublic will do. What we must strive for, as is true of most important human questions, is the right balance between what should be respected as private in our lives and what belongs to our more-or-less public and communal life. Then our lives will be neither fortified castles nor public places. ■

What do *you* think?

1. What differences in privacy behavior does the author describe between his generation and his children's generation? Between his parent's generation and his children's generation?

2. What does the author tell us about the historical development of privacy? What do you think might be the costs and benefits of a medieval absence of privacy?

3. What does the author tell us about privacy behavior on an Israeli kibbutz? How do his observations lead him to suggest a solution for the unresolved problems of modern city life?

4. How do your attitudes about privacy compare with the author's? What do you think is the right balance between the public and private parts of our lives?

Using the Lesson

1. Imagine that you are working for an architectural firm. Design a house in which you would like to live. Then explain how the house you have designed reflects your ideas about the need for privacy.

2. *Gulliver's Travels* is a famous book written by Jonathan Swift. It contains descriptions of several imaginary cultures and presents examples of the privacy behavior of the people who live in them. Read this book and compare the privacy behavior of the people in two of the cultures. Then report your findings to the rest of the class.

3. Write a story about a person living in the United States who wants to keep something private. In your story, describe what the person wants to keep private and what you think are the reasons for the person's privacy behavior.

4. In your privacy journal, write at least three questions you have about privacy.

Unit Three: What Are Some Benefits and Costs of Privacy?

What benefits and costs of privacy are illustrated by these photographs?

Purpose of Unit

Maintaining privacy entails certain consequences. Some consequences are **benefits,** or advantages; some are **costs,** or disadvantages. It is important to recognize and consider the consequences of privacy in making decisions about issues of privacy. If you are trying to decide in a particular situation whether to recognize a claim to privacy, you need to think about what the benefits and costs might be of maintaining privacy in that situation.

In this unit, you will identify some common benefits and costs of privacy, and you will explore the consequences of privacy in a number of specific situations. As you will see, different individuals may have different opinions about whether the right to privacy should be protected in a particular situation.

LESSON 6

What Are the Possible Consequences of Privacy?

<table>
<tr>
<td>

Purpose of Lesson

In this lesson you examine some of the possible consequences of privacy and classify them as benefits or costs. You also evaluate positions on issues of privacy by thinking about the consequences of privacy. When you have completed this lesson, you should be able to explain some common benefits and costs of privacy.

</td>
</tr>
</table>

Terms to Know

writs of assistance
conformity
totalitarian
creativity
intellectual stimulation

Critical Thinking Exercise

EXAMINING CONSEQUENCES OF PRIVACY

Your teacher will divide your class into small groups. Each group should read the situations below, list the possible consequences of privacy in each situation, and classify these consequences as **benefits**—advantages— or as **costs**—disadvantages. Each group should be prepared to share its lists of benefits and costs with the class.

1. Before the American Revolution, English officials in the colonies used general search warrants, called writs of assistance, to enter the colonists' homes at any time and search them for evidence of crimes. Now, because of the Fourth Amendment to the U.S. Constitution, government officials cannot use general search warrants to search for evidence of crimes. Instead, they can only get a warrant if they first convince a judge that there is good reason to believe specific evidence of a crime will be found in a particular place. Then, if the judge is convinced, he or she issues a specific search warrant particularly describing the place to be searched and the persons or things to be seized.

How did the Fourth Amendment curtail the English practice of using writs of assistance to search colonial homes and businesses?

2. Psychiatrists, psychologists, and other counselors keep records and notes of their sessions with patients and clients. These records and notes are highly confidential, and may not be disclosed to anyone under most circumstances.

3. Under most circumstances, a lawyer may not reveal what a client has said to him or her in private.

4. When Shandra's brother told her he had AIDS, she cried and cried at home. But Shandra never let her feelings show at school. When Shandra's friends asked her what was bothering her, she just shook her head.

As you can see, some consequences of privacy are benefits and some are costs. The next two sections describe some of the most common benefits and costs of privacy. As you read these sections, think about the benefits and costs that result from privacy in your life.

What are the benefits of privacy?

FREEDOM. Privacy helps people think and act freely, without unreasonable influence or control by others. This freedom may prevent a society from becoming totalitarian, that is, subject to complete control by a dictator or ruling party.

Example: In private places where they cannot be overheard, people may feel free to speak with their family and friends about ideas and beliefs that may not be popular with others.

SECURITY. Respect for privacy fosters a sense of security; if one's privacy is respected, one can feel safe and secure.

Example: If your family and friends respect your privacy, you can feel secure that they will not bother you when you want to be alone or embarrass you by revealing things you want to keep private.

INDIVIDUALITY. Without privacy, the pressure to be like others might inhibit an individual from forming his or her own values, beliefs, and opinions.

Example: Sometimes families, gangs, and whole societies do not allow their members to have much privacy. In these circumstances people often feel they have to go along with whatever the group or its leaders consider to be correct beliefs and behavior.

How were freedom, security, and individuality undermined in Nazi Germany by the absence of privacy?

PROTECTION OF ECONOMIC INTERESTS. Privacy enables people to keep their ideas, plans, and inventions secret. This may help them create and sell new products and compete with others.

Example: Suppose you designed a T-shirt that you thought would sell well and make a lot of money. Keeping your idea secret until you created the T-shirts and had them ready to sell would prevent others from taking your idea.

CREATIVITY. Privacy may be necessary for creative thought or work.

Example: Suppose you were painting a picture and someone was looking over your shoulder as you painted. You might feel as though that person was judging you, or worry about what the person would think of your painting. Or suppose people were talking near you or asking you questions. You might find it difficult to concentrate.

INTIMACY. Privacy is necessary for people to develop warm and affectionate relationships with other people.

Example: Suppose there was no place you could go to be alone with someone or there was no way to communicate in private. You might not be willing to express your innermost thoughts and feelings and you might find it difficult to develop close relationships with anyone.

Critical Thinking Exercise
IDENTIFYING AND DESCRIBING THE BENEFITS OF PRIVACY

Work with a study partner to answer the following questions. Include examples to explain or illustrate your ideas.

1. Do you think privacy is truly essential for people to develop close relationships? Why or why not?

2. What pressures to be like other people exist in your school and community? In what way does having privacy free you from those pressures and enable you to develop your own thoughts, feelings, and lifestyle?

3. How would you feel if no one respected the privacy of your personal possessions or if people did not respect your wishes when you wanted to be alone?

4. In what ways does privacy help you to be creative?

What are the costs of privacy?

LONELINESS AND ALIENATION. Too much privacy can lead to loneliness and to poor relations with others.

Example: Suppose a person always kept his or her feelings private. Others might be reluctant to share their feelings with someone who never reciprocates. With no one to talk to, the person might feel cut off and lonely.

LOSS OF STIMULATION AND INTELLECTUAL GROWTH. People correct errors in their thinking and learn new ideas through interaction with other people; too much privacy can inhibit the exchange of ideas and prevent learning from others.

Example: Some people are afraid to express their views for fear of being ridiculed. Because they keep their thoughts to themselves, it is difficult for them to become aware of errors and refine their thinking. Also, other people never benefit from their ideas.

MISBEHAVIOR AND LAWLESSNESS. Privacy enables unlawful behavior to remain undiscovered and unpunished.

Example: By acting in private, without being observed, people can plan and commit crimes and hide evidence of their crimes.

FINANCIAL COSTS. Maintaining privacy increases the cost of doing things.

Example: A company has to spend more to provide separate offices for its employees than to have them all work in a single large room.

LACK OF ACCOUNTABILITY. Privacy enables people to do things that others cannot observe; as a result, it may be impossible to hold them responsible for wrongdoing.

Example: Without supervision, people might take shortcuts in their work, cheat on a test, or steal. Other people might never discover what has been done or there may be no way to prove who is responsible.

Critical Thinking Exercise
IDENTIFYING AND DESCRIBING THE COSTS OF PRIVACY

Work with a study partner to answer the following questions. Include examples to explain or illustrate your ideas.

1. Could too much privacy inhibit your ability to be creative? Explain your answer.

2. How might too much privacy cause a person to have problems in developing friendships or in relating to other people?

3. How can maintaining privacy increase the cost of doing things?

4. Do you think privacy makes it possible for people to commit crimes and not get caught? Why or why not?

5. Do you think privacy makes it more difficult to hold people responsible for their actions? Why or why not?

Using the Lesson

1. Identify an issue of privacy in the news media or make up an example. Prepare a chart that lists the consequences of maintaining privacy in the situation and identify these consequences as benefits or costs. Be prepared to explain the issue to your class.

2. Working with your teacher, invite a law-enforcement officer or an attorney to class to discuss his or her ideas about the benefits and costs of privacy. Prepare a list of questions to ask.

LESSON 7

What Might Be Some of the Benefits and Costs of Confidentiality?

Purpose of Lesson

This lesson provides an opportunity to identify the benefits and costs of privacy in a specific situation, and to evaluate the importance of these benefits and costs. This lesson also provides an opportunity to role-play an administrative hearing concerning the privacy obligations of lawyers and therapists.

When you have completed this lesson, you should be able to identify benefits and costs and use these ideas to evaluate, take, and defend positions on issues of privacy.

Term to Know

hearsay

Why is it important to evaluate the benefits and costs of privacy?

Evaluating the benefits and costs of privacy is important before making decisions about issues of privacy. We need to decide which consequences of privacy are most important to us. Are the benefits more important than the costs? Or do we think the costs outweigh the benefits?

People may disagree about which benefits and costs of protecting privacy in a particular situation are most important. For example, consider a rule that protects the privacy of student lockers. Everyone would agree that the benefits of this rule include protection of the students' right to privacy and protection of their personal property. Everyone would also agree that the costs of this rule include interference with the school administrators' ability to find illegal drugs, weapons, or other improper things that might be hidden in lockers.

Some people might think that the benefits of this rule protecting the students' right to privacy outweigh its costs. Others might think that the costs outweigh the benefits. As you can see, it is important to consider benefits and costs when examining issues regarding privacy.

Critical Thinking Exercise
EXPLAINING SOME CONSEQUENCES OF CONFIDENTIALITY

Work in study groups to complete this exercise. As you read the following adaptation of a newspaper article, think about the consequences of requiring lawyers and therapists to keep their clients' confessions confidential. Then complete the tasks and answer the questions that have been assigned to your group in the section "Identifying Benefits and Costs." Be prepared to share your answers with the class.

A Fine Line: To Tell or Not to Tell
By Barry Siegel   *Times Staff Writer*

Los Angeles Times
Wednesday December 29, 1993

Leroy Phillips, Jr. is a criminal defense attorney in Chattanooga, Tennessee. He had always believed that the rules for being a defense attorney were very clear: you never shared your client's confidences with anyone, never gave an inch to the prosecutor, were a strong adversary of the state and an even stronger advocate of the defendant. The confidentiality privilege is a sacrosanct basis for how lawyers work. People must know they can tell their lawyer anything and it won't be divulged. Then in May, 1993, Phillips received a phone call that called his beliefs into question.

In response to the call, Phillips met the caller—an unassuming, rather awkward young man dressed in plain work clothes—who confessed to an unsolved homicide. "I did it," Phil Payne told Phillips. "I killed that store clerk last night. I thought she was my ex-girlfriend." At that point, attorney Phillips was faced with a difficult moral and legal dilemma. When an attorney is admitted to the bar, he takes an oath to keep his clients' confessions confidential. In Tennessee, a legal obligation exists as well; to divulge a client's confidence is a felony that carries a possible five-year prison term. Only if a client directly threatens to kill someone does the law oblige the attorney to inform authorities. Phil Payne never directly threatened to kill anyone; only by implication did he suggest that he might kill again. What was the lawyer to do?

Here is Phil Payne's story. Two weeks earlier, Payne had tried to visit a former girlfriend whom he had dated nine years before. The girl, however, ran him off. Distraught, Payne went to a bar and drank beer all evening, after which he went back to the girl's house planning to kill her. When she failed to answer the door, Payne began driving around, oblivious to his whereabouts. He finally stopped for cigarettes at an all-night market where he saw a female clerk making coffee. When Payne saw the clerk, he thought of his ex-girlfriend who had always fixed coffee for him; in his mind, he "saw" the girlfriend, not an unknown clerk. He pulled out a gun, shot the clerk and drove back to his mother's home where he went to bed.

What rights of privacy should be extended to persons suspected of violating the law?

The attorney asked, "What do you want me to do?" Payne, smiling, said "I know I did a terrible thing and I don't want to harm anyone else. I need to be punished but I want help, too." This request put Phillips in a quandary. If he turned Payne over to the police and Payne subsequently confessed, the young man would go to jail. Payne, however, did not appear to understand his rights, and Phillips was morally and legally obliged to explain the rights and the consequences if he turned himself in. The attorney therefore said, "If you go to the police, they might put you in a jail cell for the rest of your life. If you go through me, they might put you in a hospital. If you are mentally ill, you have a right to be treated. Do you want that?" "Yes, yes I do."

Phillips paid a visit to assistant district attorney Stan Lanzo. He told Lanzo the story of this delusional man who had admitted to murder but who seemed to be totally insane. Phillips said, "I am worried about the girlfriend but he hasn't said he plans to kill her so I cannot legally turn him in." Lanzo listened as Phillips suggested that they file a petition, put Payne in a hospital and examine him. His client would be off the street and whatever he said to the doctor would be usable only on the sanity issue and not on the question of guilt. Now Lanzo faced a dilemma as well. Phillips was a lawyer, not a psychologist. As a district attorney he couldn't commit Payne on the strength of a lawyer's analysis alone.

Phillips felt increasing concern about the ex-girlfriend who was in danger with Payne still at large. If he shared Payne's secrets, however, he could be reprimanded by the Tennessee Bar Association and perhaps even sued. Phillips turned to George Bercaw, a clinical psychologist, who administered a battery of tests. After a period of weeks, Bercaw encouraged the attorney to resolve the matter with the prosecutors although he was not too worried at that point.

In July 1993, Bercaw received a call from Payne's mother who reported that Payne had disappeared. Bercaw contacted Phillips, Phillips' first thought was to contact the ex-girlfriend. His second thought was, how could he? He'd be violating his trust with his client. Phillips' phone rang an hour later. It was Payne who explained that he had spent most of the time driving around his girlfriends house and in a cemetery talking with the girl's dead mother and listening to voices from the grave. The psychologist realized that Payne was indeed dangerous and might kill or commit suicide. Bercaw decided that moral obligations should take precedence over legal ones, especially after Payne's mother said that he talked of killing both the girlfriend and himself. Bercaw relayed this information to Phillips saying, "Leroy, I know you have an obligation as a lawyer, but I believe the law permits me to do more. The law says if I feel he's dangerous to himself or others, I can report him."

Phillips spoke to his client: "Mr. Bercaw thinks you're very ill. He believes that you need help and should turn yourself in. They will put you in jail, but eventually you will be examined to see if you should be put in a hospital." When Payne agreed, Phillips admonished him to talk only to the doctors, not the police.

Payne went to jail but refused to talk with police and because they had no hard evidence against him, Lanzo suggested to Phillips that they were ready to let him go. Phillips, by this time truly concerned about the safety of both Payne and his ex-girlfriend, responded, "If you turn him loose, the full responsibility is on you." When Payne called his attorney to say that he was back home, Phillips decided that the solution lay in bringing the situation to the media's attention and gaining the public's wrath. He also sent an investigator to visit Payne's girlfriend.

What knowledge about their clients should lawyers keep confidential?

Media attention pushed the DA into action. When Phillips would not let his client confess outright, Lanzo suggested that Payne waive his confidentiality. This action would permit Bercaw to explain his findings without fear of moral and legal recriminations. Imagine everyone's astonishment when state psychologists found Phillips sane and competent to stand trial.

Phillips realized that he had bent too far. For safety's sake, he had yielded to the prosecutor's refusal to get Payne off the streets. He had probably violated the code of ethics for letting a client waive his rights and now faced reprimand from the Tennessee Bar Association's Board of Professional Responsibility. Bercaw, too, came in for his share of criticism for letting his client waive his constitutional rights; he received a warning letter from the Tennessee Psychological Association. ■

IDENTIFYING BENEFITS AND COSTS

Group 1: Confidentiality Obligations of a Lawyer

1. List four or five possible consequences of requiring lawyers not to reveal their clients' confessions, except when the client directly threatens to kill someone.

2. Write a B next to each consequence you consider to be a benefit and a C next to each cost.

3. Do you think the defense lawyer, Leroy Phillips, acted properly in this case? Why or why not? What do you think defense lawyers should be required to do in situations like this? Use the benefits and costs you have identified in developing your opinions.

Group 2: Confidentiality Obligations of a Therapist

1. List four or five possible consequences of requiring therapists not to reveal their clients' confessions, except when the client directly threatens to harm someone.

2. Write a B next to each consequence you consider to be a benefit and a C next to each cost.

3. Do you think the therapist, George Bercaw, acted properly in this case? Why or why not? What do you think therapists should be required to do in situations like this? Use the benefits and costs you have identified in developing your opinions.

Critical Thinking Exercise

EVALUATING, TAKING, AND DEFENDING A POSITION ON THE VIOLATION OF CONFIDENTIALITY

Imagine that the Tennessee Bar Association has charged Leroy Phillips with violating the ethical rules which prohibit lawyers from revealing their clients' secrets, and that the Tennessee Psychological Association has made similar charges against George Bercaw.

Administrative hearings are to be conducted by both organizations to deal with these charges. Group 1 will role-play the Bar Association hearing, and Group 2 will role-play the Psychological Association hearing. Each group should be divided into three parts, with one part assigned to play the role of hearing officers, one part assigned to play the role of advocates for the professional organization bringing the charges, and one part assigned to play the role of defense counsel for the accused individual.

Advocates for the professional organizations should prepare arguments explaining why the accused individuals should be reprimanded or punished, and defense counsel for the accused individual should prepare arguments explaining why no discipline or punishment should be imposed. Each side should select one or two spokespersons to present its case.

While the advocates and defense counsel are preparing their arguments, the hearing officers should develop questions to ask each side, and should select a chairperson to conduct the hearing. Advocates for the professional organizations should make their presentations first; defense counsel should make their presentations second. Hearing officers may interrupt at any time to ask questions.

Each side should be allowed ten minutes for the presentation, including time spent asking and answering questions. After both sides have completed their presentations, the hearing officers should discuss the arguments presented, reach a decision, and explain their decision to the class.

Using the Lesson

1. Write a story or draw a picture that describes a time when having privacy was very important to you or to someone you know. Then list the benefits and costs of privacy in the story or picture you created. Finally, decide whether the benefits outweighed the costs, and explain why.

2. Draft a bill amending the Tennessee statute that makes it a crime for lawyers to reveal their clients' secrets, except when the client directly threatens to kill someone. Prepare arguments to support the changes your bill would make in the law.

LESSON 8

What Might Be Some Benefits and Costs of the Government Keeping a Secret?

Purpose of Lesson

This lesson provides an opportunity to examine the benefits and costs of allowing the federal government to keep secrets. Specifically, the lesson concerns a report on the Vietnam War which was "leaked" without authorization to reporters for the *New York Times* and the *Washington Post*. The lesson asks you to role-play a Supreme Court hearing in which the government seeks to prevent the newspapers from publishing the report.

When you have finished this lesson, you should be able to explain your position on the issue of privacy in this case. You also should be able to explain the usefulness of considering benefits and costs in evaluating, taking, and defending positions on issues of privacy.

Terms to Know

executive branch
injunction
prior restraint

Critical Thinking Exercise

EXAMINING GOVERNMENTAL PRIVACY

The following selection is based on an actual Supreme Court case, *New York Times Co. v. United States*, known as the Pentagon Papers case. Read the case carefully. After you have finished, the class will be divided into groups to evaluate the consequences of secrecy in the selection, and to engage in a simulated Supreme Court hearing on the case.

The Pentagon Papers Case

American involvement in the Vietnam War generated massive conflict in the United States. By 1967 more than 35,000 Americans had been killed or wounded or were missing in action, and many Americans publicly expressed their opposition to the war. President

Johnson's commitment to increase the number of troops overseas to more than 500,000 by the middle of 1968 led to increased nationwide protests. At the 1968 Democratic National Convention thousands of anti-war protesters clashed with the Chicago police; the protests grew even larger after President Nixon took office. In December, 1969, 250,000 anti-war protesters demonstrated in Washington, D.C., to oppose Nixon's plans for only a gradual withdrawal of U.S. troops, and thousands more participated in anti-war rallies around the country. Some demonstrations led to violent conflict. National Guard troops called in to maintain order at Kent State University in Ohio shot and killed four students on May 4, 1970, and on May 14, 1970, state police shot and killed two students at Jackson State College in Mississippi.

In June, 1971, *The New York Times* and the *Washington Post* obtained copies of a classified 7,000-page report entitled "History of U.S. Decision-Making Process on Vietnam Policy." The report, which showed that the government had misled the American public about U.S. involvement in Vietnam, was leaked by Daniel Ellsberg,

Daniel Ellsberg arguably broke the law by providing the "Pentagon Papers" report to The New York Times and the Washington Post. Does that make a difference in whether the government should be able to prevent publication of the report?

a former government employee, without authorization. When the newspapers began to publish excerpts from the report, the government sued for an injunction—a court order prohibiting certain conduct—to prevent further publication of the report.

The government claimed that publication of the classified report would endanger lives, undermine efforts to negotiate a peace treaty, and interfere with efforts to secure the release of prisoners of war. The government argued that the responsibility of the executive branch for the security of the nation is so basic that the president should be granted an injunction against publication of a newspaper story whenever the information to be revealed threatens grave and irreparable injury to the public interest, regardless of how the newspaper got the information it seeks to publish.

The newspapers claimed that the First Amendment prohibits any prior restraint on the publication of news, whatever the source; that the main purpose of the First Amendment was to prohibit the widespread practice of governmental suppression of embarrassing information and to safeguard the freedom of the press to criticize and expose deception in the government. The newspapers argued that the information they sought to publish would contribute to an ongoing national debate concerning the Vietnam War; that open debate and discussion of public issues are essential to preserve our constitutional form of self-government; that secrecy in government is undemocratic and perpetuates bureaucratic errors; and that the government's concerns about the possible effects of publishing the report were unproven speculations.

Conducting a Supreme Court Hearing

Your class should be organized into three groups to conduct the following activity. One group will play the role of Supreme Court justices, one group will play the role of lawyers for the newspapers, and one group will play the role of lawyers for the government. Each of the groups should list the benefits and costs of allowing the government to maintain secrecy in the above situation by prohibiting the newspapers from publishing the secret

report. The groups representing lawyers for the newspapers and for the government should prepare a brief presentation explaining why the government should or should not be permitted to keep the report secret. Use the benefits and costs you have listed in preparing your arguments. Select two or three spokespersons to present the group's position to the Supreme Court.

While the other groups are preparing their presentations, the students representing Supreme Court justices should prepare questions to ask the spokespersons for each side, and should select a Chief Justice to conduct the hearing.

After each group has presented its position, the Supreme Court justices should discuss the arguments presented and decide whether to allow the government to keep the report secret. The justices should justify their decision in terms of the benefits and costs it will entail. The class should conclude the activity by discussing the usefulness of considering benefits and costs in taking and defending positions on issues regarding privacy and other subjects.

Using the Lesson

1. Should the government be allowed to prevent the publication of information on how to make a nuclear bomb? Research the court case of *United States v. Progressive, Inc.* and report to the class how one court dealt with this issue. Explain why you agree or disagree with the court's decision.

2. Can you think of any institution (such as a school, hospital, or government agency) that has information about you or your friends that you would not want to be made public? If so, do you approve of this example of institutional secrecy? Explain your position.

3. Review the questions you wrote in your privacy notebook or journal at the end of Lesson 5. What do you think the answers to these questions might be? Write your answers down, then list three or more new questions you have about privacy.

Unit Four: What Should Be the Scope and Limits of Privacy?

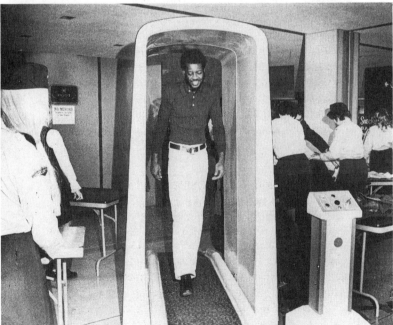

How do these photographs illustrate different issues concerning the scope and limits of privacy?

Purpose of Unit

Some of the most important issues we face as citizens involve questions about the scope and limits of privacy: What kinds of things will we allow people to keep private? When will we require privacy to give way to other values? Issues such as these arise between individuals or groups wishing to maintain privacy and others claiming the right to know something private or to regulate or interfere with an individual's or a group's freedom. In some cases it is reasonable and fair to protect privacy; at other times different values and interests may be more important. In this unit you will learn some intellectual tools—concepts and procedures—that are useful in evaluating, taking, and defending positions on questions about the scope and limits of privacy.

LESSON 9

What Considerations Are Useful in Dealing with Issues of Privacy?

Purpose of Lesson

This lesson introduces you to some considerations useful in dealing with issues of privacy, and provides an opportunity for you to apply these considerations in examining a conflict between privacy and the need to enforce the law. When you have finished the lesson, you should be able to explain how these considerations can be useful in examining issues of privacy.

Terms to Know

effects	consent
Freedom of Information Act	moral obligation
legality	interests
legal obligation	seizure
warrant	relevant considerations
values	

When should government be able to invade your privacy?

Since colonial times, Americans have believed strongly that citizens should have a right to privacy protecting them from arbitrary arrest and unreasonable searches, and protecting their homes from forced entry by government officials. The Fourth Amendment to the United States Constitution prohibits "unreasonable searches and seizures" by the government of our "persons, houses, papers, and effects [possessions]." However, it is not always easy to agree on what is unreasonable.

The Constitution's protection of privacy is not absolute. Government officials are allowed to enter our homes under certain conditions. For example, firefighters may enter our homes to put out a fire. Police may enter our homes if necessary to stop a crime in progress or one about to be committed. Police also may enter our homes if they first convince a judge that there is good reason to

believe evidence of a crime will be found inside, and the judge issues a search warrant authorizing them to search for that evidence. Government officials also may enter someone's home if that person gives them permission or invites them inside.

Should we always require a warrant for government officials to enter our homes? What examples might you cite to support your position?

Outside the home, people's expectations of privacy are not as strong. Still, the Fourth Amendment prohibits police and other government officials from unreasonably infringing on people's right to privacy. Although an officer who sees something suspicious does not need to obtain a warrant to stop and question the persons involved, he or she cannot stop and question a person arbitrarily, or just on a hunch. The conduct of the officer must be reasonable in order to comply with the Fourth Amendment.

IDENTIFYING THE CONFLICTING VALUES AND INTERESTS OF THE FOURTH AMENDMENT

As you read the following situation, think about the values and interests promoted by the Fourth Amendment, the competing values and interests at stake, and the choice that must be made between them. Work with a study partner to answer the "What do *you* think?" questions.

Jack Frost: Citizen and Suspected Criminal

Jack Frost is a citizen of the United States. Privacy is an important part of his life: it means that he is secure in his home; he can cast a secret ballot at election time; and he can think about any idea without fear that the government will try to make him conform to its point of view. Without privacy, his and all other Americans' individuality and freedom would mean very little.

Jack Frost is a suspected leader of organized crime. He may be responsible for millions of dollars in theft, drug dealing on a massive scale, scores of injuries and murders, and countless other violations of the law. The police want to end the suspected criminal career of Jack Frost, but to do so, they need information about his activities. Their job is very difficult because of every person's right of privacy.

What do *you* think?

1. What values and interests conflict with privacy in the situation described above?

2. Why might it be necessary to choose between protecting privacy and protecting other values?

3. Why is it important to have rules or a system for deciding when someone's right to privacy should give way to other values?

What things should you consider in analyzing issues of privacy?

As you can see, privacy may interfere with other important values and interests. In the situation you just considered, a conflict existed between the goals of protecting privacy and enforcing the law. In any given situation, people may have different opinions about how conflicts between privacy and other values and interests should be resolved. Following are some **relevant considerations**—things that should be considered, that are important, or that might make a difference—in deciding how to resolve conflicts about privacy.

- **Consent.** Has someone whose privacy is at issue **consented** or agreed to the invasion of his or her privacy? For example:

  - If police want to search someone's home or car, and the person gives them permission to do so, the person has consented to the search.

  - At airport security checks, airline passengers know that they will have to pass through a metal detector, and carry-on luggage will be x-rayed, before they can board the plane. Because they know this in advance, and because they could avoid the invasion of their privacy by choosing not to travel by plane, it can be said that they have consented to these security procedures.

  - Elected officials know that much of their personal history and behavior will be revealed to the public. Because they could avoid this invasion of their privacy by choosing not to run for public office, it might be said that they have consented to the public disclosure of information about themselves.

- **Legality.** Do those who wish to invade someone's privacy have a **legal right**—a right confirmed by law—to do so? For example:

  - A search warrant issued by a judge gives police a legal right to search the places described in the search warrant.

  - Customs officials have a legal right to search anyone who crosses the border into the United States.

  - The Freedom of Information Act, a law passed by Congress in 1966, gives people a legal right to obtain documents from the federal government, unless the documents contain certain types of confidential or classified information.

- **Legal obligation.** Does a person have a **legal obligation**—a responsibility imposed or enforced by law—to maintain the privacy of another? For example:

  - Certain laws impose a legal obligation on alcohol and drug abuse counselors not to disclose their clients' identities.

What do you think are the costs and benefits of expecting public officials to disclose information about themselves?

- If someone signs a contract promising to keep certain information secret, the contract may create a legal obligation not to reveal the information.

- Under the Constitution, police have a legal obligation not to invade a person's privacy without a warrant, except in certain limited circumstances.

- **Moral obligation**. Does a person have a **moral obligation**—a responsibility imposed by principles of right and wrong—to maintain the privacy of another? For example:

  - Someone who promises to keep a secret generally has a moral obligation not to tell the secret to anyone else.

  - Doctors have a moral obligation not to reveal private medical information about their patients, and counselors have a moral obligation not to reveal what people tell them in private.

  - Lawyers have a moral obligation not to reveal confidential information about their clients.

Critical Thinking Exercise
DESCRIBING RELEVANT CONSIDERATIONS

As you read the following selection adapted from the case of *Terry v. Ohio*, think about the values and interests listed in the previous section. Work in small groups to answer the "What do *you* think?" questions.

The Search

Officer Martin McFadden thought something was odd about the behavior of two men talking across the street. First one and then the other walked up the street, looked into a store window, walked a short distance, turned around, stopped again in front of the same store, and then rejoined his companion. Back and forth, almost a dozen times, the men repeated this pattern of behavior. Then both men walked toward the store.

"Stop right there," Officer McFadden shouted. "Put your hands against the wall and spread your legs."

The men complied. Officer McFadden patted down the suspects. He was not surprised to feel a hard, heavy object concealed in each man's overcoat. These objects proved to be guns.

"You're under arrest," he informed them. Later charged with carrying a concealed weapon, John Terry and Richard Chilton were represented by a skilled lawyer. Told of the circumstances of his clients' arrest, the lawyer argued that Officer McFadden's conduct violated the Fourth Amendment. Therefore, the evidence against Mr. Terry and Mr. Chilton should not be used in court.

The prosecutor disagreed. "Officer McFadden had a reasonable suspicion that criminal activity was afoot," he argued. "Mr. Terry and Mr. Chilton were 'casing' the store and were about to commit armed robbery. Officer McFadden had every right to stop the men and to frisk them for weapons they might use to attack him."

Under what circumstances should we permit law enforcement officials to "pat down" or frisk suspects for weapons?

What do *you* think?

1. Did Mr. Terry and Mr. Chilton **consent** to the search by Officer McFadden? Explain your answer.

2. Did Officer McFadden have a **legal right** to search Mr. Terry and Mr. Chilton? Why or why not?

3. Did Officer McFadden have a **legal obligation** not to search Mr. Terry and Mr. Chilton? Why or why not?

4. Did Officer McFadden have a **moral obligation** not to search Mr. Terry and Mr. Chilton? Why or why not?

Using the Lesson

1. If you believe that police never should be allowed to invade people's privacy, then how can society be protected against crime? If you believe that police always should be allowed to invade people's privacy, then how can a person feel secure and be free? If you think that police should be allowed to invade people's privacy only in certain situations, then what rules would you impose on police to tell them when the are allowed to invade someone's privacy?

2. Think about a conflict involving privacy in your school, neighborhood, or town. Use what you have learned in this lesson to evaluate this conflict. Imagine alternative ways in which the conflict might be resolved. Decide what is the best way to resolve the conflict. Then explain to the class what the conflict is, what should be done about the conflict, and why.

3. Working with your teacher, invite a person who deals with issues of privacy, such as a police officer, judge, doctor, lawyer, or city council member, to visit your classroom. Ask that person to describe a conflict involving privacy and to suggest several ways in which the conflict could be resolved.

LESSON 10

What Conflicts about Privacy May Arise from Law Enforcement?

Purpose of Lesson

In this lesson you learn and apply a set of intellectual tools to examine an issue regarding law enforcement. The issue is whether the police should have the authority to demand that a person state his or her name, and to arrest the person if he or she refuses. When you have completed the lesson, you should be able to use the intellectual tools to take and defend a position on this issue of privacy.

Term to Know

loitering

What are procedures for analyzing issues of privacy?

In the last lesson you looked at some relevant considerations that can help you think more clearly about issues of privacy; now you will use these considerations as part of a specific procedure for analyzing issues of privacy. The procedure is described below and summarized in the chart on page 98; it consists of a series of steps that you can follow each time you want to evaluate, take, or defend a position on privacy. Note that the person in each step might be a group or an institution, such as a school or government agency.

1. **Identify the person claiming privacy**. Identify the person who wants privacy and what he or she wants to keep private. How is it to be kept private? What are the reasons for wanting to keep it private?

2. **Identify the person wishing to invade the other's privacy.** Identify the person who opposes the first person's claim to privacy. Give the reasons for opposing the claim. Describe the way in which the first person's privacy is to be invaded.

3. **Examine relevant considerations.** Consider matters that are relevant to or make a difference in conflicts about privacy, such as consent, legality, legal obligations, and moral obligations. Determine how these matters apply to the situation.

4. **Evaluate alternative means of managing the issue**. Think about different ways to resolve the issue. These might include recognizing or rejecting the claim to privacy or reaching a compromise. In thinking about these alternatives, be sure to identify and evaluate the costs and benefits of each proposed solution.

5. **Take and defend a position.** Decide what you think is the best way to resolve the issue and explain the reasons for your decision.

Critical Thinking Exercise

EVALUATING A POSITION ON LAW ENFORCEMENT

As you read the following situation, think about how you would feel if a police officer asked you to stop and identify yourself. Then work in small groups to answer the questions on the intellectual tool chart that follows. Be prepared to explain your answers to the class.

The Stranger

Throughout the history of civilization, communities have sought to protect themselves from outsiders. Yet one of the cherished freedoms we enjoy as Americans is the right to go where we please and to travel from town to town. Not too long ago, these two traditions came into conflict in California.

Police officers stopped Edward Lawson as he walked down the street. Asked to identify himself, Mr. Lawson refused to cooperate, remaining silent. California law made it a crime for a person who loiters or wanders upon the streets or from place to place without apparent reason or business to refuse to identify himself and to account

Would you rather live in a society where police could stop anyone on the street and demand identification, or in a society where they could not?

violated his constitutional privacy rights guaranteed by the Fourth Amendment. His case eventually reached the United States Supreme Court.

for his presence when requested by a police officer. The police arrested Mr. Lawson and charged him with violating this law. Mr. Lawson sued to have the law declared unconstitutional. He claimed that the law

---

Using the Lesson

1. Suppose Congress was considering a law that would require every person to carry a "National I.D." card specifying whether the person is a U.S. citizen or the citizen of another country. The law would require that people present the card when seeking employment. What do you think would be the best arguments for and against such a law? What position would you take on such a law? Write a letter to your member of Congress expressing your views. Be sure to explain the reasons for your position.

2. Government agencies have used television cameras to monitor public places such as highway rest areas, parking garages, and subway stations. How do you think this compares to having police officers patrolling such areas? Which provides better protection against unlawful behavior? Which imposes a greater burden on privacy? Do you agree with the government's use of cameras in this way? Write a letter to the editor of a newspaper or give a presentation to your class expressing your opinions.

Intellectual Tool Chart for Issues of Privacy

Questions	Answers
1. Identify the person claiming privacy: ■ Whose claim to privacy was endangered in this case? ■ What objects did the person want to keep private? ■ How might the person have kept the object private? ■ Why might the person want to keep the objects private?	
2. Identify the person wishing to limit or invade the other's privacy: ■ Who wished to limit or invade the other's privacy? ■ How did that person invade the other's privacy? ■ Why did that person want to invade the other's privacy?	
3. Examine relevant considerations: ■ Did the person consent to have his or her privacy invaded? Explain. ■ Did the person who invaded the other's privacy have a legal right to do so? Why or why not? ■ Did the person who invaded the other's privacy have a legal obligation not to do so? Why or why not? ■ Did the person who invaded the other's privacy have a moral obligation not to do so? Why or why not?	
4. Evaluate alternative means of managing the issue: ■ What are the costs and benefits of recognizing the person's claim to privacy? ■ What are the costs and benefits of rejecting the claim to privacy? ■ What are alternative means of gathering information that the person who wants to invade the privacy of another might use? ■ What are the benefits of each of these means? ■ What are the costs of each of these means?	
5. Take and defend a position: ■ How do you think this issue should be resolved? Explain your position.	

LESSON 11

How Do Advances in Technology Threaten Privacy?

Purpose of Lesson

In this lesson you participate in a simulated congressional debate on a bill intended to protect the privacy of medical information, while allowing that information to be stored and transmitted on computers as part of a national health care system. When you have finished the lesson, you should be able to explain and evaluate different positions on the privacy issues this proposal raises. You also should be able to present and defend your position.

Terms to Know

data bank
retrieve

How do computers affect privacy?

Computers affect the lives of everyone in our society. People use computers not only to keep track of information, but also to increase efficiency. Computers are involved in almost everything we do:

- from the production of electricity to the production of textbooks

- from the use of telephones to the use of credit cards

- from the checkout line at the grocery store to the check-cashing line at the bank

But computers present problems for privacy in modern society because they can store information permanently and they can easily retrieve the stored information. Computers store such information as how much electricity and water you use each month, the amount of taxes you pay, your hair color, eye color, and whether you wear glasses. In fact, as you can see from the chart on this page, information about you that is stored in computers could draw a detailed picture of your life.

Although certain laws impose some restrictions, organizations usually can decide whether they will share the information they have stored in their computers, and several private companies have created large computer data banks by combining information

Information Stored in a Computer Data Bank	
Every Time You	**A Computer Stores**
use your telephone	the number you call, the date, and the length of time you talk
rent a movie from a video store	the name of that movie and the date you rented it
use a credit card	the date, amount of the purchase, name and location of the store, and a description of what you bought
subscribe to a newspaper or magazine	your name and address, the name of the newspaper or magazine, and the dates your subscription starts and ends
apply for a loan	your address and telephone number, the name, address, and phone number of the place you work, how much money you earn, the value of the property you own, how much money you already owe, and how much you pay on your debts each month
apply for car insurance	your address, driving record, the make and model of your car, how far you drive to work, and how far you drive each year
pay your bills	the date and amount of your payment

from different sources, such as the forms people fill out when they apply for a loan, credit card, or driver's license. They sell this information to businesses that use it to identify people who might buy their products. Information disclosed to one person for one reason may be retrieved by other people and used for other purposes.

Computers make it almost impossible for individuals to control who learns personal information about them. As time goes by, computers will become more powerful; they will be able to store more information and retrieve it faster. More people and organizations will use computers, and privacy problems are likely to increase.

What do *you* think?

1. Do you think computers pose a serious problem for people who want to maintain their privacy? Why or why not?

2. Do you think the advantages of computer technology outweigh the privacy problems they create? Explain your position.

3. What measures, if any, would you support to prevent private companies from compiling and storing data about the private activities of individuals?

4. How could individuals act in order to limit the ability of private companies to gather and store information about their activities?

How does technology affect privacy in health care?

Since the ancient days of Hippocrates, people have expected their doctors to keep their medical condition confidential. The concern for privacy of medical information derives in part from its personal nature, and in part from the way it can reveal our weaknesses and make us vulnerable. The doctor's obligation of confidentiality promotes health care by encouraging us to report our symptoms to our physician without fear of embarrassment. Today, that confidentiality is not only a doctor's moral obligation but his or her legal obligation as well.

Nevertheless, the privacy of medical information is far from absolute. To provide insurance benefits, health insurance companies require covered patients to consent to their doctor's disclosure of their medical condition. Even people without insurance may be required to permit their doctors to disclose their medical condition, for example if that condition is an issue in a lawsuit. Public health concerns have led to laws requiring doctors to report medical information regarding their patients to government health agencies, such as when the information is needed to prevent the spread of infectious diseases.

Now, however, new concerns have been raised about the privacy of medical information. These concerns arise from two factors.

■ The widespread use of health insurance to pay for medical care has resulted in the creation of computer files and data banks that store medical information regarding identifiable individuals.

■ A national health care program has been proposed that would require patients to present a "National Health Card" before receiving treatment. The card would make more medical information available systematically. In particular, if smart cards with magnetic strips were used for this purpose, the National Health Card could contain an individual's entire medical history.

Critical Thinking Exercise
USING INTELLECTUAL TOOLS TO EVALUATE, TAKE, AND DEFEND A POSITION

Work with a study partner or in small groups to answer the following questions about the privacy problems that would be created by the National Health Card proposal described below. Be prepared to share your answers with the class.

Imagine that you are a member of the United States House of Representatives. Legislation has been proposed that would require every individual to present his or her National Health Card in order to receive medical care. Doctors and hospitals will be able to access the individual's entire medical history with the card; the information will be stored on the card's magnetic strip. Whenever medical care is provided, the information on the card will be updated. The government will assume the responsibility of paying for medical care; information about services provided will be forwarded electronically and stored in the government's central computer data bank, and all paperwork will be eliminated.

1. **Identify the person claiming privacy.**

   ■ Whose claim to privacy would be endangered by the use of a National Health Card?

   ■ What medical information might people **not** want to have in a government data bank? Why?

   ■ How could information about individuals be kept private?

2. **Identify the person wishing to limit or invade the other's privacy.**

   ■ How might a National Health Card limit or invade people's privacy?

   ■ Why might the federal government wish to have people use a National Health Card?

3. **Examine relevant considerations.**

   - By taking advantage of health insurance benefits from the government, do people **consent** to disclosure or use of information pertaining to their health care? Explain your position.

   - Do you think the federal government has a **legal right** to require the use of a National Health Card and to maintain medical information about people in a centralized computer data bank? Why or why not?

   - In your opinion, would requiring the use of a National Health Card violate a **legal obligation** of the federal government to respect the privacy of citizens? Explain your position.

   - Do you think requiring the use of a National Health Card would violate a **moral obligation** of the federal government to respect the privacy of citizens? Explain your position.

4. **Evaluate alternative solutions.**

   - What are the costs and benefits of the federal government requiring people to use a National Health Card?

   - What are some means the federal government could use to ensure the privacy of medical information it collects? What are the benefits and costs of each of these means?

5. **Take and defend a position.**

   - What position would you take on requiring the use of a National Health Card? Explain your reasoning.

Critical Thinking Exercise

EVALUATING, TAKING, AND DEFENDING A POSITION ON A NATIONAL HEALTH CARD

During this activity, you participate in a simulated congressional hearing. You suggest alternative ways of dealing with privacy issues raised by a National Health Card. Your teacher will divide your class into the following groups:

- **Doctors United for Health Care.** Your group is in favor of a national health care program and strongly supports any plan that would do away with paperwork. You believe the benefits of the National Health Card outweigh the privacy problems it would create. While you have no objection to imposing requirements on the government to protect privacy, you do not believe any such requirements should be imposed on medical care providers, because they are not needed.

- **Citizens for Efficiency in Health Care.** Your group favors any proposal that it believes will improve government health care programs and make them more efficient. To gain support for the National Health Card proposal, you are willing to propose that severe penalties be imposed on doctors, hospitals, and the government for unauthorized or improper use or disclosure of medical information.

- **Citizens for Privacy Committee.** Your group believes that the National Health Card proposal should be opposed unless safeguards, restrictions, and penalties are enacted that would provide real protection for the privacy of medical information.

- **People United against Tyranny.** Your group thinks it would be a dangerous mistake to allow the government to have access to each citizen's medical information, regardless of the legal restrictions that might be imposed to prevent misuse of that information. You oppose the National Health Card proposal under all circumstances.

- **House Information Subcommittee.** You will decide whether to approve the use of a National Health Card as part of a national health care program and whether to enact any special provisions to secure the privacy of medical information. You will listen to all views because you want to make the best possible decision. You know your constituents are concerned about and want health care, but they also value their privacy and freedom.

Preparing and Conducting the Hearing

The first four groups should prepare arguments supporting or opposing the use of a National Health Card, and suggest how (if at all) privacy of medical information could be preserved if such cards were used. The arguments should identify and take into account the benefits and costs of a National Health Card and the benefits and costs of the privacy-securing suggestions. The arguments also should explain how the group's position would

- protect the privacy of people

- give government a way of obtaining and using needed information to run a national health care program

The first four groups should select two or three spokespersons to present their arguments to the House Information Subcommittee. While the first four groups develop their arguments, the subcommittee should prepare questions to ask each group's spokespersons. The subcommittee also should elect a chairperson to conduct the hearing.

After the four groups have presented their arguments, each member of the subcommittee should express and explain his or her views on the creation of a National Health Card and on the privacy-securing suggestions that were made.

Using the Lesson

1. Imagine that Congress was considering a law that would require everyone to have an I.D. number. The number would be used whenever a person filled out an official form, such as a tax return, hospital admission form, or an application for a passport, driver's license, or government benefits. The number also would be used if the person received a traffic ticket or was arrested. What arguments could you make in favor of this law? What arguments could you make to oppose it? Which arguments do you think are the strongest? Why?

2. Why do you think individuals and groups are willing to testify at public hearings? Think about the groups who have just been represented at your mock congressional hearing.

3. What are the benefits of holding hearings on decisions the government will make? What are the costs? Should all government decisions be made only after hearings? Why or why not?

LESSON 12

What Privacy Rights Should People Have with Regard to Their Own Bodies?

Purpose of Lesson

This lesson examines the right of privacy a person has with regard to his or her own body. The lesson provides an opportunity for your class to conduct a legislative hearing concerning the extent to which this right of privacy should be protected when the person's life is at stake. When you have completed this lesson, you should be able to evaluate, take, and defend positions on the issue of privacy it contains.

Term to Know

living will

Critical Thinking Exercise
EXAMINING PRIVACY AND BODILY INTEGRITY

Your class will be divided into four groups to complete this exercise. Each group should read the selection assigned to it and answer the "What do you think?" questions. Be prepared to share your answers with the class.

1. Henning Jacobson did not want to be vaccinated against smallpox. The Cambridge Board of Health had determined that vaccination was needed to prevent the spread of the disease, and Massachusetts law required that Jacobson submit to the Board of Health's order or face a fine. Jacobson claimed the state had no power to compel him to be vaccinated; that "a compulsory vaccination law is unreasonable, arbitrary, and oppressive, and, therefore, hostile to the inherent right of every freeman to care for his own body and health in such way as to him seems best; and that the execution of such a law against one who objects to vaccination…is nothing short of an assault upon his person."

Do you think people have especially strong privacy rights with regard to their own bodies?

2. Antonio Rochin was sitting on the edge of his bed when three deputy sheriffs burst into his room. Spying two capsules on a night stand by the bed, the deputies demanded, "Whose stuff is this?" Rochin grabbed the capsules and put them in his mouth. The three deputies jumped on him and tried to force him to open his mouth. Unable to do so, they handcuffed Rochin and took him to a hospital. There a doctor pumped Rochin's stomach by inserting a tube down his throat and forcing a liquid through the tube, making him vomit. The vomited capsules proved to contain morphine. Charged with possession of drugs, Rochin claimed the conduct of the deputies and the doctor, and the bodily intrusion by which they accomplished the seizure of the capsules, violated his rights.

3. Rudolph Lee was brought to the emergency room by police. He had a gunshot wound to the left side of his chest, and the bullet was lodged under his collarbone. Lee told the police he had been shot by two robbers, but when they arrived at the hospital the police heard a different story: a shopkeeper who had been shot in an attempted robbery that night, and who had also shot his attacker, had been brought to the same emergency room; this shopkeeper identified Lee as the man who had tried to rob him. After an investigation, Lee was charged with attempted robbery, and the government sought a court order requiring Lee to submit to surgery to remove the bullet, so that the bullet could be examined to see if it was fired from the shopkeeper's gun. Lee refused to consent to the surgery, and argued that it would violate his constitutional rights to compel him to submit to such a procedure.

4. Elizabeth Bouvia wanted her nasogastric feeding tube removed. Against her will, doctors at the hospital had routed the tube through her nose and down her throat into her stomach in order to keep her alive. Cerebral palsy had rendered Elizabeth's arms and legs useless—she could not even sit up in bed. Unable to eat solid food at all, Elizabeth was spoon-fed a liquid-like diet but was not consuming enough to avoid starving. Her weight had dropped to 65 or 70 pounds when the hospital staff determined that feeding through a nasogastric tube was necessary to save her life. Now, through her lawyers, Elizabeth was asking the court to order the doctors to respect her wishes and remove the tube they had inserted over her objections, even if that meant she would starve to death in the immediate future, and even if, as her doctors claimed, she could live another 15 or 20 years with the feeding tube in place.

What do *you* think?

1. Who is claiming a right to privacy or bodily integrity in this situation? How is the person's privacy or bodily integrity being violated? How serious are the violations or intrusions?

2. Who is opposing or limiting the claim of privacy or bodily integrity? What are the reasons for opposing or limiting the claim of privacy or bodily integrity?

3. Are the intrusions on privacy or bodily integrity necessary, or are there other ways of managing the conflict?

4. Do you think there are sufficient grounds to invade the person's privacy and bodily integrity in this situation, considering the seriousness of the intrusion and the importance of the reasons for it? Explain your position.

What are reasonable legislative limits regarding bodily privacy?

As you have seen, individual interests in privacy and bodily integrity can come into conflict with the interests of society in a number of different contexts. The government may need to intrude on a person's privacy and bodily integrity in order to obtain evidence of a crime, in order to protect the public health and prevent the spread of disease, or in order to protect the health of the very person whose privacy and bodily integrity is invaded.

Reasonable people may have different opinions about how the privacy conflicts in these situations should be resolved. In each of these situations, some might think that the interests of society are more important than the privacy interests of the individual, some might think that the individual's interests are more important than the interests of society, and some might think that the particular facts of the situation in question must be evaluated to determine which interests are more important.

In the following exercise you will engage in a simulated legislative hearing on the topic of life-preserving medical care. The issue the state legislature must resolve is whether individuals should be free to refuse such care at all, and if so, under what circumstances. In order to address this issue, the state legislature has formed a special committee which will conduct a hearing and present its recommendations to the legislature.

Critical Thinking Exercise

EVALUATING, TAKING, AND DEFENDING A POSITION ON BODILY INTEGRITY

To conduct this activity, your class should be divided into the following groups:

- **Doctors for Ethical Health Care**. Your group is in favor of letting patients make their own decisions about medical treatment in most circumstances, but only when they are capable of giving informed consent. Your group is concerned that in many cases, a person with medical problems may refuse treatment because he or she is depressed, rather than making an informed, rational decision. Particularly when the medical treatment would or could prolong the person's life, refusal is contrary to the person's best interests, and may well reflect the influence of psychological depression.

- **Association of Health Insurers**. Your group believes that doctors often go too far in attempting to prolong an individual's life, expending vast efforts and resources with little hope of success. Your group supports broad protection of an individual's right to refuse medical treatment, even in circumstances when that treatment could be life-saving.

- **Confederation of Concerned Religious Leaders**. Your group believes that it is morally wrong for an individual to refuse life-saving medical treatment, except when that refusal is based on religious conviction, as in the case of Jehovah's Witnesses refusing blood transfusions. Your group contends that the state has an absolute duty to prevent suicide, and is determined not to allow an individual's claims to privacy and bodily integrity interfere with that duty.

- **Advocates for the Elderly**. Your group thinks people should have the right to die with dignity, and that an individual's considered decision regarding medical treatment should be respected. However, your group is concerned that undue pressure might be placed on a person to refuse life-saving medical treatment, either by those who would gain financially by avoiding the cost of the treatment, or by those who are burdened by having to care for the person. Your group seeks to have the legislature approve the use of living wills, which provide clear evidence of an individual's wishes with regard to life-saving medical care, together with safeguards to ensure that the directions recorded in these documents are not influenced by undue pressure from others.

- **Committee on Life-Saving Medical Care.** You will decide whether individuals will be allowed to refuse life-saving medical care, and if so, under what circumstances. You will listen to all views because you want to make the best possible decision. You know your constituents value their privacy and freedom, but they also are concerned to protect and preserve the sanctity and value of human life, and to safeguard people from their own mistakes.

How would you balance the privacy rights of patients with the concerns of society and the medical profession?

Conducting the Hearing

The first four groups should prepare proposals specifying the circumstances, if any, in which a person may refuse life-saving medical care. These groups should also prepare arguments to support their proposals, explaining how their group's position would balance

- the individual's interest in privacy and bodily integrity, and

- society's interests in preserving life, in preventing suicide, in maintaining the ethics of the medical profession, and in ensuring that any decision to refuse life-saving medical care will be carefully considered and will be made without undue pressure.

The first four groups should select two or three spokespersons to present their proposals and arguments to the Committee on Life-Saving Medical Care. While the first four groups are working on their arguments, the committee should prepare questions to ask each group's spokespersons, and select a chairperson to conduct the hearing. The committee should review the chart on page 98 in preparing its questions.

After the four groups have presented their proposals and arguments, each member of the committee should express and explain his or her views on the circumstances, if any, in which individuals should be free to refuse life-saving medical care. The class as a whole should then conclude the activity by voting on the various proposals that were presented.

Using the Lesson

1. Should it make any difference whether a person's refusal of life-saving medical care is based on his or her religious convictions? Do research to find out how courts have dealt with efforts by Jehovah's Witnesses to refuse blood transfusions for themselves and for their children. Give a report to your class on what you learn, and explain your own views on this issue.

2. Should the government be permitted to require a person to receive mental health treatment? Under what circumstances? What forms of mental health treatment should the government be able to compel a person to receive? Can the government compel a person to take medications for mental illness? To engage in psychotherapy sessions? To submit to brain surgery? Do research to learn about your state's laws on involuntary commitment of persons for mental health treatment. Write a letter to the editor or to your state legislators expressing your views on this topic.

LESSON 13

How Should We Resolve Conflicts between Privacy and Freedom of the Press?

Purpose of Lesson

This final lesson on privacy provides an opportunity to examine issues that arise from the activities of the press. Your class will discuss these issues and establish guidelines for members of the press to follow when they investigate and report on private citizens.

When you have finished the lesson, you should be able to explain and evaluate different positions on this issue. You also should be able to explain the usefulness of establishing a policy to deal with situations that are likely to arise again and again.

Terms to Know

common law
libel
slander

Do you think there are some people or subjects that should be off limits to reporters and the media?

What privacy boundaries should be respected by the press?

The First Amendment provides that "Congress shall make no law...abridging the freedom...of the press." But under the common law, members of the press, like others, have been held liable for damages when they libel or slander someone by publishing or broadcasting false statements that injure the person's reputation. If the damaging statements are true, however, no suit for libel or slander can be maintained.

Does this mean the press is free to invade our privacy and publish the most private and intimate facts of our lives? Are there boundaries of privacy that journalists must respect? Are there some topics that should be considered off-limits?

What about the means used by journalists to investigate their subjects? Can reporters use hidden cameras and microphones to record the people they are investigating? Can they lie about their identity to get people to reveal things they would not tell a reporter? Can they search a person's garbage to gather information?

Both of these types of issues—limits on the topics reporters choose to investigate, and limits on the ways they investigate their topics—can have significant impacts on the extent of privacy we enjoy in this country. These issues also involve other values, such as freedom and human dignity. The following exercise gives you an opportunity to explore the first type of issue: what limits there ought to be on the topics reporters choose to cover. Later, your class will have a chance to formulate guidelines for reporters to follow with regard to both types of issues.

Critical Thinking Exercise

EXAMINING INVASION OF PRIVACY BY THE PRESS

Read the following selection carefully. Then work with a study partner to complete the intellectual tool chart on page 98. Be prepared to explain your position to your class.

Briscoe v. Reader's Digest Association

In the late 1960s, *Reader's Digest* published an article titled "The Big Business of Hijacking." One sentence in the article referred to Marvin Briscoe: "Typical of many beginners, Marvin Briscoe [and another man] stole a 'valuable-looking' truck in Danville, Ky., and then fought a gun battle with the local police, only to learn that they had hijacked four bowling-pin spotters." In fact, the theft had occurred in 1956, some eleven years before the article was published, and Mr. Briscoe had paid his debt to society and lived a crime-free life since then.

Mr. Briscoe sued for invasion of privacy, asserting that *Reader's Digest's* publication of "truthful but embarrassing private facts about his past life was wrongful." He claimed that he had assumed a place in respectable society and made many friends who were not aware of the incident in his earlier life; that these friends and his own 11-year-old daughter first learned of the incident as a result of the publication of the article, and that he had been humiliated and subjected to contempt and ridicule as a result.

In discussing Mr. Briscoe's claim, the California Supreme Court noted that

> In many respects a person had less privacy in the small community of the 18th century than he did in the urbanizing late 19th century or he does today in the modern metropolis. Extended family networks, primary group relationships, and rigid communal mores served to expose an individual's every deviation from the norm and to straitjacket him in a vise of backyard gossip. Yet [it is] mass exposure to public gaze, as opposed to backyard gossip, which threaten[s] to deprive men of the right of 'scratching wherever one itches'.

> Acceptance of the right to privacy has grown with the increasing capability of the mass media and electronic devices with their capacity to destroy an individual's anonymity, intrude upon his most intimate activities, and expose his most personal characteristics to public gaze.... Men fear exposure not only to those closest to them....

The claim is not so much one of total secrecy as it is of the right to *define* one's circle of intimacy....

On the other hand, the court also noted that

> The right to keep information private [is] bound to clash with the right to disseminate information to the public.... [M]en are curious about the inner sanctums of their neighbors; the public will create its heroes and villains.... The masks we wear may be stripped away upon the occurrence of some event of public interest.... [T]he risk of exposure is a concomitant of urban life.... In a nation built upon the free dissemination of ideas, it is always difficult to declare that something may not be published.

Critical Thinking Exercise
IDENTIFYING GUIDELINES FOR REPORTERS

Your class should be divided into small groups to complete this exercise. Each group will be assigned to represent one of the following organizations:

- **Association of Responsible Newspaper Editors**: Your views are summarized by the motto of *The New York Times*: All the News That's Fit to Print.

- **Broadcast Entertainment Group:** Your views might be summarized as All the News That Fits, We Print.

- **People for Protection of Privacy:** Your group seeks strong protection for the privacy rights of private citizens.

- **First Amendment Foundation**: Your group stresses the importance of a free press to a free society, and the need to permit unrestricted discussion of any matter having any importance to the public.

- **Citizens for Decency and Dignity**: Your group opposes the lack of standards of decency and decorum in the press, particularly on television, and believes that the failure of mass media to govern itself responsibly justifies the imposition of standards of decency by the government.

Each group should develop a proposed policy or set of guidelines that addresses the following two issues:

■ What limits should apply to the means used by journalists to investigate their subjects?

■ What limits should apply to the topics journalists choose to investigate and report?

Each group should select two or three spokespersons to present each component of its proposed guidelines to the class. First, using a roundtable format, the groups should take turns presenting their views on what limits should apply to the topics journalists choose to investigate and report. Following discussion of this subject, the groups should take turns presenting their views on what limits should apply to the means used by journalists to investigate their subjects. The teacher should moderate the roundtable discussions. The class should conclude the activity by evaluating the usefulness of developing guidelines or policies to deal with privacy issues that are likely to arise again and again.

Using the Lesson

1. The film Absence of Malice presents a number of issues regarding the conduct of the press, including the propriety of a newspaper editor's decision to identify a source who was promised confidentiality. View the film and give a report to your class describing the issues it raises, and explain your position on these issues.

2. Some schools have used cameras to monitor hallways, outdoor campus areas, and problem classrooms. What do you think are the best arguments for and against this practice? Do you agree with the school's use of cameras in this way? Write a letter to the school board expressing your opinions.

3. Businesses such as banks and stores often have video cameras that tape persons doing business there. Make a chart of the costs and benefits of this practice. What alternatives can you think of for banks and stores to use? What are the costs and benefits of these alternatives? If you wanted to, how could you persuade the stores to stop using the cameras? Present your suggestions to the class.

RESPONSIBILITY
Table of Contents

Introduction

This statue in front of the United States Supreme Court building symbolizes the responsibility of government to make and enforce the law. What might happen if government failed to fulfill this responsibility?

We the People of the United States, in order to form a more perfect Union, establish justice, insure domestic tranquility, provide for the common defense, promote the general welfare, and secure the blessings of liberty to ourselves and our posterity, do ordain and establish this Constitution for the United States of America.

The Preamble to the Constitution of the United States clearly states the purposes for which we, the people, have created our government. We have given it the responsibility to treat all people fairly, provide for the common defense, promote the general welfare, and safeguard our freedoms. We have given our government a great deal of power to carry out these responsibilities.

What can we do to make sure our government fulfills its responsibilities? What responsibilities do we have to ourselves and to our government? We, as citizens, have the right to determine how our government uses its power. We have the responsibility to ensure that our government protects the rights of all people and promotes the general welfare. To be effective citizens, we need to understand both the responsibilities of government and the responsibilities of citizens and we should be able to make informed decisions about those responsibilities.

What you study here will help you deal with issues of responsibility as they arise in your life. You will learn some intellectual tools to help you make informed and wise decisions about issues of responsibility. The knowledge and skills you gain will help you assume the responsibilities of citizenship in our democratic society and help you ensure that our government fulfills the purposes for which we, the people, created it.

Unit One: What Is Responsibility?

What responsibilities are illustrated by these photographs?

Purpose of Unit

No man is an island, entire of itself; every man is a piece of the continent, a part of the main; ... any man's death diminishes me, because I am involved in mankind; and therefore never send to know for whom the bell tolls; it tolls for thee.

John Donne (1572–1631), the English poet, penned these lines in the early seventeenth century. The ideas he raises about responsibility are not new. For centuries, people have been writing about responsibility—responsibilities to themselves, to others, and to their country.

You probably are reminded often of your responsibilities to your family, school, or job.

What is responsibility? Where does it come from? Why is it important to society? What is its importance to you?

The purpose of this unit is to help you answer these questions and to clarify and develop your ideas about what responsibility involves. You will learn to identify certain responsibilities, their sources, and the rewards and penalties for fulfilling or not fulfilling them. This unit lays the groundwork for considering the issues involving responsibility that you will face later.

LESSON 1

What Is Responsibility?
Where Does It Come From?

Purpose of Lesson

This lesson introduces you to the concept of responsibility and its importance in everyday life. You examine several common sources of responsibility, and explore different ways people acquire responsibilities—whether they are freely chosen, imposed by others, or assumed unconsciously.

When you have completed the lesson, you should be able to identify different sources of responsibility and explain how and why people assume specific responsibilities.

Terms to Know

contract
responsibility
moral principles

constituents
obligation
civic principles

Critical Thinking Exercise

DETERMINING SENATOR SMITH'S RESPONSIBILITIES

Read the selection below about Senator Smith and answer the "What do *you* think?" questions.

To Ban or Not to Ban?

Cigarette smoking is a serious national problem. Every year thousands of Americans die from lung cancer. Studies have shown a direct link between cigarette smoking and cancer; even breathing the smoke from someone else's cigarette has proved dangerous. The issue of banning cigarette smoking in public places has become increasingly controversial as smokers defend their rights to individual freedom and nonsmokers argue about their rights to a healthy environment.

Senator Jean Smith represents a tobacco growing state in which the cigarette industry plays a key role. There is a bill before Congress to ban smoking in public places. Passage of this bill could cause many people in Senator Smith's state to lose their jobs. It would have a major impact on the economy of the state.

Senator Smith personally believes smoking is dangerous and would prefer that people not smoke in public. She herself is a nonsmoker. On the other hand, she is fully aware that passage of this bill would have a negative impact on her state. Senator Smith is faced with the dilemma common to many members of Congress: is it her responsibility to vote for the general good of the country or to represent the interests of her state?

What do *you* think?

1. What reasons can you think of for Senator Smith to vote against the bill, even if she thinks it would make a good law?

2. What reasons can you think of for Senator Smith to vote for the bill, even if she thinks it would have a negative impact on her state?

3. If Senator Smith votes for the bill, what might be the consequences for herself, her state, and the nation?

4. If Senator Smith votes against the bill, what might be the consequences for herself, her state, and the nation?

5. If you were Senator Smith, what would you do? Can you think of a way to accommodate the interests of both the state and the nation?

6. Generally speaking, do you think elected representatives have a responsibility to follow the wishes of their constituents, or to exercise their best judgment for the good of the country? Explain.

The questions you have just considered involve issues of **responsibility**. They are difficult to answer. To make wise choices you will need some tools that can help you analyze the complex issues involved. This section of the book gives you these tools and challenges you to consider issues of responsibility.

What is responsibility?

What do we mean by responsibility? In the first three units that deal with this concept we use the word in a very specific way.

- **Responsibility is the duty or obligation of a person to do something or to behave in a particular way.** For example, you have the responsibility to attend school.

- **Responsibility is also the duty or obligation of a person not to do something or not to behave in a particular way.** For example, you have the responsibility not to steal merchandise when you go shopping.

Perhaps when you hear the word **responsibility** you think of having to do something that you do not want to do. You know that if you do not fulfill your responsibility, you might have to take the consequences. You also know, however, that if you do fulfill your responsibility, you might be rewarded. Typically, although not always, those who fulfill responsibilities are rewarded in some way. Usually, those who fail to fulfill responsibilities incur penalties of some sort.

We sometimes have mixed feelings about responsibility and the burdens that it may impose on us. Yet we often take for granted that those around us will carry out their responsibilities. Imagine what your life would be like at home, at school, and in your community if no one accepted or fulfilled their responsibilities. How would you feel, for example, if you had to fly in an airplane but could not be certain that the flight crew, maintenance personnel, and control tower operators had fulfilled their responsibilities to protect your safety?

Where does responsibility come from?

Responsibilities may come from a variety of sources. They may develop as a result of our jobs, our school, the law, or our moral principles. Some responsibilities may come from only one source, others from two or more sources.

Nine important sources of responsibility are described in the next column and on page 115. As you read about each category, think of responsibilities you have that might have a similar source. In each case, answer the following questions. Did you chose the responsibility freely? Was the responsibility imposed on you? Did you assume the responsibility without consciously thinking about doing so?

1. **UPBRINGING.** People take on responsibilities as a result of the influence of their parents, family members, and others close to them, such as friends and teachers. Obligations such as helping with household chores, taking care of younger children, and obeying family rules are typical responsibilities for many young people. Families also can pass to their children religious and moral beliefs that call for the performance of certain duties.

How are religious responsibilities and traditions passed from generation to generation?

2. **PROMISES.** When we make promises to others, we are expected to fulfill them, to live up to our word. We understand from an early age that a promise should be kept. That is why very young children can be heard complaining, but you promised! Promises may be stated explicitly or they may be implied. A promise may be a private verbal agreement, such as a pledge to help a friend, or a written legal contract such as an agreement to repay a loan.

3. **ASSIGNMENT.** Whether you are going to school or working at a job, others will most likely assign certain responsibilities to you. For example, in school your teacher may assign homework or give you the responsibility to develop a computer program; in a job, your boss might assign you the responsibility of cleaning the shop or managing other employees.

4. **APPOINTMENT.** In some instances, people are appointed to positions that carry certain responsibilities. For example, the president of the United States appoints people to serve as ambassadors to foreign countries; a club president might appoint a member to take minutes at a meeting. Appointments differ from assignments in that they can usually be refused without penalty.

What are the responsibilities of a United States ambassador to a foreign country and what are the sources of those responsibilities?

5. **OCCUPATION.** Each job carries certain responsibilities. For example, an auto mechanic is responsible for repairing automobiles expertly and efficiently. A police officer is responsible for enforcing the law and protecting people's safety. A legislator is responsible for representing his or her constituents and working for the general welfare.

6. **LAW.** The legal system imposes many responsibilities on us, including the obligation to attend school, serve on a jury, obey traffic laws, and pay taxes. The Constitution—the supreme law of our land—also places a number of responsibilities on members of the legislative, executive, and judicial branches of our government.

7. **CUSTOM.** Many responsibilities come from custom. Traditions that have been followed for a long time often become obligations. Examples include waiting in line in public places, taking turns, and observing religious holidays.

8. **CIVIC PRINCIPLES.** Our society places on citizens obligations that include voting, serving on juries, serving in the armed forces in case of national emergency , and obeying the law. As citizens we are responsible for keeping informed about public issues and for monitoring the conduct of political leaders and governmental agencies, to ensure their compliance with constitutional values and principles.

9. **MORAL PRINCIPLES.** Some of the strongest obligations that people feel come from their moral principles. Such principles may be based on personal values or religious beliefs. Examples include the responsibility to treat others as you would like to be treated, to avoid telling lies, to refrain from cheating, and to respect others.

Using the Lesson

1. While you are studying the concept of Responsibility, you should keep a journal. Begin by observing all the responsibilities you have during the next twenty-four hours. Write an essay describing these responsibilities and their sources. For each responsibility you identify, label those you chose voluntarily, those you were required to assume, and those you assumed without conscious or deliberate thought.

2. Suppose you see a friend shoplifting. Is it your responsibility to report the theft? What is your responsibility to help your friend? What are the sources of each responsibility?

3. Read today's newspaper or listen to the news on radio or television. List three instances or events involving responsibility. In each instance, describe the source or sources of the responsibility.

LESSON 2

How Can You Examine Issues of Responsibility?

Purpose of Lesson

In this lesson you learn intellectual tools to use in examining responsibilities. You also apply what you learn to specific situations. When you finish this lesson, you should be able to use the intellectual tools to analyze situations and reach decisions about responsibilities.

Terms to Know

warranty
summons
Fourth Amendment
unreasonable search and seizure
Hippocratic oath

How can you examine responsibilities?

Every day you are confronted with questions about fulfilling certain responsibilities. Whether it is a homework assignment, an after-school job, or a parental curfew, you need to decide if you will do what is expected of you. To make this decision, you need tools to help you

Why might it be important to use appropriate intellectual tools to analyze issues of responsibility?

consider what is involved. This lesson provides you with these tools. Different problems require the use of different tools. You would not try to bake a cake with the same tools that you use to repair a car. Likewise, there are tools of the mind "intellectual tools" that can help you deal with issues of responsibility.

Intellectual tools include ideas, questions, and observations about society that are useful in analyzing situations and reaching decisions. Here is the first set of intellectual tools, a series of questions you can ask when examining issues of responsibility:

- What is the responsibility?

- Who has the responsibility?

- To whom is the responsibility owed?

- What are the sources of the responsibility?

- What might be the rewards for fulfilling the responsibility? Examples include feelings of satisfaction, increased self-esteem, approval, praise, payment, or awards.

- What might be the penalties for failing to fulfill the responsibility? Examples include shame, guilt, blame, fines, imprisonment, or physical punishment.

- Is the responsibility freely chosen, imposed by others, or assumed without conscious or deliberate thought?

In the next section you examine responsibilities in the context of a town meeting. The intellectual tools you have just learned will help you answer the "What do you think?" questions.

What responsibilities accompany your right to free speech at public meetings?

In the United States, a number of traditions govern public meetings. These traditions originated from customs practiced for hundreds of years in the New England colonies and in other societies.

Today people meet to discuss and take action on various matters, such as school problems, neighborhood crime, traffic safety, environmental policies, and national and

What responsibilities do you have when you participate in a town meeting?

international issues. Our tradition of constitutional democracy guarantees each person the right to attend meetings, to be considered a political equal, to have freedom of expression, and to hear the positions of other people.

The right to freedom of speech is a basic principle of such meetings. Yet, unless those attending agree to limit their talking and remain quiet when proceedings are about to start, the meeting cannot even begin. Someone must preside over the meeting and maintain order.

Certain rules are necessary for the meeting to run in an orderly way. For example, those attending usually agree that no one may speak unless called on by the chairperson. Also, those who are called on are responsible for speaking on the point under discussion and not on some irrelevant issue, such as the most recent movie they have seen or their vacation plans. People also are required to take turns expressing their views and to let others have their turns.

The purpose of public meetings is not merely to speak out, but to do so intelligently and concisely to get something accomplished, to explore ideas, or to make decisions.

If a speaker wanders from the subject under discussion, treats others abusively or rudely, or threatens to defeat the purpose of the meeting, then the chairperson may declare him or her out of order. At that time the speaker must either step down or correct his or her behavior. If such a person refuses, then as a last resort, the person may be removed from the meeting.

Public meetings have the specific purpose of providing for and protecting the right of all people to have a voice on issues that concern them.

What do *you* think?

1. What responsibilities are involved in the tradition of public meetings?

2. Who has these responsibilities?

3. To whom are they owed?

4. What are the sources of the responsibilities?

5. What might be the rewards for fulfillment of the responsibilities?

6. What might be the penalties for nonfulfillment?

7. Would such responsibilities be freely chosen, be imposed by others, or be assumed without conscious or deliberate thought?

Critical Thinking Exercise

IDENTIFYING RESPONSIBILITIES

For this exercise, your teacher will divide your class into five groups. Each group should read the selection assigned to it, complete a Responsibility Study Chart like the one on page 120, and select a spokesperson to report the group's answers to the class.

Group 1: What responsibilities does the Fourth Amendment place on school administrators?

The Fourth Amendment to the Constitution protects against unreasonable searches and seizures. Two questions have arisen as to how this protection should be applied in school situations. First, should the Fourth Amendment protect students against school authorities opening and searching purses and backpacks without permission? Second, what should be the responsibility of the school to protect its students from the sale, possession, or use of illegal drugs on school property?

A 1985 Supreme Court case (*New Jersey v. T.L.O*) involved a fourteen-year-old girl found smoking in the lavatory with a friend. Both girls were taken to the principal's office where they met with the assistant vice-principal. One girl admitted she had been smoking; the other, known as T.L.O., denied it. The assistant vice-principal took T.L.O. into a private office and examined her purse. He found a package of cigarettes and a pack of rolling papers which he associated with marijuana. He then conducted a more thorough search of T.L.O.'s purse and found the following: a small quantity of marijuana; a pipe; several empty plastic bags; a substantial sum of money, mostly one-dollar bills; notes indicating she had been selling marijuana to fellow students; and two letters implicating T.L.O. as a marijuana dealer.

T.L.O. confessed to selling marijuana and the state began proceedings against her. Her attorney sought to suppress the evidence found in her purse by arguing that the search was an unreasonable infringement of T.L.O.'s Fourth Amendment rights.

Group 2: What responsibilities of the president are described in this selection?

In the summer of 1945, Harry S. Truman, president of the United States, faced a terrible decision. In May of that year, Germany had officially surrendered, ending six years of fighting in Europe. In the Pacific, World War II dragged on. Some U.S. military experts believed that the war might continue for another year or more, at great human cost to both sides. They predicted as many as one million additional American casualties if the fighting continued.

On July 15, American scientists conducted a successful test of an atomic bomb. The success of this test set the stage for Truman's decision. He had to decide whether or not to use this horrendous weapon against the Japanese as a means of hastening their surrender, or to continue fighting in a conventional manner, in the face of the dire predictions of his military experts.

President Truman chose to use the bomb. On August 6, a B-29 aircraft named the Enola Gay dropped an atomic bomb with the destructive force of approximately four million pounds of TNT on the Japanese city of Hiroshima, killing or injuring more than half the 344,000 residents of that city. On August 9, a second bomb was dropped on Nagasaki, with similarly devastating results. On August 15, Japan surrendered.

Widespread devastation followed the August 6, 1945, bombing of Hiroshima. What responsibilities should a president consider in making decisions as commander in chief?

President Truman believed that he had made the right decision. Public reaction, however, has been deeply divided. Truman has been praised by some for saving hundreds of thousands of lives and condemned by others for causing terrible death and suffering. Few have failed to recognize the overwhelming weight of the responsibility he had to bear.

Group 3: What responsibilities do these quotations imply?

I often wonder whether we do not rest our hopes too much upon constitutions, upon laws and upon courts. These are false hopes; believe me, these are false hopes. Liberty lies in the hearts of men and women; when it dies there, no constitution, no law, no court can save it; no constitution, no law, no court can even do much to help it. While it lies there it needs no constitution, no law, no court to save it....

Judge Learned Hand, 1944

A student in China protests government violations of freedom of expression. What responsibilities do individuals have to stand up for liberty?

In Germany, the Nazis first came for the Communists, and I didn't speak up because I wasn't a Communist. Then they came for the Jews, and I didn't speak up because I wasn't a Jew. Then they came for the trade unionists, and I didn't speak up because I wasn't a trade unionist. Then they came for the Catholics, and I didn't speak up because I was a Protestant. Then they came for me, and by that time there was no one left to speak up for me.

Attributed to Rev. Martin Niemoeller (c. 1949)

Group 4: What responsibilities does this oath place on doctors?

The following excerpt is from the Hippocratic oath taken by physicians as they enter into the practice of medicine.

I swear by Apollo, the Physician....and all the gods and goddesses that, according to my ability and judgment, I will keep this oath and stipulation; I will follow that method of treatment which, according to my ability and judgment, I consider for the benefit of my patients, and abstain from whatever is deleterious and mischievous. I will give no deadly medicine to anyone if asked, nor suggest any such counsel....Whatever, in connection with my professional practice, or not in connection with it, I may see or hear in the lives of men which ought not to be spoken abroad I will not divulge, as reckoning that all such should be kept secret. While I continue to keep this oath inviolated may it be granted to me to enjoy life and the practice of the art, respected by all men at all times but should I trespass and violate this oath, may the reverse be my lot.

Group 5: What responsibilities does the Civil Rights Act of 1964 place on government and private citizens?

The Civil Rights Act of 1964 prohibits discrimination on the basis of race, color, religion, or national origin in places of public accommodation. The Act applies not only to places of public accommodation operated by government, such as public parks, swimming pools and beaches, but also to restaurants, hotels, stores, movie theaters and other businesses operated by private individuals and companies. Violations of the Act are punishable by fines and criminal penalties, and violators are also subject to civil suits by persons who have suffered discrimination in violation of the Act. Largely as a result of the Act, segregation on the basis of race no longer exists in facilities open to the public in the United States.

Responsibility Study Chart

Questions	Answers
1. In the above selection, what responsibilities are involved?	
2. Who has these responsibilities?	
3. To whom are they owed?	
4. What are the sources of the responsibilities?	
5. What might be the rewards for fulfillment of the responsibilities?	
6. What might be the penalties for nonfulfillment?	

Using the Lesson

1. Choose one of the selections on responsibility that your group did not read. Read the selection and complete a Responsibility Study Chart for the selection. Explain how your answers differ, if at all, from those of the group that reported on this selection to the class.

2. Make a list of the responsibilities of a classroom teacher. Analyze these responsibilities by completing a Responsibility Study Chart for them.

3. The Nineteenth Amendment to the U.S. Constitution provides: "The rights of citizens of the United States to vote shall not be denied or abridged by the United States or by any State on account of sex. Congress shall have the power to enforce this article by appropriate legislation." On whom does the Nineteenth Amendment place responsibilities? What responsibilities are imposed? To whom are they owed? What are the related rewards and penalties? Would you say the responsibilities are chosen freely, imposed by others or assumed without conscious deliberate thought? Explain your views.

Unit Two: What Are the Benefits and Costs of Fulfilling Responsibility?

What benefits and costs of fulfilling responsibility are illustrated by these photographs?

Purpose of Unit

In Unit One, you learned to use intellectual tools when considering issues of responsibility. In this unit you examine in greater depth the consequences of fulfilling responsibility. You learn to identify the various results of fulfilling responsibility and how to classify these results as benefits or costs. What is meant by the benefits and costs of fulfilling responsibility? A **benefit** is an advantage to others or to the person carrying out the responsibility. A **cost** is a loss or disadvantage. You also

learn that people with different values and interests might weigh the benefits and costs of fulfilling responsibility differently.

Understanding the consequences of fulfilling responsibility helps you decide whether or not to assume a particular responsibility. It also allows you to set priorities among different responsibilities.

LESSON 3

What Are the Consequences of Assuming Responsibility?

Purpose of Lesson

If you assume a responsibility you must be prepared to deal with the benefits and costs of fulfilling that responsibility. This lesson helps you learn to identify the benefits and costs. When you have completed the lesson you should be able to explain some common benefits and costs of responsibility and to identify the benefits and costs of fulfilling responsibility in a specific situation.

Terms to Know

benefits	security
costs	efficiency
predictability	resentment

Critical Thinking Exercise

IDENTIFYING CONSEQUENCES AS BENEFITS OR COSTS

What happens when you assume a responsibility? There are consequences to your choices. Some of these consequences may be **benefits**, and some may be **costs**. It is important to recognize these benefits and costs in deciding whether to take on a particular responsibility.

Read the story below and complete a chart like the one that follows. Then answer the "What do *you* think?" questions. Be prepared to share your answers with the class.

What should Selina do?

Selina, a junior at Elkwood High School, was well liked by her classmates and her teachers. Outgoing and friendly, with a sharp sense of humor, Selina got along well with most everyone. Yesterday, the assistant principal had asked Selina if she would be willing to take on the responsibility of serving as a peer mediator in the school's new violence-prevention program. Peer mediators helped to resolve disputes between students by listening to each student involved and by suggesting ways to resolve the dispute. The peer mediator cannot require the students to agree to any particular solution, but can help the students reach agreement by discussing the dispute with them. Peer mediators are not paid for their services, but they do receive a certificate of appreciation from the school, and their participation in the program can be helpful in applying to college. Peer mediators must participate in a two-week training course, which develops their abilities to listen, to defuse conflicts, and to get people to agree to proposed solutions. They must be available for at least one hour every day after school to conduct peer mediation sessions with students involved in disputes.

As Selina considered the assistant principal's request, she decided to list the consequences of taking on the responsibility, to help her decide what to do.

Consequences	Benefit or Cost

What do *you* think?

1. What responsibility was Selina asked to fulfill?

2. What would be the benefits and costs of fulfilling this responsibility?

3. If you were Selina, would you agree to take on the responsibility of serving as a peer mediator after school? Why or why not?

Critical Thinking Exercise

DESCRIBING BENEFITS AND COSTS

In thinking about the consequences of fulfilling responsibility, you, like Selina, should be able to identify and weigh the benefits and costs involved. Work with a study partner to read the following descriptions of benefits and costs of fulfilling responsibility. For each one, identify an example from your own experience which illustrates the benefit or cost. Be prepared to share your examples with the class.

Benefits

■ **Predictability.** When people consistently fulfill responsibilities, others know what to expect from them.

■ **Security.** Knowing that others will fulfill their responsibilities enables a person to feel more secure.

■ **Efficiency.** Work can be accomplished more efficiently when the people involved fulfill their responsibilities.

■ **Cooperation.** When people working together on a task fulfill their responsibilities, cooperation increases.

■ **Fairness.** If responsibilities are distributed fairly, and everyone fulfills his or her share, it is unlikely that some people will need to do more or less than their share.

■ **Community Spirit.** If all members of a group fulfill their responsibilities, a sense of community spirit or group pride is likely to develop.

■ **Individual Rewards.** Rewards may include a sense of independence and self-esteem; feelings of satisfaction; approval from others; increased recognition, status, or payment; and gains in knowledge, skills, and experience.

Costs

■ **Burdens.** It may be necessary to spend time, effort, or money to fulfill a responsibility.

■ **Resentment.** People may resent an unwelcome responsibility even though they have agreed to accept it. Others may feel resentment towards someone who has the responsibility they wanted.

■ **Fear of Failure.** If people are unsure that they can fulfill a particular responsibility, they may be anxious and uneasy.

■ **Sacrifice of Other Interests.** When people accept particular responsibilities, they may need to put aside other values, needs, or interests.

■ **Abdication of Responsibility by Others.** If one person or group seems to have primary responsibility for a task, it is easy for others not to do their fair share.

Critical Thinking Exercise

EVALUATING POSITIONS IN TERMS OF BENEFITS AND COSTS

In this activity you analyze the consequences of fulfilling responsibility. Your teacher will divide your class into small groups. Each group should read one of the situations described below and answer the "What do *you* think?" questions. Each group may make a chart like the one Selina made to help examine the benefits and costs involved. Each group should then share its answers with the rest of the class.

1. To bring the nation's attention to laws that unfairly discriminated against African Americans, Martin Luther King, Jr. deliberately broke those laws and went to jail.

Martin Luther King, Jr., a prominent leader of the civil rights movement in the 1960s, shouldered heavy responsibilities in that struggle. What were the benefits and costs of fulfilling these responsibilities?

2. Maria Rodriguez, who had been taking classes in automobile repair, volunteered to help her friend Thomas tune up his car on the weekend.

3. Berta heard of an on-the-job training program designed to help unemployed people learn computer skills. She applied for the program and was given a job on the condition that she complete the training.

4. The Public Issues Committee of Kennedy High School decided to sponsor a seminar on the prevention of violence among high school students. The committee opened the meeting to speakers representing a wide range of opinions on topics such as the use of drug testing and the right of the school to search students' possessions.

5. The congregation of the Community Church of Saticoy voted to establish a day-care center for children of working parents.

6. As the fighting in Lebanon worsened, the United States government made plans to evacuate American citizens.

7. Despite the warnings of environmentalists, oil companies sailing tankers through the Alaskan harbors assured the Environmental Protection Agency that the ships posed no threat to the fisheries and wildlife in the area.

What do *you* think?

1. In the situation your group has studied, who has responsibility?

2. What responsibilities did the person or groups involved in the situation fulfill or intend to fulfill?

3. What might be some of the consequences of fulfilling responsibility in the situation?

4. Which of these consequences do you consider to be benefits?

5. Which do you consider to be costs?

Using the Lesson

1. Imagine that you are considering an after-school job. Make a chart of the benefits and costs involved. Describe how you would reach a decision whether or not to accept the job based on the consequences of fulfilling such a responsibility.

2. Read a recent news article about a government decision involving responsibility that was made at either the national, state, or local level. Make a list of the consequences involved in that decision, and label each as either a benefit or cost.

LESSON 4

How Do You Evaluate the Benefits and Costs of Assuming Responsibility?

Purpose of Lesson

In this lesson you see how a consideration of benefits and costs of responsibility can be used in decision making. Your class conducts a public hearing on the issue of using solar energy in a hypothetical community called Gibsonville. The main purpose of the hearing is to give community groups the opportunity to express their opinions on the solar energy plan proposed by the mayor.

When you have completed this lesson you should be able to use the ideas of benefits and costs in evaluating, taking, and defending positions on issues of responsibility.

Terms to Know

agenda   relative importance
public hearing   ex officio

Critical Thinking Exercise

EVALUATING, TAKING, AND DEFENDING A POSITION ON THE USE OF SOLAR ENERGY

To begin preparing for this activity, read the description of the solar energy project and the agenda for the public hearing. The instructions for conducting the hearing follow the agenda.

The Solar Project

The U.S. Department of Energy, in an experimental program, announced it would offer grants to ten cities interested in partially converting their public buildings to the use of solar energy for heating and air conditioning. The grants would cover half the total cost of buying and installing solar energy equipment. When the mayor of Gibsonville, a medium-sized city in the Midwest, heard of the grant program, he asked the city engineer's office to study the subject and recommend whether or not the city should apply for a grant.

The city engineer's office found that the total cost of the project would be about $12 million. Since grant funds would pay for only half that amount, the city would have to find another source for the $6 million needed to complete the project. The needed funds would most likely have to come from increased city taxes. During a twenty-year period, however, the city engineer projected that the system would be cheaper to run and provide a small savings to taxpayers.

The engineer's office examined the effectiveness of solar energy in Gibsonville. A solar energy system works best when there is plenty of sunshine or a light cloud cover. Gibsonville usually has harsh winters with heavily overcast skies. Weather patterns during the past seventy-four years indicated that, in the long run, there should be enough days in the year with sufficient solar power for the city to save money—provided there were few variations in climate in future years. During the days when solar energy was inadequate, the old sources of heating and air conditioning could still be used.

How would you evaluate the benefits and costs of converting buildings to solar energy?

When the mayor read the city engineer's report, he decided to recommend to the city council that Gibsonville apply for the federal grant. The response to the mayor's decision was mixed; some groups supported his position while others strongly opposed it. The city council decided to hold a public hearing before acting on the mayor's recommendation. The hearing would allow interested groups to present their opinions. The date for the hearing was set, and several groups asked to be placed on the agenda.

Preparing for the Public Hearing

The class should be divided into five groups. One group will play the part of the city council. Another will act as the members of the city engineer's office. The other three will each represent one of the interested groups appearing on the agenda. At the end of the presentations, the city council will vote on the solar energy proposal and announce its decision.

With the exception of the group representing the city council, each of the other groups should take a stand for or against the mayor's plan. Use the instructions and background information provided on the following pages. In developing your group's position, you should consider the following questions:

1. If the U.S. Department of Energy awarded a grant, what responsibility would the government of Gibsonville take?

2. What would be the probable consequences of the city government taking this responsibility?

Notice of Public Hearing

Monday, 9:00 a.m., September 24
Gibsonville City Hall

The city council of Gibsonville is holding a public hearing on the proposed plan to apply for federal funds to be used, along with matching funds, for partially converting public buildings to the use of solar energy.

Agenda

1. Opening remarks by city council chairperson (2 minutes)

2. Introduction by the mayor (1 minute)

3. Presentation of proposed plan by the office of the city engineer (5 minutes)

4. Responses by interested groups
   a. Coalition for Conservation and Use of Alternative Energy Sources (5 minutes)
   b. Taxpayers' Union (5 minutes)
   c. Chamber of Commerce (5 minutes)

5. Open meeting with question-and-answer period and comments from the floor

6. Summation by chairperson of city council

7. Secret ballot by council members

8. Announcement of result by council chairperson

9. Adjournment

3. Which of these consequences would you consider to be benefits?

4. Which would you consider to be costs?

5. From the point of view of your group, which benefits or costs would be most important?

6. On the basis of your position on the relative importance of the benefits and costs, would your group recommend approval or disapproval of the mayor's plan?

When your group meets, select a chairperson to lead your discussion, a recorder to take notes on ideas to be used in your presentation, and one or more persons to present your group's position. You also may prepare posters or charts to use in your presentation. Do not hesitate to add ideas that come up in your group's preparation period.

Group 1: City Council

Your chairperson presents the agenda at the public hearing. You also select a mayor as an ex officio member of the council; he or she makes a brief statement at the hearing and introduces the city engineer. Your group is responsible for conducting the hearing and reaching a decision on whether or not to approve the mayor's plan.

Your main purposes are to gather enough information to make a wise decision and provide interested individuals and groups the opportunity to present their points of view.

Your group should consider the issue and develop a list of questions to ask the representatives of the groups making presentations.

Group 2: City Engineer's Office

Your group is proposing the plan. Select someone to take the role of the city engineer. Then help develop the presentation by reviewing the facts about the proposed project. Set forth the reasons you think the city government should take the responsibility for partially converting public buildings to the use of solar energy. Include an analysis of the benefits and costs of the project in your presentation.

Group 3: Coalition for Conservation and Use of Alternative Energy Sources

Your overall position presented at the hearing should be that the benefits outweigh the costs, and you should recommend approval of the mayor's plan. In supporting this position, your group should include an explanation of the various benefits of using solar energy.

Group 4: Taxpayers' Union

Your group's overall position should be that the costs of the plan outweigh the benefits, and you should recommend disapproval of the mayor's plan. In supporting this position, your group should include a description of the financial costs of the project, and the impact these costs will have on taxpayers.

How can you use an analysis of benefits and costs to argue for or against taking on a responsibility?

LESSON 5

What Considerations Are Useful in Deciding Among Competing Responsibilities?

<table>
<tr>
<td>

Purpose of Lesson

In this lesson you add to your set of intellectual tools. You consider factors useful in making decisions among competing responsibilities, values, and interests. When you have completed this lesson, you should be able to use these tools to evaluate, take, and defend positions about situations in which choices must be made among competing responsibilities, interests, and values.

</td>
</tr>
</table>

How can you choose among competing responsibilities?

Choosing among competing responsibilities is often complicated. It can be hard to decide what is most important. Making such decisions often involves setting priorities and seeking alternatives. It may mean rejecting certain responsibilities or postponing them until you fulfill other responsibilities. In making choices among competing responsibilities, consider these important factors:

- **Urgency.** Deciding the degree of urgency of a responsibility allows you to set priorities—to put some responsibilities before others—and to decide which one to fulfill first. For example, it would be more urgent to work on an assignment that is due tomorrow than on one that is due in a week.

- **Relative Importance.** You need to consider the importance of each responsibility in relation to other ones. For example, you might drive into a parked car if necessary to avoid running over a pedestrian.

- **Time Required.** You need to think about the time it would take you to fulfill a responsibility and the time that you have available. For example, before taking on an after-school job you would need to consider whether you can afford to devote the time required to fulfill the job's responsibilities.

- **Resources Available.** The availability of resources such as equipment, experience, or financial means is a major factor in decision making. Without the necessary resources, you may be unable to fulfill a responsibility. For example, to take on a delivery job you need a driver's license and a car.

- **Competing Interests and Values.** You also may need to consider other things you are interested in doing or other values you believe in to decide which responsibilities to fulfill. For example, you might decide not to take on an after-school job if it would prevent you from playing in the school band.

Terms to Know

urgency	interests
resources	compromise
values	

Have you ever been in a situation in which you believed that you had more responsibility than you could possibly manage? How did you decide what to do?

■ **Alternative Solutions.** You may not always need to decide between competing responsibilities. Instead, a creative solution or compromise may allow you to resolve your dilemma. For instance, do you need to fulfill the responsibility yourself or can you get someone else to do it?

Critical Thinking Exercise
EVALUATE AND TAKE A POSITION ON WHICH RESPONSIBILITY TO FULFILL

Read the following story and then work in small groups to complete the Intellectual Tool Chart for Deciding Among Responsibilities on page 133. Be prepared to share your answers with the rest of the class.

Drugs, Danger, and Political Responsibility

The drug lords sent a chilling message to the people of the small South American country: We declare total and absolute war on the government...and everyone else who has attacked us. The lines had been drawn. On one side stood the drug cartel, its leaders wealthy, armed, and without compunction about destroying all who would hinder them. On the other side were the members of the government, the journalists, and all those citizens willing to risk their lives to protect their nation. It was truly a struggle for the future of the country. Was law or terror to rule the nation?

No one had any doubts that the drug lords were deadly serious in their threats. Murder and assassination had become a way of life. In the last few months they had killed one presidential candidate, numerous judges and legal officials, and several prominent journalists. A climate of fear pervaded the country, especially in the capital city. The drug lords had proclaimed a war that extended to the families of those threatened. Public officials were particularly concerned about their children. Some sent their families to live abroad, but even that did not offer complete protection. Assassinations had taken place outside the country, in Europe and in the United States. There was no real safety for those marked by the drug lords.

High on the most-wanted list of the drug cartel was the young justice minister of the country, Elana Gonzales. Only thirty-two years old, known as a brilliant lawyer, she had taken the post when no one else would accept it.

How might your personal safety or your other interests conflict with your political responsibilities? How could you decide what to do?

Of her six predecessors in the last three years, two had been killed and two had left the country. She also had been threatened repeatedly and the previous week her brother had been kidnapped and was feared dead.

Gonzales came from a well-known family long involved in the leadership of the nation. She had built her reputation on defending the law. Now that the judicial system was under siege, she proclaimed, "We must protect the law and the government in any way we can. My responsibility is to my country and its people."

Despite her public proclamations, however, Gonzales was deeply worried about the effect her job would have on her family. She was married and had three young children. She knew that she was endangering their lives every day she continued to serve as justice minister. The situation reached a climax when she received, almost simultaneously, a new job offer and word of the attempted kidnapping of her youngest daughter from school.

The call from New York came first. She was asked to serve as chair of a special United Nations commission created to examine the international consequences of the drug trade. It was clearly a chance to leave her nation and remove herself and her family from the constant threat of death.

Gonzales had two weeks to decide about the job offer. The prospect of a safe haven, while still working to combat the drug problem, was tempting. It would certainly help her fulfill her responsibility to protect her family. On the other hand, she had an equally strong sense of responsibility to her nation and its future. If she left, she would be admitting defeat, admitting that the rule of terror was stronger than that of the government. She would undermine the courage of all those who had committed themselves to fight the drug lords at any cost. If she stayed, she might endanger herself and the lives of her family. Which responsibility should she fulfill?

What do *you* think?

1. Review the information you have written on the chart. What do you think Elana Gonzales should do? Why?

2. Your decision shows that you consider certain values or responsibilities to be more important than others. What are those values or responsibilities?

3. Why might another person, using the same information you have considered, arrive at a different conclusion?

Using the Lesson

1. In your journal, describe a situation in which you had to choose among competing responsibilities. How did you decide what to do? Why did you make this choice?

2. Identify an issue in the news in which a decision was made among competing responsibilities. Write an explanation of the issue involved, the decision that was made, and the reasons for that decision.

3. Assume that you have been nominated for a top position in your student government that will involve after-school activities each week. This position would look impressive on your college applications. You also have been offered a job in the local video shop that would be very helpful financially but would conflict with the student government position. Which position would you choose to take? Why?

Intellectual Tool Chart for Deciding Among Responsibilities

Note: Sometimes questions 7, 9, 10 or 11 may not be applicable in the situation you are trying to resolve. If this is the case, write "not applicable" or "NA" in the appropriate box.

	RESPONSIBILITY 1:	RESPONSIBILITY 2:
1. What are the responsibilities?		
2. What are their sources?		
3. What are the rewards for fulfilling them?		
4. What are the penalties for not fulfilling them?		
5. What are the benefits of fulfilling them?		
6. What are the costs of fulfilling them?		
7. How urgent are they?		
8. What is their relative importance?		
9. What is the time required to fulfill them?		
10. Do I have the resources needed?		
11. What other values or interests are involved?		

LESSON 6

How Would You Resolve the Conflicting Responsibilities in This Situation?

Purpose of Lesson

In Lesson 5 you learned some intellectual tools to help you decide among competing responsibilities. Now you apply these tools to make a decision between conflicting responsibilities. When you have completed the lesson you should be able to use the intellectual tools you have learned to evaluate, take, and defend positions on how to resolve competing and conflicting responsibilities, values, and interests.

Term to Know

dilemma

Critical Thinking Exercise

EVALUATING, TAKING, AND DEFENDING A POSITION ON WHO HAS RESPONSIBILITY

Your teacher will divide your class into small groups of three to five students for this activity. Each group will read the story below and use the chart on page 133 to analyze the responsibilities involved. On the basis of the information presented in the chart, each group should reach a decision about which responsibility should be fulfilled. Each group should then present its decision to the class, explaining the reasons for its choice.

Javert's Dilemma

Adapted from *Les Miserables*
by Victor Hugo (1802–1885)

Jean Valjean had been imprisoned some years before for stealing a loaf of bread to feed his starving sister. After his release from prison, Valjean became a respected member of the community under another name. He was forced to reveal his true identity to save another man who was falsely accused of being Valjean.

Since an ex-convict was not permitted to change his name at that time in France, the authorities returned Valjean to prison. He escaped and once again assumed a new name and became a respected citizen.

How can you decide what to do when legal responsibilities conflict with responsibilities imposed by your own conscience?

During the years following Valjean's escape from prison, Javert, a police inspector, doggedly pursued him. Javert had an inflexible devotion to his duty as a member of the police force. Then, ironically, circumstances occurred in such a way that Javert became indebted to Valjean for saving his life.

Later, when Javert apprehended Valjean, he allowed Valjean to have a few minutes to conclude his affairs. Javert had time to reflect on the task ahead of him: to return a man to prison who had distinguished himself as a selfless and compassionate humanitarian and to whom Javert was in debt for his very life.

Javert was suffering frightfully. He saw before him two roads, both equally straight. But the fact that he saw two roads terrified him. He had never in his life known but one straight line. One of these two straight lines excluded the other.

What should he do now? Imprison Jean Valjean? That was wrong. Leave Jean Valjean free? That was wrong. In the first case, the man of authority would fall lower than a common criminal, in the second, a convict rose higher than the law and trampled on it. In both cases Javert must look into his conscience and render an account of himself to himself.

What he had just thought made him shudder. He had considered setting Valjean free, which was against all the regulations of the police, against the whole social and judicial organization, against the entire legal code. On what should he resolve now? To return immediately to police headquarters and have Jean Valjean arrested? It was clear that was what he must do. Yet, he could not.

He was compelled to recognize the existence of kindness. This convict had been kind.

Javert put questions to himself, and he made answers, and his answers frightened him. He asked himself, "This convict, this desperate man, whom I have pursued to the point of persecution, and who could have avenged himself, granted me life. In sparing me, what has he done? His duty? No. Something more. And I, in sparing him in my turn, what have I done? My duty? No. Something more. There is then something more than duty."

One thing overruled all else for him. He had set a convicted second offender at large.

An honest servant of the law could find himself suddenly caught between two crimes, the crime of letting a man escape, and the crime of arresting him!

Using the Lesson

1. Design a collage of news clippings, magazine articles, advertisements, and other illustrations that demonstrates competing sources of responsibility in your life.

2. Does a soldier have a responsibility to obey an order if he believes it is morally wrong to do so? Why or why not? Write an essay in your journal defending your position on this question.

LESSON 7

Which Responsibilities Should the Court Uphold?

Purpose of Lesson

In this lesson you take part in a simulated court hearing based on an actual case decided by the U.S. Supreme Court, *Wisconsin v. Yoder*. The case deals with a conflict between a parent's responsibility to educate his children according to his religious beliefs and a state's responsibility to ensure adequate education for all school-age children.

When you have completed the lesson you should be able to use the intellectual tools you have learned to evaluate, take, and defend positions on how to resolve competing and conflicting responsibilities, values, and interests.

Terms to Know

Amish   freedom of religion

Critical Thinking Exercise

EXAMINING RESPONSIBILITY AND FREEDOM OF RELIGION

From time to time a person's responsibility to obey the law may come into conflict with his or her religious beliefs. Because freedom of religion is protected by the United States Constitution, these situations may come before the United States Supreme Court. In *Wisconsin v. Yoder*, the Supreme Court had to decide whether a state law requiring school attendance through age 16 could be applied to Amish families, who argued that the law interfered with and threatened the destruction of the practice of their religion. As you read the following description of the case, think about the conflicting responsibilities involved. Then work in small groups to complete the chart on p. 137.

Wisconsin v. Yoder (1972)

At the time of this case, the State of Wisconsin required parents to send their children to public or private school until the age of sixteen. The purpose of the law was to provide all children with educational opportunities. The authorities could fine or imprison any parent convicted of violating this law.

Jonas Yoder was a member of an Old Order Amish community in Wisconsin. The members of this community believe that they must raise their children according to the principles of the Old Order Amish religion. After completion of the eighth grade (usually by age fourteen), Amish teenagers are expected to leave school and continue their education by working with their parents. This allows Amish youth to acquire the specific skills needed to perform the adult roles of Amish farmers or housewives. They also acquire Amish attitudes favoring manual work and self-reliance. At the same time, the Amish teenager has opportunities to deepen his or her religious faith so that he or she can prepare to accept the religious obligations of adult members of the Amish community. In this way Amish life is maintained and strengthened.

Amish children are required to attend school until age 16 contrary to their religious beliefs. How should courts balance the interests of society and the interests of groups that wish to maintain a separate way of life?

The Amish believe that their children cannot be prepared for adult Amish life by attending high school. They feel that students would be drawn away from traditional religious beliefs and occupations by exposure in high school to science, machines, and modern lifestyles.

The state of Wisconsin believes that high school attendance until the age of sixteen is important for all children and that the Amish should not be treated differently from other residents of Wisconsin. Furthermore, the state of Wisconsin argued, suppose that some of the Amish children decide to leave their religious community. Wouldn't they be ill-prepared for life in American society?

Jonas Yoder refused to allow his fifteen-year-old son to attend high school. In 1968 Mr. Yoder and several other Amish parents who had refused to send their children to school were arrested, tried, and convicted of breaking the state law. They asked the Wisconsin Supreme Court to reverse their convictions. The case eventually reached the United States Supreme Court.

		Yoder		State of Wisconsin	
1.	What responsibilities are involved in this case?	To educate his children according to Amish religious beliefs	To obey the laws of the state of Wisconsin	To enforce its laws providing for the education of children	To allow its citizens religious freedom
2.	What are the sources of these responsibilities?				
3.	What might be some rewards for fulfilling these responsibilities?				
4.	What might be some penalties for failing to fulfill these responsibilities?				
5.	What are the benefits of fulfilling these responsibilities?				
6.	What are the costs of fulfilling these responsibilities?				
7.	How important is each responsibility?				
8.	How urgent is the decision?				
9.	What is the time required?				
10.	What resources are required?				
11.	What other values or interests are involved?				
12.	What alternative solutions are possible?				

Conducting a Moot Court
Hearing on The Yoder Case

A moot court hearing is like an appellate court or supreme court hearing. In the hearing a panel of judges decides whether or not to uphold a lower court's decision. No one calls witnesses or argues about the basic facts in a case, that is, about what happened. In this modified form of moot court hearing, your arguments do not have to be limited to the present law or be based on legal decisions that have been made in similar cases. They can be based on the principles found in the Constitution or on any reasonable position that you take.

Your teacher will divide your class into three groups. One group will act as the panel of judges hearing the case. The second group will represent the position of the Yoders, and the third group will take the position of the State of Wisconsin. To prepare for the hearing, each group should meet and select one or more persons to speak for the group and a recorder to take notes. Then the class should conduct the hearing as follows:

1. The chairperson of the panel of judges should open the hearing and make sure the procedures are followed. During the presentation of arguments, judges may interrupt speakers to ask questions.

2. The spokespersons for the State of Wisconsin should present their arguments and respond to questions the judges may ask.

3. The spokespersons for the Yoders should present their arguments and respond to questions the judges may ask.

4. The judges should discuss the case among themselves and reach a decision. They should present and explain their decision to the class.

5. The class should then discuss the hearing, its procedures, and the issues of responsibility raised by the case.

Using the Lesson

1. Write an editorial opposing the decision reached by the judges at the moot court hearing.

2. Imagine that you have just discovered that one of your best friends has been selling drugs at school. Even though you strongly oppose drug use, you feel an obligation to your friend not to report him. On the other hand, you also feel a responsibility to the school and to your community. Should you report your friend? Why or why not? Make a chart like the one on p. 133 to help you decide among the conflicting responsibilities involved.

3. Do you believe a newspaper reporter should take part in political demonstrations? Which is more important, the right of a reporter to freedom of expression or the responsibility of the media to try to preserve objectivity in their news coverage? Write an essay describing the issues involved, and applying the intellectual tools you have learned, state which responsibility you think should have greater priority.

Unit Four: Who Should Be Considered Responsible?

How can you decide who should be considered responsible for an accident or injury? How can you decide who should be considered responsible for an achievement? How can you decide who should be considered responsible for war crimes?

Purpose of Unit

In the first three units dealing with this concept, you have been concerned with one meaning of responsibility—responsibility as it involves the duties or obligations of people.

In this unit, you are introduced to a different aspect of responsibility. You will learn ways of determining who should be considered responsible for something that has happened. Being able to decide who should be held responsible allows us to do the following:

■ reward individuals for positive accomplishments

■ determine if a remedy is needed when a wrong or injury is involved

■ use the information as a guide for our future actions

In many instances, it is relatively easy to determine who is responsible. At other times, however, it can be far more difficult. In this unit, you will determine who should be held responsible in a number of complex situations. You will learn additional intellectual tools to help you make such decisions.

LESSON 8

How Can You Determine Responsibility?

Purpose of Lesson

When should individuals be considered responsible for an achievement or a wrongdoing? In this lesson you examine a new set of intellectual tools useful in deciding such issues. When you have completed the lesson, you should be able to use these intellectual tools in making decisions about responsibility.

Terms to Know

state of mind
intent
recklessness
carelessness
knowledge of probable consequences
control or choice

Who should be considered responsible for a collision between two automobiles?

Critical Thinking Exercise

EVALUATING INFORMATION TO DETERMINE RESPONSIBILITY

We often are quick to accuse or praise someone by saying, Well, you did it. It's your responsibility. What do we really mean? How can you decide who should be considered responsible?

Read the two stories below. One involves holding someone responsible for an injury and the other concerns giving credit for an achievement. In both cases, we want to determine who is responsible.

Who is responsible for the accident?

Early one morning Charlotte was driving her small sports car down a narrow residential street. Just then George backed his station wagon out of his driveway into the path of the sports car. He could not see the oncoming car, because a large moving van parked on the street blocked his vision. A cat running across the road distracted Charlotte who did not notice the station wagon until it was too late. The cars crashed.

What do *you* think?

1. Who, if anyone, should be held responsible for the collision?

2. Is there a general agreement among class members on the answer?

3. How should one decide such issues?

Who deserves credit for finding a cure?

For the past several decades, scientists all over the world have been working on a cure for cancer. Slowly, they are making progress. Much of it is due to the exchange of ideas among scientists who report on their progress— their successes and failures—through correspondence, articles in professional journals, and presentations at meetings and conventions. Step by step, the medical field is getting closer to a solution. Each advance is built on the experiences of individual scientists and their combined knowledge of the work of others. When the cure or cures are finally discovered, those held responsible will receive a great deal of credit, along with public praise and financial rewards.

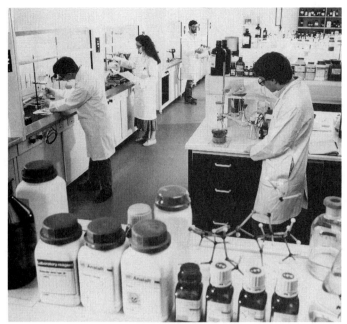

Which member of a scientific team should be considered responsible for an important medical discovery?

What do *you* think?

1. Given a situation in which a great number of scientists have worked for many decades searching for a solution, how can we decide who is responsible for finally finding a cure for cancer?

2. If you were on the Nobel Prize committee and wished to give a prize to those who found a cure for cancer, how would you reach a fair decision?

What intellectual tools are useful in determining responsibility?

Every day people in your school, community, and government face problems of deciding who should be considered responsible for one thing or another. Sometimes such decisions are easy to make, but in certain situations, reaching reasonable and fair decisions can be more difficult.

The following intellectual tools can help you decide in a systematic, thoughtful way who is responsible for something that happened. The first three tools will help you to make reasoned decisions about when persons should be considered responsible for a situation. All seven tools should be used when you want to determine responsibility for some wrongdoing.

1. **What is the event or situation for which someone might be considered responsible?**
   A good first step in determining responsibility is to identify the event or situation.

For example: An event or situation for which you might want to determine responsibility could be the following:

- an automobile accident
- the discovery of a cure for a disease
- the soccer team winning the state championship
- vandalism at a school

2. **Who are the people involved who might be considered responsible for what happened?**
   Once you have identified the event or situation, you can list the people who might be responsible for the event or situation.

For example: The people who might be considered responsible for the automobile accident described at the beginning of this lesson would be the following:

- Charlotte
- George
- the person who parked the moving van
- the cat's owner

3. **How might each person be considered to have caused the event or situation?**
   Once you have listed all the people who might be considered responsible for an event or situation, you need to evaluate how each person's conduct contributed to or caused the event or situation. That is, was the person's conduct one of the main reasons the event or situation happened? Or would the event or situation have happened even if the person had acted differently?

For example: You might say the automobile accident described at the beginning of this lesson was caused or contributed to by the following:

- Charlotte, because she did not keep her eyes on the road
- George, because he backed out of his driveway without making sure the road was clear
- the person who parked the moving van, because the van blocked George's view of the road
- the person who let the cat out, because the cat distracted Charlotte's attention

4. **Did the person's conduct violate or fail to fulfill a duty or obligation he or she had?**

Once you have determined how each person's conduct contributed to or caused the event or situation, you should evaluate whether or not the person had a duty or obligation to act differently. That is, did the person fail to fulfill a duty or obligation and, therefore, was the person guilty of wrongdoing? Or was the person acting within his or her rights?

For example: In connection with the automobile accident described at the beginning of this lesson

- Charlotte may have violated an obligation to drive carefully and safely

- George violated an obligation to yield the right of way when entering a street

- the person who parked the moving van did not violate a duty or obligation unless he or she parked the van illegally or carelessly in a dangerous position

- the person who let the cat out did not violate a duty or obligation, since cats are not required to be kept inside or on leashes

5. **What was the individual's state of mind in causing the event or situation?**

To answer this question, consider the following points:

- **Intent.** Did the person or persons intentionally or deliberately cause the event or situation? That is, did they act on purpose? For example, a driver who purposely runs another car off the road.

- **Recklessness.** Was the person who caused the event **reckless**? Recklessness means deliberately ignoring obvious risks of serious harm. For example, speeding at 60 miles per hour on a busy city street.

- **Carelessness.** Was the person who caused the event careless or negligent? Carelessness (or negligence) means not paying sufficient attention to risks of harm or damage that should have been foreseen. It is the failure to use reasonable care to avoid injury to yourself or others. For example, leaving a small child unattended next to a pool or lake.

- **Knowledge of probable consequences.** Did the person or persons know (or should they have known) the probable results of their actions? Knowledge of probable consequences means being aware of the sorts of things that are likely to happen as a result of what you do.

Why should we examine state of mind in determining responsibility? A person's state of mind can make a difference in how we evaluate their conduct.

For example: Fred caused an automobile accident. Does it make a difference if he crashed into the other car:

- on purpose (acted with intent),

- because he was drunk (acted recklessly), or

- because he failed to notice a stop sign (acted carelessly)?

For example: Katrina set fire to the drapes with a cigarette lighter. The entire house burned to the ground. Does the following make a difference:

- she was only two years old (acted with no knowledge of probable consequences),

- she was ten years old, and thought she could put the fire out (acted recklessly with knowledge of probable consequences), or

- she was thirty years old, and hoped to collect insurance money from the fire (acted intentionally, with knowledge of probable consequences)?

6. **Did the person or persons have control over their actions? Did they have a choice to do something other than what they did?**

Without control or choice, a person usually cannot be held responsible for his or her conduct.

For example: Juanita walked into the bank to deposit her paycheck. A group of masked robbers came in, robbed the bank, put a gun to Juanita's back, and forced her to drive their getaway car.

For example: While walking down the stairs at school, George bumped Avi. As Avi fell, he could not avoid hitting Susan, who then fell and injured her ankle.

7. **Did the person or persons have more important values, interests, or responsibilities that caused them to act as they did?**

Sometimes important values, interests, and responsibilities justify or excuse conduct for which a person might be held responsible.

For example: Juan broke down his neighbor's door to save three children from a fire.

For example: When the fire broke out in the theater, an usher knocked out a hysterical man who had begun to shout, then calmly directed the audience to leave by the exits.

Critical Thinking Exercise

APPLYING INTELLECTUAL TOOLS TO DETERMINE RESPONSIBILITY

Applying the intellectual tools you have just learned is not always as easy as it might seem. How would you apply them in the following imaginary situation to determine who should be held responsible?

The Accident

Peter, Mario, and Marty looked older than they were. The three high school seniors played in a band they called Marley's Ghost; they played well enough to get gigs at local nightclubs. Although the state's minimum drinking age was 18, these 17-year-old students had no trouble buying drinks with their fake IDs.

After a particularly energetic performance at the Ace of Clubs one Friday night, Peter, Mario, and Marty stayed at the bar drinking beer for an hour or two. As they stumbled to the van at two-thirty in the morning, Marty said, "I don't think I should drive. I've had too much to drink." But Peter replied "Come off it. You're okay. Besides, Mario and I have had just as much as you. Just take it easy on the road, and we'll be home before you know it."

The three young men climbed into the van, with Marty behind the wheel, Peter in the passenger seat, and Mario passed out in the back. The short drive home was never completed. Swerving to avoid an oncoming car, Marty lost control of the van and crashed into a huge oak tree by the side of the road. Fortunately, he had his seatbelt on, and merely suffered a concussion and some cuts and bruises. Mario was not so lucky. He was thrown into the back of the front seats, separating his shoulder and seriously injuring his back. With therapy, he should recover most of his prior mobility, although he can expect back pain for the rest of his life. Peter, however, will not have to deal with any pain in the future. He was thrown through the windshield into the tree, and his injuries were fatal. He died before the ambulance arrived to take the victims to the hospital.

Using the Lesson

1. Working with your teacher, invite an attorney or judge to visit the class and discuss what he or she takes into account in determining responsibility.

2. Working with your teacher, arrange to visit a courtroom to observe a trial. Is the trial an attempt to determine responsibility for an event or situation? What is the event or situation being considered? Which of the intellectual tools seem to be important in the trial. Report your findings to the class.

3. Imagine you are a member of the committee selecting the student for the "Community Leadership Award" at your school. What criteria would you use to decide who was responsible for making the greatest contribution to school spirit? Write a short essay in your journal describing how you would make your selection.

LESSON 9

Who Should Be Held Responsible for the Oil Spill?

Purpose of Lesson

In Lesson 8 you learned to use some intellectual tools to help you determine responsibility. In this lesson you use these tools in a specific situation. When you have completed the lesson, you should be able to explain how you used the intellectual tools to decide who should be considered responsible.

Critical Thinking Exercise
IDENTIFYING WHO IS RESPONSIBLE

Your teacher will divide your class into small groups of three to five students for this activity. Each group should read the story, "The Wreck of the *Exxon Valdez*," and complete the chart that follows the lesson.

Each group should develop a position on who should be considered responsible for the damage caused by the crash of the oil tanker. Each group should then present its report to the class. At the conclusion of the group reports, class members should analyze and evaluate the positions taken by each group.

The Wreck of the *Exxon Valdez*

The facts of the grounding of the *Exxon Valdez* on March 24, 1989 have been fairly well documented. The tanker ran aground shortly after midnight on a well-charted, well-marked reef about 25 miles from the Trans-Alaska Pipeline terminal at Valdez. The tanker lost about 11 million gallons of North Slope crude oil from its tanks. The state and federal governments agree that the on-the-water response by industry was slow and inadequate. Cleanup on all or part of nearly 1,300 miles of Alaska shoreline continued from 1989 through June 1992.

The ship left port at 9 p.m. on March 23 with a crew of twenty, two-thirds the size of some other oil tanker crews. Exxon claimed that new technology enabled the smaller crew to handle the ship safely, and the Coast Guard had approved Exxon's decision to reduce the size of the crew.

Nevertheless, crew members often had to work for long stretches with little sleep, and averaged 140 hours of overtime work per month. Exhaustion was common.

For two hours the *Exxon Valdez* was guided out of port by a harbor pilot, who turned control of the vessel over to Captain Hazelwood and left the ship at 11:24 p.m. At 11:25 Captain Hazelwood radioed the Coast Guard and received permission to steer south to the in-bound shipping lane. Approximately fifteen minutes later, Captain Hazelwood turned control of the ship over to his third mate, Gregory T. Cousins, and returned to his cabin after giving Cousins directions on how to steer clear of the ice in Prince William Sound. Though prohibited by Coast Guard regulations, Hazelwood had been drinking in town within four hours of the ship's departure, and was found to be legally drunk when tested ten hours after the grounding. Third Mate Cousins did not have the license required to pilot the ship in Prince William Sound, but he was now in charge of the tanker.

The passage through the Sound is so narrow that ships rely heavily on the Coast Guard when they sail that particular area. The Coast Guard, however, had lost track of the *Exxon Valdez*. The Guard claimed that difficult weather conditions, poor equipment, and a change-of-shift prevented the watchman from following the tanker on radar.

The Exxon Valdez *and an unloading barge after the grounding. Who should be considered responsible for the Alaskan oil spill in 1989?*

Shortly after midnight the *Exxon Valdez* ran aground. Following Captain Hazelwood's instructions, Third Mate Cousins had steered the ship outside the established shipping lanes in order to avoid ice floes; he acted too late in turning back toward the channel, and the ship ran hard aground on Bligh Reef. Oil began rapidly leaking into Prince William Sound.

The damage done by the wreck of the *Exxon Valdez* was devastating. The harm to the fish and wildlife in the area was enormous. Beaches and shoreline were blackened and recovery would be slow. Despite previous assurances by the oil companies that operated in the area that they could control any oil spill, months and even years later the effects of the oil spill could still be seen along the Alaska coastline.

Who should be responsible for cleaning and caring for wildlife and the environment during and after an oil spill?

Using the Lesson

1. Write a letter to the editor defending the actions of one of the four individuals or groups involved in the story you have just read.

2. Do library research to find out more about the *Exxon Valdez* oil spill and the damage it caused. Write an analysis of the incident and explain you conclusions as to who should be held responsible.

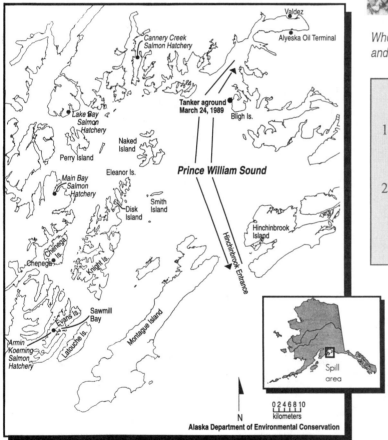

Who should be responsible for safely navigating an oil tanker through treacherous waters off the coast of Alaska? The ship's captain? The Coast Guard? The Third Mate? The ship's owner?

Intellectual Tool Chart for Deciding Who Is Responsible

1. What is the event or situation in question?				
2. Who are the persons who might be considered responsible?				
3. How might each person be considered to have caused the event or situation?				
4. What duty or obligation, if any, did the person's conduct violate or fail to fulfill?				
5. What was the person's state of mind? Consider a. Intent b. Recklessness c. Carelessness d. Knowledge of probable consequences				
6. Did the person lack control? Could he or she have acted differently? Explain your answer.				
7. What important values, interests, or responsibilities, if any, excuse the person's conduct?				

LESSON 10

Who Should Be Considered Responsible for Achieving the Peace Treaty?

Purpose of Lesson

We often want to determine responsibility to punish a person or prevent the person or others from wrongdoing. There are other times, however, when we want to decide responsibility to give recognition or a reward to someone who deserves it. In this lesson you evaluate and take a position on who deserves the credit for an achievement.

When you have completed the lesson, you should be able to explain how you used the intellectual tools you have learned to decide who should be rewarded for achieving a peace treaty.

Critical Thinking Exercise

EVALUATING, TAKING, AND DEFENDING A POSITION

Your class will conduct a meeting of an imaginary organization, the International Peace Award Committee. Each year this committee gives a prestigious award, along with a sizable grant of money, to the individuals or groups most responsible for contributing to world peace that year.

The class will be divided into small groups of three or five students to complete this exercise. Each group should read "The Peace Treaty" and then review the section "Information to Be Considered in Determining Responsibility." Next, each group should answer the "What do *you* think?" questions. Follow the instructions in "Preparing for and Conducting the Hearing."

The Peace Treaty

The Valley of Potomus is one of the most fertile parts of the Planet Scone. Since before recorded history, the valley has been populated by people drawn by its rich resources. From earliest times to the present day, diverse groups—from small tribes to modern nations—have disputed ownership of the land.

During the past thirty years, two industrialized nations, Sarnia and Ganges, have dominated the area. Although constantly at war with each other, neither country is able to achieve complete victory over the other. Each nation devotes the bulk of its resources to war.

In both countries, opinion is divided over how to achieve peace. There are some in each nation who believe that peace can not be accomplished without total surrender of the other. Others believe that continued fighting is inevitable and must be endured. Some people, sickened by the continual destruction of life and property, want peace at any price. Some people believe that compromise is the key; they want to negotiate a peace that will meet the needs of both nations.

The Situation in Sarnia. In a recent election, the people of Sarnia elected Artemis, a moderate who favored a peace treaty. During the election, Artemis was opposed by a number of powerful groups, including the owners of the major newspapers and television stations.

Sarnia's legislature is composed of representatives of five parties; none has a majority. It is clear that for a treaty to be passed by the required two-thirds vote, members of the different parties would have to cooperate.

The Situation in Ganges. Three years ago in Ganges, Porter, who like Artemis favored a negotiated peace treaty, was elected by a narrow margin over a more militant opponent. As in Sarnia, the legislature of Ganges is split among a number of parties; none has a controlling vote. Unlike Sarnia, in Ganges the news media favor a negotiated settlement of differences. However, a militant religious sect that represents a large segment of the population, opposes a peace settlement.

Since Artemis's election, representatives of both governments have met often. They are drafting a peace treaty that they hope will receive the support of the majority of each country's legislature and citizens.

The negotiation process is not an easy one and extremists in both nations are attempting to undermine the peace efforts. At the same time, supporters of the negotiations are working hard to build support for the forthcoming treaty.

How can you decide who should be considered responsible for successfully negotiating a peace treaty between two hostile nations?

Artemis's and Porter's associates have circulated drafts of the proposed treaty to key members of each nation's legislature. Artemis's staff is working to convince the opposing members of the news media to reduce their violent opposition to the treaty. Porter's associates are making similar attempts to soften the opposition in Ganges among the militants.

Finally the negotiators called a summit meeting amid great ceremony, and with worldwide news coverage, Artemis and Porter met, accompanied by the negotiators and the major dignitaries of both nations.

Although members of each group knew the treaty could not be put into effect until ratified by the legislatures of each nation, they believed that most of the necessary groundwork had been done. Two months later, after considerable effort and negotiation within each nation, the treaty was ratified. After years of struggle and the loss of thousands of lives, the nations finally achieved a peace treaty that provided a solution to the major problems that divided them.

Information to Be Considered in Determining Responsibility

Listed below are some principal persons and groups involved in the peace process between Sarnia and Ganges. Review the list and add any others that you think should be included. Then answer the "What do *you* think?" questions.

Sarnia

Artemis

Government

Negotiators and assistants

Artemis's staff

Leaders of minority parties who convinced their members to support the treaty

Newspaper owners

TV station owners

Interest groups opposed to the treaty

Interest groups favoring the treaty

Ganges

Porter

Government

Negotiators and assistants

Porter's staff

Leaders of minority parties who convinced their members to support the treaty

Newspaper owners

TV station owners

Interest groups opposed to the treaty

Interest groups favoring the treaty

What do *you* think?

1. Who should be considered responsible for achieving the peace treaty? Why?

2. To whom should an International Peace Award be presented? Why?

Preparing for and Conducting the Hearing

Each group should select a spokesperson and a recorder, then decide whom it considers primarily responsible for achieving the peace treaty, and prepare a presentation explaining why its nominee should receive the award.

The group assigned to represent the International Peace Committee should choose a chairperson and a recorder. The committee should prepare a list of questions and considerations to ask about each nominee.

Each group will have two to three minutes to present its nomination for the International Peace Award. The class as a whole should then analyze and discuss the nominations made by each of the groups and vote on which nominee should receive the award.

What responsibility do citizens have for monitoring and influencing changes in public policy?

Using the Lesson

1. Imagine that you are a newspaper reporter covering the ceremony announcing the peace treaty between Sarnia and Ganges. Write an article based on the interview you have conducted with participants from both countries.

2. Write a short journal entry opposing the choice made by the International Peace Award Committee. Describe who you think should be considered responsible for achieving the peace treaty and explain your decision.

JUSTICE
Table of Contents

Introduction

What issues of justice were raised by Martin Luther King, Jr.'s "I Have a Dream" speech during the 1963 civil rights march on Washington?

I have a dream that my four little children will one day live in a nation where they will not be judged by the color of their skin, but by the content of their character.

Martin Luther King, Jr.'s speech from the steps of the Lincoln Memorial on August 28, 1963 quoted above, was a call for justice that continues to inspire us. It is almost impossible for a day to go by in which we do not think of something that is just or unjust; for issues of justice arise in our daily lives, in the news media, on entertainment programs, and in the actions of our government and others. The Preamble to the U.S. Constitution states that one of the main purposes of our government is to establish justice in our nation; and the Pledge of Allegiance ends with the phrase with liberty and justice for all.

The central idea of justice is fairness, but despite our belief in justice, it is not always easy to decide what is fair in many situations. This course of study will provide opportunities for you to examine and make decisions about justice in a number of specific situations. In this way, you will learn to apply several sets of intellectual tools to different types of problems of justice.

Intellectual tools are ideas and sets of questions useful in examining issues and making decisions. They are tools of the mind that, if used thoughtfully and with skill, will build understanding. Your use of these tools should help you gain a better understanding of the subject of justice and a greater ability to deal effectively with issues of justice when they arise in your daily life.

Unit One: What Is Justice?

How do these photographs illustrate the difference between distributive justice, corrective justice, and procedural justice?

Purpose of Unit

What is justice? How can you decide whether or not something is just?

This unit will sharpen your ability to deal with such questions. As you will see, the essence of justice is fairness, and situations can be fair or unfair in different ways. For example, someone may not get his or her fair share of something that is being distributed; someone may not get a fair chance to explain his or her side of the story; or someone may suffer a punishment that is unfair in relation to his or her wrongful conduct.

Issues of justice can be divided into three categories: **distributive justice**, **corrective justice**, and **procedural justice**. This unit introduces you to these three categories of justice. When you have completed this unit, you should be able to identify issues of justice and explain why it is useful to do so. You also should be able to identify examples of issues of distributive, corrective, and procedural justice in your daily life.

LESSON 1

What Are the Different Kinds of Issues of Justice?

Purpose of Lesson

This lesson introduces you to three types of issues or problems of justice that you will examine and discuss. When you have completed the lesson, you should be able to classify issues of justice and explain the usefulness of doing so.

Terms to Know

distributive justice
benefits
corrective justice
burdens
procedural justice

The law, in its majestic equality, forbids the rich as well as the poor to sleep under bridges, to beg in the streets and to steal bread.

Anatole France, *La Lys Rouge*, 1894

Can justice always be achieved by treating people equally?

Critical Thinking Exercise

EXAMINING ISSUES OF JUSTICE

We think of the essence of justice as fairness, and the essence of fairness as treating people equally. But as the Anatole France quotation shows, issues of justice can arise even if everyone is subjected to the same rules, and even if everyone who breaks the rules receives the same punishment. Issues of justice are often complex and multifaceted, and they require careful analysis. At the outset, it is important to recognize and to be able to distinguish different types of issues of justice. As you read the following situations, ask yourself what is fair or unfair about them. Then answer the "What do *you* think?" questions. Be prepared to share your answers with the class.

- At the end of the week, Jane received her paycheck. It was for $275. She was upset and angry when she learned that Paul had received $410 for doing the same type and amount of work.

- During the riot, the secret police arrested Hans, dragged him off the street, and threw him into a small cell. That night he was taken to a room and three angry men questioned him for about ten minutes. Just as he began to realize that they were trying him, the man in the center banged a gavel on the table and declared, "Guilty of rebellion against the government. Sentenced to death by firing squad at once!" They took Hans outside, stood him against a wall, and shot him.

- Jean Valjean, the principal character in Victor Hugo's novel *Les Miserables*, was sentenced to prison for stealing a loaf of bread to feed his sister and her children who were starving.

What do *you* think?

1. What is fair or unfair about each of the situations above?

2. What similar experiences have you had or observed?

3. How are each of the situations similar to things that happen in your community?

4. What customs, rules, or laws do you know that are designed to promote justice or fairness in the kinds of situations described?

5. In the situations, are the issues of justice similar in any way? Are they different in any way? Explain.

Why do we divide issues of justice into different categories?

As you read each of the situations on page 153, you may have had a common reaction: "That's not fair!" or "That's not just!" Each example illustrates a type of issue of justice. The intensity of our feelings about justice and our desire to achieve it have helped to shape history and have led to numerous controversies in both private and public life in our communities, our nation, and the world.

For more than 2,000 years, scholars dealing with the subject of justice have divided issues of justice into three categories. These categories are the following:

DISTRIBUTIVE JUSTICE. Issues of distributive justice concern the **fairness** of **the distribution of something** among several people or groups. Whatever is distributed or divided can be a benefit, such as pay for work or the right to speak or vote, or it can be a burden, such as taxes, household chores, or homework.

CORRECTIVE JUSTICE. Issues of corrective justice concern the **fairness** of **the response to a wrong or injury** to a person or group. Common responses include making a person who has wronged or injured another suffer some form of punishment, give back something that was stolen, or pay for damages.

PROCEDURAL JUSTICE. Issues of procedural justice concern the **fairness** of **how information is gathered** and/or **how a decision is made**. For example, a person suspected of a crime might give information through careful, unbiased investigation or by torture. People making a decision might hear from all people interested in an issue or might make the decision without such a procedure. It is important to emphasize that procedural justice deals with the fairness of **how** we gather information or make decisions, not with **what** information we gathered or decision we make.

This division of issues of justice into different categories is helpful because each category requires the use of a different set of ideas or intellectual tools. In other words, to determine whether a situation is fair from the standpoint of distributive justice, you need to ask a different set of questions than the questions you would ask to determine whether the situation is fair from the standpoint of corrective justice. This explanation might be illustrated best by an analogy. Suppose you wanted to repair an automobile engine, paint a picture, or mend some clothing. Obviously, you would not use a paintbrush to mend the clothing or a sewing machine to repair the automobile engine. Each task would require the use of different tools.

It is the same with issues of justice. Dealing with issues in each of the three categories requires the use of a different set of ideas or intellectual tools. Fortunately, you do not have to reinvent all the tools because they have been developed during the past several thousand years by such people as philosophers, judges, political scientists, and statesmen.

Before trying to use the intellectual tools to analyze issues of justice, however, it is important to identify those issues as being distributive, corrective, or procedural so you will not try to use a sewing machine to repair an automobile engine.

Critical Thinking Exercise

IDENTIFYING ISSUES OF DISTRIBUTIVE, CORRECTIVE, AND PROCEDURAL JUSTICE

Work with a study partner or in small groups to complete this exercise. As you read each of the following examples, identify whether it raises an issue of distributive, corrective, or procedural justice. Then answer the "What do *you* think?" questions.

1. In a recent court case, a man sued the driver who ran into his car for $5,000 in damages to his automobile, $4,300 in medical bills, and $1,000 for inconveniences caused by the accident.

2. Police departments usually hire only those people who are physically able and who have had adequate education and experience for the police force.

3. Five boys were accused of vandalizing a school on a weekend. On the following Monday, they were brought to the principal's office and asked if they were guilty. Two boys said they were not and had been at the homes of friends at the time of the incident. The principal questioned their friends to check on the boys' stories. He then called the parents of the boys to his office to further verify their stories.

4. Before hiring a person to fill a vacancy in a governmental agency, the agency must advertise the availability of the position and provide all applicants the opportunity to take a written examination and to have an interview.

5. Each year the federal government gives fellowships to outstanding students under the Fulbright Act. These fellowships pay for American students to study, conduct research, or teach in foreign countries.

6. In the 1880s, thousands of Irish immigrants came to the United States. Often they were denied employment opportunities because of their Irish ancestry.

What might be some ways to fairly distribute employment opportunities among citizens and recent immigrants to the United States?

7. During the Middle Ages, people were sometimes forced to confess to crimes by the use of torture.

8. Tom borrowed his friend's car and dented a fender. He agreed to pay for the repair.

9. If you are accused of a crime, the government has the obligation to provide a lawyer to assist you at public expense if you cannot afford one.

10. Before making a decision on which textbooks to adopt, a state curriculum commission must hold public hearings to enable interested persons or groups to present their views on the textbooks being considered.

11. In some cities, unauthorized parking in a handicap zone is punishable by a fine of $330.

12. To qualify for a driver's license you must have an adequate knowledge of traffic laws, adequate driving skills, and be at least a certain age.

What do *you* think?

1. Which examples raise issues of the following:

   - distributive justice?
   - corrective justice?
   - procedural justice?

2. What do you think is fair or unfair about each of the above situations? Explain your reasoning.

3. Think about your reasoning in the twelve examples involving issues of justice. How did you evaluate whether the situation was fair or just?

   - What questions did you ask or what things did you consider in the situations involving issues of distributive justice?
   - What questions did you ask or what things did you consider in the situations involving issues of corrective justice?
   - What questions did you ask or what things did you consider in the situations involving issues of procedural justice?

4. What situations have you experienced or observed that raised issues of justice similar to those in the examples?

Using the Lesson

1. Write a brief description of a situation you have observed or experienced that raised an issue of distributive, corrective, or procedural justice.

2. Watch a television news program and identify reports on issues that involve distributive, corrective, and procedural justice. Describe those issues to your class.

3. Review newspapers and newsmagazines for articles that deal with situations involving distributive, corrective, and procedural justice. Bring these clippings to class and be prepared to explain them.

LESSON 2

How Do Our Nation's Founding Documents Promote Justice?

Purpose of Lesson

The Founders of our nation were dedicated to the ideal of justice. In this lesson, you have a chance to look at excerpts from the two most important founding documents of the United States—the Declaration of Independence and the Constitution—and evaluate which types of issues of justice the excerpts address.

When you have completed this lesson, you should be able to explain how the Declaration of Independence and the Constitution promote issues of distributive, corrective, and procedural justice.

Terms to Know

naturalized
jurisdiction
bill of attainder
ex post facto law
common law
habeas corpus
corruption of blood

indictment
grand jury
compulsory process
poll tax
probable cause
oath or affirmation

Critical Thinking Exercise
EXAMINING JUSTICE—A NATIONAL IDEAL

Each of the following excerpts from the Declaration of Independence and the Constitution of the United States is designed to protect and promote one or more of the kinds of justice you have been studying. Your teacher will divide your class into groups to complete this exercise. Each group should examine the excerpts they have been assigned and do the following:

■ Decide whether the excerpts are designed to deal with issues of distributive, corrective, or procedural justice. Some may deal with more than one type of issue.

■ Develop answers to the "What do *you* think?" questions that follow the list of excerpts and be prepared to report your group's answers to the class.

Group 1
An Excerpt from the Declaration of Independence

We hold these truths to be self-evident, that all men are created equal; that they are endowed by their Creator with certain inalienable rights; that among these are life, liberty, and the pursuit of happiness.

Excerpts from the Constitution of the United States

AMENDMENT I (Bill of Rights, 1791)
Congress shall make no law respecting an establishment of religion, or prohibiting the free exercise thereof; or abridging the freedom of speech, or of the press; or the right of the people peaceably to assemble, and to petition the Government for a redress of grievances.

AMENDMENT VIII (Bill of Rights, 1791)
Excessive bail shall not be required, nor excessive fines imposed, nor cruel and unusual punishments inflicted.

Do the First Amendment rights of assembly and petition promote distributive, corrective, or procedural justice?

Group 2
Excerpts from the Constitution of the United States

AMENDMENT XIV, Section 1 (1868)
All persons born or naturalized in the United States, and subject to the jurisdiction thereof, are citizens of the United States and of the State wherein they reside. No State shall make or enforce any law which shall abridge the privileges or immunities of citizens of the United States; nor shall any State deprive any person of life, liberty, or property, without due process of law, nor deny to any person within its jurisdiction the equal protection of the laws.

Does the Fourteenth Amendment guarantee of equal protection of the laws promote distributive, corrective, or procedural justice?

ARTICLE I, Section 9, Clause 3
No bill of attainder or *ex post facto* law shall be passed.

AMENDMENT VII (Bill of Rights, 1791)
In suits at common law, where the value in controversy shall exceed twenty dollars, the right of trial by jury shall be preserved, and no fact tried by a jury, shall be otherwise re-examined in any Court of the United States, than according to the rules of the common law.

Group 3
Excerpts from the Constitution of the United States

ARTICLE I, Section 9, Clause 2
The privilege of the writ of *habeas corpus* shall not be suspended, unless when in cases of rebellion or invasion the public safety may require it.

ARTICLE II, Section 2
The President... shall have power to grant reprieves and pardons for offenses against the United States, except in cases of impeachment.

AMENDMENT V (Bill of Rights, 1791)
No person shall be held to answer for a capital, or otherwise infamous crime, unless on a presentment or indictment of a grand jury, except in cases arising in the land or naval forces, or in the militia, when in actual service in time of war or public danger; nor shall any person be subject for the same offense to be twice put in jeopardy of life or limb; nor shall be compelled in any criminal case to be a witness against himself, nor be deprived of life, liberty, or property, without due process of law; nor shall private property be taken for public use, without just compensation.

AMENDMENT XXVI, Section 1 (1971)
The right of citizens of the United States, who are eighteen years of age or older, to vote shall not be denied or abridged by the United States or by any State on account of age.

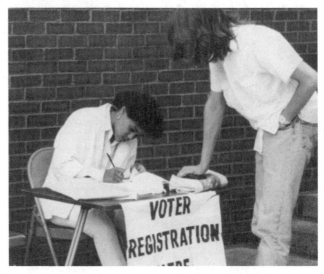

Does the Twenty-sixth Amendment guarantee of voting rights for eighteen-year-olds promote distributive, corrective, or procedural justice?

Group 4
Excerpts from the Constitution of the United States

ARTICLE III, Section 3, clause 2
The Congress shall have power to declare the punishment of treason, but no attainder of treason shall work corruption of blood, or forfeiture except during the life of the person attainted.

AMENDMENT VI (Bill of Rights, 1791)

In all criminal prosecutions, the accused shall enjoy the right to a speedy and public trial, by an impartial jury of the State and district wherein the crime shall have been committed, which district shall have been previously ascertained by law, and to be informed of the nature and cause of the accusation; to be confronted with the witnesses against him; to have compulsory process for obtaining witnesses in his favor, and to have the assistance of counsel for his defense.

Does the Sixth Amendment protection of the right to counsel promote distributive, corrective, or procedural justice?

AMENDMENT XIII, Section 1 (1865)

Neither slavery nor involuntary servitude, except as a punishment for crime whereof the party shall have been duly convicted, shall exist within the United States, or any place subject to their jurisdiction.

AMENDMENT XXIV, Section 1 (1964)

The right of citizens of the United States to vote in any primary or other election for president or vice president, for electors for president or vice president, or for senator or representative in Congress, shall not be denied or abridged by the United States or any state by reason of failure to pay any poll tax or other tax.

Group 5
Excerpts from the Constitution of the United States

ARTICLE III, Section 2, Clause 3
The trial of all crimes, except in cases of impeachment, shall be by jury; and such trial shall be held in the state where the said crimes shall have been committed; but when not committed within any state, the trial shall be at such place or places as the Congress may by law have directed.

ARTICLE IV, Section 2
A person charged in any State with treason, felony, or other crime, who shall flee from justice, and be found in another State, shall on demand of the executive authority of the State from which he fled, be delivered up, to be removed to the State having jurisdiction of the crime.

AMENDMENT IV (Bill of Rights, 1791)
The right of the people to be secure in their persons, houses, papers, and effects, against unreasonable searches and seizures, shall not be violated, and no Warrants shall issue, but upon probable cause, supported by oath or affirmation, and particularly describing the place to be searched, and the persons or things to be seized.

Does the Nineteenth Amendment guarantee of voting rights for women promote distributive, corrective, or procedural justice?

AMENDMENT XIX, Section 1 (1920)
The right of citizens of the United States to vote shall not be denied or abridged by the United States or by any State on account of sex.

What do *you* think?

1. Which of the excerpts deal with the following:

   Distributive Justice–For the excerpts focusing on distributive justice, what benefits or burdens do they deal with? What values or interests does each excerpt seem to protect or promote?

   Corrective Justice–For the excerpts focusing on corrective justice, what responses do they deal with? What values or interests does each excerpt seem to protect or promote?

   Procedural Justice–For the excerpts focusing on procedural justice, what procedures do they deal with? What values or interests does each excerpt seem to protect or promote?

2. Which excerpts deal with more than one type of issue of justice?

Using the Lesson

1. Ask a lawyer or judge to help you find a court opinion or excerpts from an opinion that deals with an issue of justice. Read and analyze the opinion to determine the principles, values, and interests that underlie the position reflected. Some landmark cases of the Supreme Court which might be analyzed include the following:

   ■ *Brown v. Board of Education* (347 U.S. 483; 1954)

   ■ *In re Gault* (387 U.S. 1; 1967)

   ■ *Stanford v. Kentucky* (492 U.S. 361; 1989)

2. Each of the following novels contains situations that raise issues of justice. Read one and then describe to the class the situations in the novel that involve issues or questions of distributive, corrective, or procedural justice.

   ■ *To Kill a Mockingbird*, by Harper Lee

   ■ *Animal Farm*, by George Orwell

   ■ *The Adventures of Huckleberry Finn*, by Mark Twain

Unit Two: What Is Distributive Justice?

How do these photographs illustrate issues of distributive justice?

Purpose of Unit

In Unit One you learned that we divide issues of justice into three categories: distributive justice, corrective justice, and procedural justice. This unit deals with the issues (or problems) of **distributive justice**, that is, how fairly we distribute benefits or burdens among persons or groups in society.

In some situations it can be relatively easy to decide what is fair when a benefit or a burden is distributed among several people. For example, it is usually considered fair for all students in a class to have the right to take part in a discussion, provided they respect the right of others to speak. In other situations, however, fair decisions can be

more difficult to make. For example, how good should a student's work be to earn an **A**? How much money, if any, should people who earn moderate incomes contribute to help support people who need help?

Some of the most difficult problems we face in our daily lives have to do with distributive justice. This unit will help you develop the knowledge and skills that will be useful to you in dealing with such issues. It provides you with a set of intellectual tools you can use to examine issues of distributive justice and take reasoned positions on those issues.

LESSON 3

What Intellectual Tools Are Useful in Examining Issues of Distributive Justice?

Purpose of Lesson

This lesson introduces you to a set of intellectual tools helpful in dealing with issues of distributive justice. When you have completed this lesson, you should be able to use these tools and explain how they are useful.

Terms to Know

principle of similarity   relevant
need   values
capacity   interests
desert

What are some issues of distributive justice?

As you have learned, distributive justice deals with the **fairness of the distribution of benefits and/or burdens among two or more people or groups in society.**

Benefits may be such things as pay for work or the right to speak or to vote. They may include almost anything that can be distributed among a group of people that would be considered useful or desirable, such as praise, awards, opportunities for education, jobs, membership in organizations, or money.

Burdens may include obligations, such as homework or chores, working to earn money, paying taxes, or caring for another person. They may include almost anything that can be distributed among a group of people that would be considered undesirable, such as blame or punishment for wrongdoing.

Making decisions about what is fair may be relatively easy in some situations, for example, when a decision has to be made about what members of a team can play in a game or what students can vote in school elections. In other situations, however, deciding what is fair is not easy and requires careful thought. In some instances, a solution that is distributively just may not be proper when considering other values and interests.

Difficult problems of distributive justice may arise over such questions as the following:

- Should all people have to pay the same amount of taxes or should the government require some to pay more than others? If so, how much more and why?

- Should all people receive the same educational opportunities at public expense, or should some people receive greater assistance and opportunities than others?

- Should part of the income of people who work go to those who are not working for one reason or another? If so, why? How? To whom? How much?

- Should the wealth of developed nations be used to assist developing nations?

These questions raise a few of the difficult issues of distributive justice that face all of us as individuals and as a society, within our nation and in other nations.

How can you decide issues of distributive justice?

Once you have identified an issue of distributive justice (as different from issues of corrective or procedural justice), there are several useful intellectual tools to aid you in examining and in making decisions about such issues. The first of these tools is the **principle of similarity**. Stated briefly, the principle means that in a particular situation, people who are the same or similar in certain important ways should be treated the same, or equally. In that situation, people who are different in certain important ways should be treated differently, or unequally. For example, suppose that out of ten people stranded on an island, three are sick and there is a limited amount of medicine. The three sick people are similar in an important way: **need**. They all have equal needs for the medicine and it would be fair to give each of the three persons the same amount. The seven other people are different from the sick people in an important way: **need**. They do not need the medicine, so it would be fair to treat them differently from the sick people and not give them the medicine.

How is the consideration of need useful in resolving issues of distributive justice?

What considerations are useful in applying the principle of similarity?

In the previous section, we looked at similarities and differences among people in terms of their **needs**. In other situations, we may look at similarities and differences in terms of people's **capacities** (or **abilities**), and also in terms of **desert**—in other words, how deserving they may be. One or more of these three considerations—**need**, **capacity**, and **desert**—are necessary when we use the principle of similarity.

Following are brief definitions of these terms and some simple problems that show the use of each consideration. In reality, many common problems of distributive justice are not as simple as the examples, and more than one of the following considerations should be used to develop a reasonable position on an issue of distributive justice.

NEED. To what degree are the persons or groups being considered similar or different in terms of their **need** for whatever is being distributed? Types of needs that might be considered include: physiological needs, such as hunger; psychological needs, such as affection or security; economic needs, such as money; or political needs such as influence.

Example: Suppose you have food to distribute among fifty people. Seventeen have not eaten for three days and the rest have eaten regularly.

1. All other things being equal, how should you distribute the food? Why?

2. How is the consideration of need useful in applying the principle of similarity in making such a decision?

CAPACITY. To what degree are the persons or groups being considered similar or different in terms of their **capacity** to deal with whatever is being distributed? Types of capacities that might be considered include physical, psychological, intellectual, economic, and spiritual.

Example: Suppose ten men and six women apply for jobs with the fire department. Eight men and three women pass the department's rigorous physical strength and conditioning test that establishes their ability to satisfy the physical demands of the job.

1. All other things being equal, if there are three jobs available, who should be hired? Why?

2. How is the consideration of capacity useful in applying the principle of similarity in making such a decision?

DESERT. Consider the degree to which the persons or groups described are similar or different in terms of **deserving** whatever is being distributed, either because of their conduct or because of their status (position). Do similarities in the conduct or status of the persons or groups justify similar treatment? Or do differences in their conduct or status justify different treatment?

Example: Suppose that in the America's Cup boat race sailboats from Australia and the United States qualified for the finals, a series of seven races. At various stages of the competition each day, different boats were ahead, but at the finish the boat from the United States was first over the line four times, and the boat from Australia was first over the line three times.

1. Which team should receive the America's Cup trophy? Why?

2. How is consideration of desert useful in applying the principle of similarity to make the decision?

Example: The Twenty-Sixth Amendment to the Constitution of the United States includes the following statement: The right of citizens of the United States, who are eighteen years of age or older, to vote shall not be denied or abridged by the United States or any State on account of age.

1. What reasoning might underlie giving all who have the status of being eighteen years or older the right to vote? Does the Amendment prohibit exceptions being made on the basis, for example, of capacity? Might it be fair in some situations to deny the right to vote to those eighteen years or older in consideration of capacity or desert?

2. How is the consideration of desert useful in applying the principle of similarity in deciding who should have the right to vote?

What difficulties may arise in applying the principle of similarity?

Two of the most common areas in which disagreements arise about issues of distributive justice are

- deciding what kinds of similarities or differences (need, capacity, or desert) should be used or considered relevant in a particular situation

- determining to what degree members of a group are similar or different in terms of their needs, capacities, or desert

The following exercise illustrates these difficulties.

Critical Thinking Exercise
IDENTIFYING RELEVANT CONSIDERATIONS

Work with a study partner to complete both parts of this exercise. Be prepared to share your answers with the class.

1. Discuss and identify which considerations (need, capacity, or desert) are most relevant in the distribution of the following:

- welfare benefits
- fines
- driver's licenses
- political rights
- college scholarships

2. Suppose 100 people were to apply for twenty-five openings in the freshman class of a college. What considerations (need, capacity, or desert) should you use in determining whom to admit? How could you determine to what degree applicants were similar or different in terms of the considerations you decided were relevant?

What values and interests should be considered?

Deciding what would be just or fair using the principle of similarity and the consideration of need, capacity, or desert is essential in many situations. Before taking action on a decision regarding what would be just, however, it is important to take into account **values** and **interests** other than distributive justice. A value is something that you think is worthwhile and important, something that is right or good, that you ought to try to achieve, such as kindness, honesty, loyalty, privacy, and freedom. An interest is something that you want or that you are concerned about, such as free time, good health, or rewards of one kind or another.

Example: Suppose a state created a program to help local communities finance the construction of flood-control systems. Under the program, the state would pay half the cost of needed improvements, provided the local community paid the other half with property taxes. Suppose that voters in a particular town repeatedly had rejected proposals to raise taxes to construct a flood-control system that would protect the town from a nearby river. After a series of heavy rains one spring, the river overflowed its banks and flooded the town. It destroyed thousands of homes and businesses, and the people of the town appealed to the state government for help in dealing with the disaster.

What important interests and values should be considered when deciding whether to help victims recover from a national disaster?

A narrow, or limited, idea of distributive justice might call for the state government to reject the request for help. However, the consequences of such a decision would include vast suffering by many people. Thus, considering such other values as kindness, the state government might decide to provide some relief.

Critical Thinking Exercise

USING INTELLECTUAL TOOLS TO EVALUATE A LEGAL CASE

The following case arose before Congress passed the Civil Rights Act of 1964. That act, and other federal laws and court decisions, now prohibit racial discrimination in employment and in public accommodations. Read the case and work in small groups to complete the chart that follows it. The chart contains the intellectual tools you have just studied. Be prepared to explain your position to the class.

Colorado Anti-Discrimination Commission v. Continental Airlines, Inc.

Marlon D. Green, an African-American, had served as a pilot in the United States Air Force for several years. In 1957, when he was about to leave the Air Force, he wrote to several airline companies, including Continental Airlines, seeking employment as a pilot.

An executive of Continental Airlines told Green to fill out an employment application. They accepted his application and he took Continental's employment tests for pilots along with other applicants.

Green was one of the six people who passed the employment tests. He had more flying experience than the other five qualified applicants who were all white. Yet Green was not hired. He was put on the waiting list, while the other five applicants joined the company and entered the pilots' training program immediately. In the next two months, Continental accepted seventeen more white men into the training program. Green was still on the waiting list.

At this time Green filed a complaint with the Colorado Anti-Discrimination Commission. At the hearing held by the Commission, Green argued that Continental Airlines had refused to hire him solely because of his race. He argued that the airline company had violated the Colorado Anti-Discrimination Act of 1957. This act provided that it was unfair for any employer to refuse to hire any qualified applicant because of that person's race, creed, color, national origin, or ancestry.

Continental Airlines officials argued that the hiring of Green would cause great problems. His presence in the cockpit of an airplane might create arguments, which could be a safety hazard. They also said they would have a problem housing and feeding a black pilot because of racial discrimination in some cities. Furthermore, the company was afraid that the pilots' union would reject Green. This rejection would cause labor problems for the company. Therefore, they argued that the airline company could legitimately refuse to hire Green.

Using the Lesson

1. Identify an issue of distributive justice in a newspaper or newsmagazine. Determine how the ideas of need, capacity, or desert were used in dealing with the issue. Be prepared to discuss the issue with your class.

2. Before 1920, the laws of most states did not allow women to vote. Do you think these laws were based mainly on ideas of need, capacity, or desert? Explain your answer.

   Since 1920, women have been guaranteed the right to vote by the Nineteenth Amendment to the U.S. Constitution. Do you think this provision of the Constitution is based mainly on ideas of need, capacity or desert? Explain your answer.

3. Interview persons who are responsible for hiring decisions. Ask them to describe the considerations they use in choosing among candidates. Compare their ideas with those you have just studied.

4. Describe a situation in which someone made a decision about distributive justice that you think was unfair. Explain why you think the decision was unfair, and what you think the right decision would have been. Explain the considerations you used in reaching your position.

Intellectual Tool Chart for Issues of Distributive Justice

Questions	Answers
1. What benefit or burden is to be distributed?	
2. Who are the persons being considered to receive the benefit or burden?	
3. What important similarities or differences are there among the persons in terms of ■ need ■ capacity ■ desert	
4. Which of the similarities and differences listed above should be taken into account in deciding who should receive the benefit or burden? Explain your position.	
5. Based on the similarities and differences you have decided to take into account, what would be a **fair** way to distribute the benefit or burden?	
6. What might be the advantages and disadvantages of doing what is fair? Would other values and interests be served by a different distribution of the benefit or burden?	
7. How do you think the benefit or burden should be distributed? Explain your position.	

LESSON 4

How Should State Governments Distribute Financial Assistance?

Purpose of Lesson

In this lesson you use intellectual tools to decide who should be eligible to receive financial assistance. You will give your opinion on the issue and defend it. When you have completed this lesson, you should be able to explain how you have used the intellectual tools you have learned in evaluating, taking, and defending positions on the issue of distributive justice.

Who should be eligibile for state financial assistance?

Each year state governments distribute millions of tax dollars to people in the form of income subsidies and welfare payments. The basic principle involves providing assistance to people who are in need to enable them to maintain at least a minimal standard of living.

Although various states are different in terms of the types of persons eligible to receive government financial assistance, the following are some of the kinds of categories or groups of people commonly eligible:

- People who are too old to work and do not have enough income to support themselves.

- Adults who are blind and do not have enough money to support themselves.

- Adults who are so physically or emotionally disabled that they cannot earn enough to support themselves and have no other means of support.

- Families with young children who do not make enough money to adequately provide for their needs and those of their children.

- Adults who, for one reason or another, cannot find a job and have no other means of support.

- Mothers of young children who cannot work because they have to take care of their children and who do not have other means of support.

- Adults who, although they may be working, cannot earn enough money to support themselves and their families at a minimum level.

How would you decide who should be eligible for state financial assistance?

What do *you* think?

1. What considerations (need, capacity, desert) appear to have been used to establish these categories or groups?

2. Should people in each of the categories be eligible for financial assistance? Why?

3. What might be the consequences of providing financial assistance to all eligible people in these categories? Which consequences would be classified as advantages? Which would be disadvantages?

4. What values and interests underlie your position?

Critical Thinking Exercise

EVALUATING THE ELIGIBILITY OF APPLICANTS FOR STATE FINANCIAL ASSISTANCE

A number of applicants are applying for financial assistance, and you will help determine which ones are eligible by applying the principle of similarity and considerations of need, capacity, and desert and other values and interests. Your teacher will divide your class into six groups to role-play a hearing before the Governor's Assistance Eligibility Board. One group will play the role of the Eligibility Board, and will hear testimony from representatives of the other groups. Each of the other groups will be assigned to represent one of the five applicants described below, and will present arguments to the Board explaining why they should be eligible to receive benefits.

First, each group should read the descriptions of the five hypothetical cases described below. Next, the groups representing the applicants should prepare their arguments and select one or two spokespersons to present them to the Board. The Board should use the Intellectual Tool Chart for Issues of Distributive Justice on page 165 in making its decision. The groups representing the applicants should refer to the chart and prepare arguments focusing on need, capacity, desert, and other values and interests to present their applicant's best possible case. While the other groups are preparing their arguments, the Board should use the intellectual tool chart from Lesson 3 to reach some preliminary impressions about which applicants should be eligible to receive benefits, and select a chairperson to conduct the hearing.

After the groups representing each of the applicants have presented their arguments, the Eligibility Board should reach a decision on which applicants are eligible for benefits, and explain its decisions to the class. The class as a whole should then discuss the "What do *you* think?" questions on page 169.

Group 1: Eccentric Creator

Boris Axelrod was by common standards eccentric in his habits. He slept all day and worked throughout the night on his creative projects. These included composing music, inventing various machines, and writing philosophical essays on the nature of love and patriotism, which he hoped to publish.

Boris was thrifty and liked gaudy secondhand clothes. He had not been successful at earning money with any of his creations, not because he lacked talent, but mostly because he did not understand business matters.

Boris's father left the family when Boris was young and had not been seen or heard from since. When his mother was alive, she supported Boris. After she died, Boris found it necessary to support himself. He had a mechanical mind and sometimes found work as a handyman, but he preferred night work and had

difficulty getting it. Once he had a regular job as a night watchman, but he became so absorbed in composing a musical suite that he forgot to go to work, and he was unaware for two weeks that he had been fired.

Which consideration—need, capacity, or desert—should be evaluated in deciding whether Boris Axelrod should receive state financial assistance?

Boris had no relatives and scarcely any friends. The few people who knew him said, "He'll never be able to hold a job." Finally, a neighbor suggested that he apply for state financial assistance.

Group 2: Unskilled Worker

John Harwood and his wife, Louise, struggled continually to feed their eight children, aged one to twelve. Both parents were poorly trained and uneducated, which made it very difficult for them to find jobs. Louise was unable to work outside her home because child care was unaffordable.

John had applied at more than seventeen factories and at various community agencies, but there were no openings in manual labor categories. The Harwoods could not provide a minimal level of shelter, food, or other necessities for themselves or their children, so they applied for government financial assistance.

Group 3: Unemployed Engineer

Andrea Baer had been an engineer in the aerospace industry. She had worked for Aero Labs for seven years. As a result of a government cancellation of a contract, Aero Labs laid off several hundred employees, among them Andrea. Andrea's specialization was hydrology; she worked on designs for undersea missile launching devices. After losing her job, she spent several hundred dollars on a job resume and distributed it to prospective employers. She received a few vague responses and finally a job offer at a much lower salary than she had been making at Aero Labs. The offer came from a firm in another state, and her family was against moving from their home.

After several months, Andrea had used her twenty-six weeks of unemployment compensation and her personal savings. With great reluctance, she applied for state financial assistance to support her family.

Which consideration—need, capacity, or desert—should be evaluated in deciding whether Andrea Baer should receive financial assistance?

Group 4: Paraplegic Worker

Donald Pierce, whose legs were paralyzed at birth, moved about in a wheelchair. To maintain his health he visited his doctor frequently and received regular physical therapy.

Educated in his home through tutoring, Donald excelled in English and political science. Due to his interest in civic matters and current events, he began writing letters to the editor of his local newspaper. The editor of the newspaper recognized Donald's ability to analyze community problems and provide good ideas. He asked him to work part-time as a staff writer.

Which consideration—need, capacity, or desert—should be evaluated in deciding whether Donald Pierce should receive financial assistance?

Donald received the same pay as others for this type of work; however, because of his special needs, he could work only a few hours a week. Although Donald was able and willing to contribute to his own support, he still needed help and found it necessary to apply for state government financial assistance.

Group 5: Abandoned Children

Mary Jones was a 26-year-old mother of two who suffered from drug addiction. She had already been jailed for one year on a narcotics offense. While in jail she attended Narcotics Anonymous meetings and learned that addiction is a disease recognized by the American Medical Association. She vowed to stay away from drugs when she was released.

After getting out of jail, Mary and her husband George had a third child. This increased the pressures that they both felt and they again became involved in drugs. Mary's job did not pay enough to support her and George's drug habit as well as their other needs. As a result Mary wrote some bad checks and was seriously overdrawn at the bank.

The Joneses frequently left the children alone while they searched for money and drugs. Since the children were young they could not look after themselves. Neighbors often heard them crying and could see that they were dirty and improperly fed.

One evening George became ill and lost consciousness from an overdose. Mary called an ambulance, but later that night he died. Believing that she was unable to care for her children and work at the same time, Mary applied for state government financial assistance.

What do *you* think?

1. Which ideas—need, capacity, desert—were most important in deciding which applicants should be eligible? Which ideas were least important? Why?

2. What might be some benefits and costs of deciding eligibility for benefits using the principle of similarity?

3. What values underlie your position on the eligibility of the five applicants?

Using the Lesson

1. Identify an issue of distributive justice in a newspaper or newsmagazine. Determine how the ideas of need, capacity, or desert were used in dealing with the issue. Be prepared to discuss the issue with your class.

2. Ask a school administrator to visit the class and explain school policies on the distribution of special educational opportunities. Discuss how the school policies take into account the ideas of need, capacity, and desert.

3. Ask your teacher, a librarian, or an attorney to help you find a written account of the Supreme Court's decision in *Fullilove v. Klutznick*, 448 U.S. 448 (1980), *San Antonio Independent School District v. Rodriguez*, 411 U.S. 1 (1973), or another court case dealing with an issue of distributive justice. Read the facts in the case and the decision of the court, and summarize them for class discussion.

LESSON 5

How Can We Achieve Distributive Justice in Public Education?

Purpose of Lesson

In this lesson you evaluate an issue of distributive justice raised by the financing of public education in the United States. Your class role-plays a legislative debate on the subject and votes to uphold or to change the present system. When you have completed the lesson you should be able to evaluate, take, and defend positions on the issue of distributive justice.

Term to Know

caucus

Critical Thinking Exercise
EVALUATING THE ROLE OF THE TAXPAYER IN PUBLIC EDUCATION

Some people have doubts about the fairness of the system most states use for collecting tax money to support public schools. An issue of distributive justice that is raised may be stated as follows: How should the burden of paying taxes to support public education be distributed? Any solution must involve consideration of distributive justice and other values and interests of our society.

Distribution of the Property Tax Burden

Throughout our country the property tax is the most common way local communities raise money to support public schools. Most property tax money comes from taxes placed on houses, apartment buildings, stores, factories, other commercial and industrial buildings, and on open land. In most states, people who own these types of property must pay a tax each year that is based on the property's market value. For example, if a person's house had a market value of $75,000, and if the tax rate for residential property was two percent of market value, then the tax to be paid would amount to $1,500 ($75,000 x .02) each year. Most of that tax money would support the local school system.

Who should have to pay taxes to support public schools?

Homeowners must pay property taxes directly from their income or savings. Owners of apartments, stores, businesses, and industries usually pay property taxes from the income they receive from people who rent their property or who buy their goods and services. Thus, even people who do not own property pay property taxes indirectly through payments for rent, goods and services, or both.

This form of taxation raises some basic problems of distributive justice. In 1978, a tax revolt began in California. The people who started the revolt believed that the rates of property tax for homes and businesses were unfair. The state legislature passed a law to limit the amount of property tax that local governments could charge. This action caused a crisis in the support of public schools. It also has had repercussions throughout the nation as people began reexamining the ways they were being taxed and the fairness of the property tax and other means of taxation.

A Problem in Taxation

Many people claim that how taxes are now collected to support public schools and other local government services is unfair and unreasonable. In particular, they argue that a family's tax burden should depend on the number of school-age children in the family. These claims raise questions about the basic principles and practices of taxation presently used by our government.

To understand and evaluate these claims, consider the following example:

> The Browns, the Franks, the Davidsons and the Smiths are neighbors. Their houses have the same market value, and they each pay the same amount of property taxes. The Browns have no children. The Franks have two children who are now grown and attend college. The Davidsons have three children who attend public school, and the Smiths pay for their three children to go to a private school operated by their church.

What do *you* think?

1. What similarities or differences are there between the Browns, the Franks, the Davidsons and the Smiths in regard to their tax burden?

2. What similarities or differences are there between the Browns, the Franks, the Davidsons and the Smiths with regard to the benefits they receive from public schools?

3. How, if at all, can the present distribution of the tax burden between the Browns, the Franks, the Davidsons and the Smiths be justified in terms of similarities or differences in relation to any of the following considerations: need, capacity, or desert?

4. What other considerations might be taken into account to support the present distribution of the tax burden between the families?

5. What might be the advantages and disadvantages of the present distribution?

6. Taking into account your responses to the above questions, is the present distribution of the tax burden fair? Why? Is it desirable? Why?

7. What changes, if any, would you suggest to the distribution of the tax burden between the families? Why?

Critical Thinking Exercise

TAKING AND DEFENDING A POSITION ON TAXATION TO SUPPORT PUBLIC SCHOOLS

In this exercise your class engages in a simulated debate in the state legislature on the subject of financing public education. Specifically, you will debate whether the system of financing public education should be changed to make a family's tax burden depend on the number of school-age children in the family. To conduct the exercise, your teacher will divide the class into four groups, and each group should prepare for the debate according to their instructions.

Group 1: Committee on Property Taxation

You are the members of the state legislature who have been asked to evaluate the fairness of the present system of property taxation. Report your recommendations for changing the system or for keeping it as it is to the entire legislature. Your group should do the following:

1. Select a chairperson to moderate your committee meeting.

2. Discuss the fairness of the present system of property taxation, focusing on the issue of whether a family's tax burden should depend on the number of school-age children in the family.

3. Discuss possible changes that might make the system of property taxation more fair.

4. Vote on whether to recommend changing the present system of property taxation or to recommend keeping it as it is.

5. Prepare a three-minute presentation (the majority report) to make to the entire legislature to support your recommendation.

6. If you wish, prepare a three-minute presentation (the minority report) to explain to the entire legislature the views of those members of the committee who oppose the committee's recommendation.

7. Select spokespersons to present the committee's reports to the legislature.

Group 2: Urban Legislative Caucus

You are the members of the state legislature who represent people from the largest cities in your state. Your constituents include many families with low or moderate incomes and some wealthier families. Although some residential parts of your district have low property values, certain large commercial areas have high values and provide substantial property tax revenues. Your district includes some of the most crowded schools and some of the oldest schools in the state. Several schools in your

*What arguments should state legislators consider in deciding
who should have to pay taxes to support public schools?*

district, however, have special programs that are not available in the suburban or rural schools in your state. Your group should do the following:

1. Select a chairperson to moderate your meeting.

2. Discuss how your constituents would view proposals to change the present system of property taxation, focusing on proposals to make the amount of taxes depend on the number of school-age children in a family.

3. Decide whether you would support any proposals to change the present system of property taxation, given the interests of your constituents and your views on the issue.

4. Prepare arguments to support the positions you think you should take.

Group 3: Suburban Legislative Caucus

You are the members of the state legislature who represent people from the suburbs in your state. Your constituents include many families with moderate incomes and many wealthier families. Most residential neighborhoods in your district have high property values and generate substantial property tax revenues. Your

district includes some of the most well-equipped schools in the state, and most of the schools in your district are new. Your group should do the following:

1. Select a chairperson to moderate your meeting.

2. Discuss how your constituents would view proposals to change the present system of property taxation. Focus on proposals to make the amount of taxes depend on the number of school-age children in a family.

3. Decide whether you would support any proposals to change the present system of property taxation, given the interests of your constituents and your views on the issue.

4. Prepare arguments to support the positions you think you should take.

Group 4: Rural Legislative Caucus

You are the members of the state legislature who represent people from the rural areas of your state. Your constituents include many families with moderate incomes and some poorer families. Most of the property in your district has low property values and generates little property tax revenues. Your district includes some of the most poorly funded schools in the state, and most of the schools in your district are old. Your group should do the following:

1. Select a chairperson to moderate your meeting.

2. Discuss how your constituents would view proposals to change the present system of property taxation. Focus on proposals to make the amount of taxes depend on the number of school-age children in a family.

3. Decide whether you would support any proposals to change the present system of property taxation, given the interests of your constituents and your views on the issue.

4. Prepare arguments to support the positions you think you should take.

Conducting a Legislative Debate

To conduct the debate, the spokespersons for the Committee on Property Taxation should give their reports first. Members of each legislative caucus should then present their views. If time permits, the committee members should have a chance to respond to the arguments presented by the other legislators. Following the debate, the class should vote on the proposal presented by the committee.

Using the Lesson

1. Should tax credits or vouchers be given to parents who send their children to private school? Proponents of such measures argue that parents who send children to private school reduce the cost of the public school system and should receive a tax credit to help offset the expense of private school. Opponents claim such measures could undermine the public school system, and that they amount to a tax subsidy mainly for wealthy families.

   In 1993, Californians voted on such a voucher proposal. Do research to find out which groups supported or opposed the proposal, each group's arguments, and the outcome of the vote. Evaluate the issue and decide whether you would have voted for or against the voucher proposal. Report the results of your research and explain your position on the issue to the class. You may create a poster of other visual aid to enhance your report.

2. Do state lotteries provide a fair and effective way to increase funding for public education? Do research to find out how lotteries have affected funding for public education in one or more states and what arguments have been made for and against their use. Evaluate the issue and present a report explaining your views to the class.

Unit Three: What Is Corrective Justice?

How do these photographs illustrate issues of corrective justice?

Purpose of Unit

This unit deals with corrective justice, that is with issues of fair or proper responses to wrongs and injuries. In this unit you will learn the goals of corrective justice. You also will learn a new set of intellectual tools that are useful in evaluating, taking, and defending positions on issues of corrective justice.

When you have completed this unit, you should be able to define corrective justice and explain its goals. You also should be able to use the intellectual tools to evaluate issues of corrective justice and make thoughtful decisions about how to respond to wrongs and injuries.

LESSON 6

What Are the Goals of Corrective Justice?

Purpose of Lesson

This lesson introduces you to the goals of corrective justice and examines the difference between wrongs and injuries. When you have completed the lesson, you should be able to define corrective justice, explain its goals, and identify wrongs and injuries in different situations.

Terms to Know

wrong   correction
injury   prevention
deterrence

What is corrective justice?

The Code of Hammurabi is the most complete extant collection of Babylonian laws. Developed during the reign of Hammurabi (1792–1750 BC), these 282 case laws include economic provisions dealing with prices, tariffs, trade, and commerce; family law including marriage and divorce; criminal law; and civil law dealing with issues such as slavery and debt. The code was intended for application to a wider realm than a single country.

Do you think the principle of "an eye for an eye" is a fair response to a wrong or injury?

Each of the following situations involves an issue of corrective justice. Corrective justice refers to the fairness of responses to wrongs or injuries. A wrong is conduct that violates a duty or responsibility imposed by laws, rules, customs, or moral principles. An injury is harm or damage to persons or property, or violation of a person's rights.

- Convicted of theft, Mustafa was taken into the public square where the executioner chopped off his right hand with a sword.

- While Paul was stopped for a red light, Sarah crashed into his car. The court ordered Sarah to pay $5,500 for damages to Paul's car and $8,376 for his medical bills.

- Three members of a gang beat and robbed a 60-year-old woman standing at a bus stop. The woman was hospitalized for two months and permanently crippled by the beating. The gang members were arrested and placed in Juvenile Hall for six months where they were given psychological counseling, released, and placed on probation for one year.

What do *you* think?

1. What is fair or unfair about each response to the wrong or injury described?

2. What values and interests, other than fairness, are important to weigh in choosing a proper response to a wrong or injury?

What is the need for corrective justice?

In all societies there are situations in which one individual or group **wrongs** or **injures** another. In some cases the wrong or injury may be accidental and in other cases intentional. Since the earliest civilization, human beings have felt that if someone commits a wrong or causes an injury to another, things should be set right in some way. Ideally, this would mean restoring things to the way they were before the wrong or injury occurred. In some cases this may be possible, but in most cases it is not. For example, one cannot restore a life. Since it is not always possible to restore things to the way they were before, people have developed other ways to respond to wrongs and injuries.

Corrective justice is concerned with **fair or proper responses to wrongs and injuries.** Proper responses to wrongs and injuries may vary widely. In some instances, one may ignore what has happened, forgive the person causing the wrong or injury, or use the situation to educate the person to prevent a repetition of the event. In other situations, one might wish to require a person to compensate in one way or another for a wrong or injury done to others. In some instances, courts of law may punish wrongdoers by fines, imprisonment, or even death.

The most desirable or proper response to a wrong or injury may not satisfy our need for corrective justice in some situations, but it may serve other purposes such as the wish to forgive or pardon a person or to deter or prevent further wrongs or injuries. For example, if a friend with little money accidentally broke something you owned, you might not want to ask the friend to replace the object or compensate you for the loss. You might expect an apology, however.

Corrective justice has one principal goal—the fair correction of a wrong or injury. Additionally, we may want to prevent or discourage future wrongful or careless conduct by teaching a lesson to the wrongdoer or by making an example of him or her. Thus, the purposes or goals of corrective justice are

- **correction**–providing a remedy or imposing a penalty to set things right in a **fair** way

- **prevention**–responding to wrongdoing in a way that will prevent the person from doing wrong again

- **deterrence**–discouraging people from committing wrongs and causing injuries, for fear of the consequences

Correction, deterrence, and prevention are essential to the very existence of society. Without efforts to serve these goals, disorder and chaos may result. Ensuring proper responses to wrongs and injuries is important not only with regard to criminal behavior and civil matters but also in families, schools, and other areas of the private sector. Of course it goes without saying that one must first determine who should be considered responsible for a wrong or injury before evaluating what the proper response would be.

What do *you* think?

1. Make a list of the most common responses to wrongs or injuries that you have observed.

2. What are some situations in which a response to a wrong or injury has been fair? Why was it fair?

3. What are some situations in which a response to a wrong or injury was unfair? Why was it unfair?

4. What might happen in a family, school, community, or nation if no attempts were made to provide fair responses to wrongs or injuries, or to deter or prevent them? Why?

5. In what types of situations might it be right to let a wrong or injury go uncorrected, but still do something to make sure such wrongs or injuries do not occur again?

Do you think assigning community services to persons convicted of minor offenses is a fair response to a wrong?

How should we deal with issues of corrective justice?

Deciding how to respond to a wrong or injury may be simple in some situations, such as when a young child takes away the toy (property) of another child. Our sense of justice may be met by merely restoring the toy to the owner. Our interest in preventing such things from happening again may be met by informing the child that it is wrong to take another person's property without permission. It is hoped these actions will teach the child proper behavior.

In other situations, finding a fair response to a wrong or injury may be more difficult. Unfortunately, there is no simple formula for deciding on proper responses in difficult situations. There are a number of intellectual tools, however, that can be useful when making such decisions. They form the following procedure that you can use to make thoughtful decisions about how to respond to a wrong or injury:

1. Identify the important characteristics of the wrong and/or injury.

2. Identify the important characteristics of the person or persons causing the wrong or injury.

3. Identify the important characteristics of the person or persons who were wronged or injured.

4. Examine common responses to wrongs or injuries and their purposes.

5. Consider other values and interests and decide what the proper response(s) would be.

Each step and the intellectual tools it involves will be examined in detail in lessons 7 and 8. First, however, let's look at the difference between wrongs and injuries.

What is the difference between wrongs and injuries?

In examining issues of corrective justice it is important to understand the difference between wrongs and injuries. As you have learned,

■ A **wrong** is conduct that violates a duty or responsibility imposed by laws, rules, customs, or moral principles.

■ An **injury** is harm or damage to persons or property, or violation of a person's rights.

In some cases, conduct may be wrong and also cause an injury, such as when someone robs a store and shoots the cashier. In other cases, conduct may be wrong but not cause an injury, such as when someone drives with a suspended license. There also may be injuries caused without wrongful conduct, such as when a football player is injured by a clean hit. The following exercise asks you to determine whether situations involve a wrong, an injury, or both.

Critical Thinking Exercise

EXAMINING WRONGS AND INJURIES

Work with a study partner. Read each of the following situations and then answer the questions at the end of the exercise. Be prepared to share your answers with the class.

1. Dozens of people died and hundreds of homes were destroyed when a campfire set by a transient got out of hand.

2. Valerie pushed Monica in the volleyball finals to save the point. Monica suffered a broken wrist.

3. George drove his car through a red light. Fortunately, no accident occurred.

4. Will, a mechanic, forgot to tighten the wheels after he changed the tires. The left front wheel came off while the customer was driving and the car crashed into a parked truck.

5. The security guard shot at the bank robber, but missed. The bank robber took a hostage to ensure his escape. Later, the hostage was released.

What do *you* think?

1. In each situation, what were the wrongs, if any? What were the injuries, if any?

2. In which situations does your sense of fairness or justice make you want to respond in some way to set things right?

3. In those situations, what do you think would be a fair and just response?

4. What purposes or goals would be served by your proposed responses?

Critical Thinking Exercise

EVALUATING AND TAKING A POSITION ON RESPONSES TO WRONGS AND INJURIES

The class should be divided into small groups to review the following situations. For each situation the group should answer the "What do *you* think?" questions at the end of the exercise. Be prepared to share your answers with the class.

1. Leslie went into a department store and tried on a shirt. She really liked the way it looked, but she didn't have enough money to pay for it. Leslie decided to steal the shirt. She put it in her purse and walked out of the store. Suddenly, a security guard grabbed her by the arm. She was caught.

2. Arman drank too many beers while watching the football game with his friends. On the way home he failed to stop as the traffic light turned red. Arman's car smashed into the side of a small pickup truck, killing the passenger and seriously injuring the driver. Frank also suffered injuries, and is not expected to gain full use of his legs again.

3. Anita and her one-year-old daughter had just left the house. Suddenly, two men appeared at the side of the car and opened the door. "Get out they shouted. We're taking this car." Anita screamed, "My baby!" The men grabbed Anita, pulled her out of the car, jumped inside, and started to drive. Anita's arm was caught in the seat belt. She was dragged along the side of the car. The man who was driving wouldn't stop. He drove the car against a fence to brush Anita off the car. Anita was killed. The men stopped, put the baby on the side of the road and sped away. Four hours later they were caught.

What do *you* think?

1. What are the wrongs and injuries described?

2. Given the information you have, what do you think would be fair or proper responses to the wrongs and injuries described in each selection?

3. What purposes or goals are your responses designed to promote?

4. What additional information would you like to help you decide on a fair or proper response to the wrongs and injuries described? Why might this information be important?

Using the Lesson

1. Interview people responsible for dealing with wrongs and injuries as a part of their profession. You might consider police officers, lawyers, judges, probation officers, or school principals. Ask them to describe some situations they have handled. Find out their ideas on the best responses to wrongs and injuries.

2. Law number 125 of Hammurabi's code states: If any one place his property with another for safe keeping, and there, either through thieves or robbers, his property and the property of the other man be lost, the owner of the house, through whose neglect the loss took place, shall compensate the owner for all that was given to him in charge. But the owner of the house shall try to follow up and recover his property, and take it away from the thief.

In your opinion is the Code's response to the injury fair? Why or why not?

LESSON 7

What Intellectual Tools Are Useful in Making Decisions About Issues of Corrective Justice?

Purpose of Lesson

This lesson introduces you to some intellectual tools which are useful in examining issues of corrective justice. When you have completed this lesson, you should be able to use these tools to evaluate, take, and defend positions on issues of corrective justice.

Terms to Know

proportionality	recklessness
extent	negligence
duration	probable consequences
impact	justification
offensiveness	remorse
intent	regret

What is the first step in evaluating issues of corrective justice?

STEP 1.

Identify the important characteristics of the wrong and/or injury.

a. What was the wrong or injury?

Since corrective justice deals with the fairness of responses to wrongs and injuries, identifying the wrongs and injuries in a particular situation is a logical first step in evaluating issues of corrective justice. Identifying the wrongs and injuries also is important because it helps us evaluate whether an injury was caused by wrongful conduct, that is, by the violation of a duty.

Whether or not an injury was caused by someone's violation of a duty makes a crucial difference in deciding what a fair or proper response would be.

Example: Suppose a young child dashed into the street and was run over by a car. In deciding on a fair or proper response, would it make any difference if the driver was driving carefully and obeying all traffic laws, or if the driver could not stop in time to avoid the accident because he or she was speeding?

Why is it important to determine if an injury was caused by wrongful conduct?

b. How serious was the wrong or injury?

Evaluating the seriousness of the wrongs and injuries in a particular situation is important, because the response to a wrong or injury should be **fair in relation to the seriousness of the wrong or injury**.

We call this **the principle of proportionality.** This principle means that a response to a wrong or injury should be in proportion to the seriousness of the wrong or injury. This is what we mean when we say the punishment should fit the crime.

The principle of proportionality implies that the seriousness of a wrong or injury must be taken into account in deciding what response would be fair or proper.

Why is it important to consider the seriousness of a wrong or injury in deciding what the response should be?

Example: Suppose Michael was driving too fast on the freeway when he saw police lights flashing in his rear view mirror. Would it make any difference if the driver slowed down immediately and pulled over as soon as he could, or if he drove even faster trying to get away, running several cars off the road in the process?

As you can see, it is important to evaluate how serious a wrong or injury is when you are trying to decide what would be a fair or proper response. How can you make this evaluation? There are a number of ideas that you can use to evaluate the seriousness of a wrong or injury.

- **Extent**–How many people or things were affected?

- **Duration**–How long did the wrongful or injury-causing conduct last?

- **Impact**–How severe was the harm or damage? Will it be permanent?

- **Offensiveness**–How objectionable was the wrong in terms of your sense of right and wrong, human dignity, or other values?

Critical Thinking Exercise
EVALUATING THE SERIOUSNESS OF WRONGS AND INJURIES

Work with a study partner. Read the situations in "Two Foul Factories." Evaluate the seriousness of the wrongs and injuries each factory caused by answering the "What do *you* think?" questions. Be prepared to discuss your answers with the class.

Two Foul Factories

Suppose two factories have been charged with violating environmental laws dealing with the disposal of potentially harmful wastes.

Mondo Corporation has polluted the air of a large residential area where about 10,000 people live. The company has been allowing harmful pollutants to fill the air for five years. The pollutants can cause respiratory ailments such as emphysema, and may be a cause of cancer. The company has refused to do anything to control its emissions, despite verified reports of people in the area who have become severely ill.

What factors would you consider in deciding the seriousness of wrongs or injuries caused by industrial pollution?

Zenon Utility Co. is located on the outskirts of a city. It discharges air pollutants that are annoying, but do not threaten life. The pollutants have affected about 1,000 people living nearby who claim the smell from the power plant makes it unbearable to live in their homes. The plant has been discharging pollutants for two months. The company has made efforts to control the pollution caused by its operations, but its efforts do not satisfy the local residents.

What do *you* think?

1. How **extensive** was each factory's wrong or injury? How many people or things were affected?

2. What was the **duration** of each factory's wrong or injury? How long did the wrongful or injury-causing conduct last?

3. What was the **impact** of each factory's wrong or injury? How severe was the harm or damage? Will it be permanent?

4. How **offensive** was each factory's wrong or injury? How objectionable was it in terms of your sense of right and wrong, human dignity, or other values?

Critical Thinking Exercise

EVALUATING THE NEED FOR PUNISHMENT

In the previous exercise you examined the intellectual tools that are useful for evaluating the seriousness of a wrong or injury. But issues of corrective justice cannot be resolved just by evaluating the seriousness of the wrong or injury. Other factors or considerations also need to be taken into account.

The class should be divided into small groups and each group should read "The Fire," and then discuss the "What do *you* think?" questions. Be prepared to share your answers with the class.

The Fire

George and his friend Dan were seven years old. Both boys had played many times in the house, yard, and garage of their neighbor. They also had watched him burn leaves in a lot next door. When they asked if they could help him, he told them to keep away from the fire.

One day when the neighbor was out of town, the boys pulled aside a sheet of canvas that covered the entrance

to his garage. They went inside to play, but after a while they felt cold. They noticed a charcoal grill in the garage and decided to build a fire to keep themselves warm. They moved the grill close to the garage's entrance and then went outside and gathered leaves to make a fire. Dan went home to get some matches.

The boys lit the fire in the grill and stood with their backs to it trying to get warm. Then the canvas sheet caught on fire. They tried to put the fire out, but failed. The fire spread from the garage to the attached house and caused $28,000 in damages.

Both boys were of average intelligence. Both had been told by their parents not to play with matches and fire.

What factors or considerations might be important in deciding how to respond to the wrongs and injuries described in this case?

What do *you* think?

1. What factors or considerations suggest that George and Dan should be punished? What suggests that they should not be punished?

2. What other information would you like to have in deciding whether George and Dan should be punished? Why would this information be important?

3. What do you think would be a fair response to the wrongs and injuries described in this story?

4. Is the response you have suggested designed to correct the wrongs and injuries? How?

5. Is the response you have suggested designed to prevent further wrongs and injuries? How?

What factors are important in deciding how to respond to a wrong or injury?

In "The Fire" exercise, you evaluated whether to respond to a particular wrong and injury by punishing the wrongdoers. You also identified some important things to consider in making such decisions. As you have learned, it is not always necessary to respond to a wrong or injury by punishing the wrongdoer. Other responses are possible, and in some situations other responses may be better than punishment.

In the first place, injuries which are not caused by the careless or wrongful conduct of another do not require a response to set things right. In some cases, we decide not to punish a wrongdoer because the wrong or injury is not very serious, and we do not want to take the time or effort to try to correct it.

In other situations, we decide not to punish a wrongdoer because we believe that punishment is not the best way to prevent similar conduct in the future. A better way to prevent future wrongful conduct would be to inform the wrongdoer that he or she has committed a wrong, or to provide treatment or education. We might think future wrongful conduct is unlikely even if the wrongdoer is forgiven or pardoned.

What reasons might we have for believing that punishment is not necessary to teach a lesson to the wrongdoer? In some cases, **evaluating the wrongdoer's conduct** may persuade us that the wrong or injury was not caused with wrongful intent or purpose. In some cases **evaluating the nature or character of the wrongdoer** may persuade us that the person should be given a chance to mend his or her ways. And in some cases **evaluating the conduct of the person or persons who were wronged or injured** may persuade us that the wrongdoer's conduct was justified or excused to some degree.

The following critical thinking exercise explains the next two steps in the procedure for evaluating issues of corrective justice. It introduces the intellectual tools you can use to evaluate the important characteristics of the person or persons who caused the wrong or injury, and the important characteristics of the person or persons who were wronged or injured.

Critical Thinking Exercise
IDENTIFYING IMPORTANT CHARACTERISTICS BY USING INTELLECTUAL TOOLS

Directions: After you have read each step in the following procedure, be prepared to

■ discuss the usefulness of each step

■ give examples of its application to situations you have experienced or observed

STEP 2.

Identify the important characteristics of the person or persons causing the wrong or injury.

Questions a-e in Step 2. should be answered before deciding what to do about the person or persons causing a wrong or injury.

a. State of mind: What was the person's state of mind at the time he or she caused the wrong or injury?

A person's state of mind is one of the most important things to consider when trying to find a fair response to a wrong or injury. To determine the person's state of mind, a number of things should be considered.

■ **Intent:** Did the person act intentionally (on purpose) to bring about the wrong or injury?

■ **Recklessness:** Did the person deliberately (or knowingly) ignore obvious risks of serious harm?

■ **Carelessness:** Did the person act in a thoughtless manner, without paying enough attention to risks that were foreseeable?

■ **Knowledge of Probable Consequences:** Did the person know, or have the capability of knowing, that what he or she was doing was wrong or likely to cause an injury?

■ **Control:** Did the person have physical and mental control over his or her actions?

■ **Duty or Obligation:** Did the person have a duty to act, or not act, in a certain way in order to prevent the wrong or injury?

What factors should a judge consider in deciding what sentence to impose?

■ **More Important Values and Interests:** Did the person have any other important values, interests, responsibilities, or motives that might justify or excuse his or her actions?

Example: Consider the story of "The Fire" from the previous exercise. Would it make any difference if George and Dan set fire to the canvas sheet on purpose? Would it make any difference if they were older, and knew what might happen?

Example: Consider the case of someone speeding on the freeway. Would it make any difference if the driver was rushing an injured person to the hospital, or if he was exceeding the speed limit simply because he liked to drive fast?

b. **Past history: Has the person committed similar wrongs or caused similar injuries in the past?**

c. **Character and personality traits: Is the person generally trustworthy, careful, considerate of other's rights, and non-violent?**

d. **Feelings of regret or remorse: Is the person sorry for his or her conduct, or unconcerned about the wrong or injury he or she caused?**

e. **Role: Did the person act alone or with others, as a leader or as a minor participant?**

Example: Consider again the story of "The Fire" from the previous exercise. Would it make any difference if George and Dan had damaged homes by setting fires in the past? Would it make any difference if they were

sorry or not sorry about the damage the fire caused? Would it make any difference if they had been encouraged by older children to start the fire?

STEP 3.

Identify the important characteristics of the person or persons who were wronged or injured.

Besides looking at the relevant characteristics of the person or persons causing the wrong or injury, there may be important characteristics about the person or persons who suffered the wrong or injury that should be considered. The following two questions are designed to focus your attention on this aspect of the issue.

a. **Did the person or persons who were wronged or injured contribute to causing the wrong or injury?**

b. **What is the person's ability to recover from the wrong or injury?**

Example: Consider again the story of "The Fire" from the previous exercise. Would it make any difference if the neighbor had been home, and had specifically told the boys they could burn leaves in the charcoal grill? Would it make any difference if the fire had destroyed the neighbor's irreplaceable family heirlooms?

What do *you* think?

1. Why might it be important to consider the wrongdoer's state of mind in deciding how to respond to a wrong or injury? Why might it be important to consider the justifications or excuses for the wrongdoer's conduct?

2. What arguments can you make to support the position that a person's past history, character, personality traits, and feelings of remorse or regret should be considered in deciding how to respond to a wrong or injury he or she caused? What arguments can you make to support the position that responses to wrongs and injuries should not depend on the nature or character of the wrongdoer, but should be the same for anyone who commits a particular wrong?

3. Are the three steps in the procedure you have studied in this lesson adequate to resolve issues of corrective justice, or should other considerations also be taken into account? Explain your answer.

Using the Lesson

1. Bring excerpts from newspapers to class, or descriptions of television news or entertainment programs, in which issues of corrective justice are raised. Explain to the class which intellectual tools were used to decide how to respond to the wrongs and injuries.

2. Working with your teacher, invite a judge or attorney to class to discuss how the intellectual tools you have studied are used in court cases.

3. Draw a cartoon to illustrate a situation involving an issue of corrective justice, specifically showing one or more of the intellectual tools you have studied.

LESSON 8

What Values and Interests Should We Consider in Deciding How to Respond to Wrongs and Injuries?

Purpose of Lesson

This lesson introduces you to the remaining two intellectual tools useful in examining issues of corrective justice. You learn some common responses to wrongs and injuries and the goals these responses serve. You also examine some values and interests that are important in deciding on proper responses to wrongs and injuries.

When you have completed the lesson, you should be able to explain the purposes served by common responses to wrongs and injuries. You also should be able to use the intellectual tools you have learned to evaluate issues of corrective justice in different situations.

Terms to Know

pardon
restore
compensate

What are the final steps in the procedure for examining issues of corrective justice?

So far, you have considered the first three steps in the procedure to be used in deciding issues of corrective justice: Step 1 – Identifying important characteristics of the wrong or injury; Step 2 – Identifying important characteristics of the person or persons causing the wrong or injury; Step 3 – Identifying important characteristics of the person or persons wronged or injured. Two steps remain in this procedure: Step 4 – Examining common responses to wrongs and injuries and their purposes; and Step 5 – Considering related values and interests to decide what would be the best response.

As you have learned, there are many possible responses to wrongs and injuries. To make sure you select the best response or responses, you should evaluate all the possibilities and examine related values and interests.

STEP 4.

Examine common responses to wrongs and injuries and their purposes.

As mentioned earlier, the principal goal of corrective justice is to provide a fair or proper response to a wrong or injury, to set things right. Responses may be used not only to correct wrongs or injuries, but also to prevent those responsible from causing further wrongs or injuries, and to deter or discourage others from causing wrongs or injuries. In some cases, a response may be chosen to serve other values and interests, rather than to serve the goals of corrective justice. The following is a list of common responses to wrongs and injuries and a brief explanation of the purposes of each. Often more than one response may be chosen, and often more than one purpose may be involved.

a. **We may inform or tell the wrongdoer that what he or she did was wrong or caused injury.**

The purpose of this type of response is to prevent future wrongs and injuries by explaining to the wrongdoer how his or her conduct was wrong or caused injury. In these cases, the wrong or injury goes uncorrected, unless some other response is also chosen.

Example: After stopping a motorist with an out-of-state driver's license, the officer informed the driver that in this state making a right turn on a red light was illegal, but allowed the driver to proceed without giving him a ticket.

Example: Craig, age six, was playing with matches and started a small grass fire, which his parents put out. Later, a member of the fire department called on Craig and his parents and informed Craig of the danger he had created to himself and others and the damage he had caused by his wrongful conduct.

b. **We may overlook or ignore a wrong or injury.**

Sometimes we decide to overlook or ignore a wrong or injury because it is not worth the time and effort to try to correct it. Sometimes we may believe the wrongdoer is just trying to get attention. Ignoring the wrongful act may deter such conduct in the future. In these cases the wrong or injury goes uncorrected.

Example: When the J-M Company truck was delivering a new television set to Kevin's house, the driver accidentally ran over Kevin's prize rose bush. Although Kevin was upset, he chose to do nothing about it.

Example: Mrs. Johnson was a nursery school teacher. One of her younger students repeatedly clapped his hands while she read a story to the class. Mrs. Johnson generally ignored his behavior.

c. We may forgive or pardon the wrongdoer for a wrong or injury.

Sometimes we decide to forgive or pardon wrongful acts in the hope that this will cause the wrongdoers to regret their actions and mend their ways. Sometimes we decide to forgive or pardon a wrongdoer out of the belief that he or she has already suffered enough; we understand that everyone makes mistakes and we would want others to forgive our mistakes. In these cases the wrong or injury goes uncorrected.

Example: When Thomas accidentally fell against Paul, causing him to sprain his ankle, he apologized and indicated how sorry he was. Paul told him not to worry; he realized it had been an accident and he forgave Thomas completely.

Example: Sue loaned $1,000 to her friend, Mike. Mike agreed to repay Sue over a period of one year. Mike lost his job and was unable to repay the loan. Instead of pursuing the matter in court, Sue decided not to make Mike repay her.

d. We may punish the wrongdoer for a wrong or injury.

One purpose of punishment is corrective justice, that is, to avenge or get even for a wrong or injury. Punishment also may prevent future wrongs and injuries by teaching the person a lesson. It also may deter others from wrongdoing by setting an example.

Example: When Martin and Lorenzo started fighting in class, the principal suspended them from school for five days.

Example: Convicted of burglarizing two homes, Sylvia, Marie, and Sam were sentenced to six months in jail.

e. We may require the wrongdoer to restore or give back something he or she has taken.

When a wrongdoer has taken things that can be returned to their owner, we may require the wrongdoer to restore or give back the items in order to set things right. Requiring a wrongdoer to restore what he or she has taken also may serve to prevent or deter future wrongs and injuries.

Example: When David was convicted of fraud in the purchase of the Hausers' home, the judge required him to return the property deed to them.

Example: When the security officer caught Jason spray painting the side of the gym, he had to spend the next Saturday repainting the wall he had decorated.

What might be a fair and proper response to the wrongs and injuries caused by graffiti artists who paint the property of others without permission?

f. We may require the wrongdoer to compensate or pay for a wrong or injury.

In many cases a wrong or injury cannot be undone in the sense that the items taken, damaged, or destroyed cannot be restored or put back. In such cases, we may require the wrongdoer to compensate for the loss by paying money or giving something of value to the wronged or injured person. Requiring a wrongdoer to compensate or pay for a wrong or injury also may serve to prevent or deter future wrongs and injuries.

Example: After borrowing a book from the library, Mr. Burns lost it. He had to pay the price of a new book to compensate for the one he had lost.

Example: A driver's family sued an automobile manufacturer for damages when one of its cars exploded, killing the driver. After a trial, the jury awarded $1 million to the driver's wife to compensate for the loss of her husband. The court made the manufacturer pay this amount to the driver's wife.

Do you think monetary awards are appropriate to compensate for losses that cannot be restored?

g. We may provide treatment or education to the wrongdoer.

Providing treatment or education to wrongdoers is not intended to correct the wrong or injury they caused. Its purpose is to prevent them from causing further wrongs or injuries by giving them the knowledge and skills to become self-sufficient and responsible members of society.

Example: In Topeka, Kansas, all persons sentenced to prison receive tests and treatment from psychiatrists and other mental health experts. Studies show that these prisoners are 25 percent less likely to return to prison after release than prisoners who do not receive treatment.

Example: Carlo was driving too fast and got a ticket for speeding. The court allowed Carlo to attend driving school instead of paying a fine because it was his first offense.

How might education serve the goals of corrective justice?

What do *you* think?

1. What are some situations in which you might decide not to punish someone for committing a wrong or causing an injury? What other responses would you choose in these situations? Why?

2. In your opinion, what should be the response if someone carelessly injures another person or damages another person's property? What should be the response if the injury or damage was caused on purpose?

3. If an adult has committed a wrong in the past and he or she has been warned not to do it again, what should be the response if the person commits the wrong again? Would your answer be different if the wrongdoer were an infant? A teenager? Explain your answers.

STEP 5.

Consider related values and interests and decide what the proper response would be.

As you have learned, the basic goal of corrective justice is to set things right in a fair way when a wrong or injury has occurred. Often, we also wish to prevent similar wrongs or injuries from happening because we want to live in an orderly and just society. Thus, we should consider the goals of correction, prevention, and deterrence in deciding on responses to wrongs and injuries. To ensure that the responses are fair, we should consider the principle of proportionality.

We also should consider other values and interests. On the one hand, we might want to satisfy our sense of human dignity and respect for life. On the other hand, we might want retribution.

It is often difficult to weigh all these considerations, some of which might be contradictory. Sometimes we choose a response to serve the goals of corrective justice, and sometimes we design a response to serve other values and interests. In deciding what the proper response(s) would be, you should consider the following:

a. What responses would correct the wrong or injury?

Our need for corrective justice might be satisfied by responses that set things right in one way or another, such as those that require a person to give back something taken from another person, compensate a person for a loss, or those that place a burden or punishment on a wrongdoer.

However, it is important to remember that a response may be chosen to serve other values and interests, rather than to serve the goals of corrective justice.

Example: If a friend were to break something of yours by accident, you might not ask or allow her to replace it or pay for it.

b. How might a response deter or prevent future wrongs or injuries?

In many situations, one of the main reasons for selecting a particular response to a wrong or injury is that the response probably will prevent the wrongdoer from committing such actions in the future and will deter other people from committing such actions.

Example: Sending someone who has committed a crime to prison removes the person from society. It is hoped that when the person is released, he or she will refrain from such actions in the future. Others, who value their freedom, may be deterred from wrongdoing because they do not wish to be imprisoned.

c. How might a response affect distributive justice?

Distributive justice requires that like cases be treated alike. Cases that are different in important ways should be treated differently.

Example: Suppose two persons with similar backgrounds and criminal records were caught stealing. Both were tried and convicted. If one of the persons was sentenced to prison and the other was placed on probation, the response might be considered a violation of distributive justice.

d. How might a response affect human dignity?

An important belief held by many people is that all persons, no matter what their actions, should be treated with dignity—as persons of value with basic rights, deserving respect as human beings. For example, responses that are cruel should not be used no matter how offensive a person's crime may be.

e. How might a response affect promotion of the value of human life?

Human life has a basic worth or value that should be protected. Some people say that the death penalty conflicts with this value, even when it is imposed for taking the life of another person. Others argue that the death penalty deters potential murderers and promotes the value of human life.

f. What responses are practical given the resources available?

Individuals and society—the public—need to make efficient use of their time, energy, and property when making responses to wrongs and injuries. The costs of various responses must be considered and, in some instances, a response that sets things completely right may prove too costly.

Example: Under our system, society pays for the costs of gathering evidence against criminal wrongdoers, trying them in a court, and, if they are found guilty, sometimes placing them in a prison or other institution. However, society usually does not pay the victim for any losses he or she may have suffered as a result of criminal wrongdoing.

g. How might a response affect freedom?

Our society, like many others, places a high value on individual liberty, choice, movement and expression. In selecting a response, one should consider the value of freedom—both of the wrongdoer and of the rest of society.

h. How might a response affect proportionality?

A fundamental consideration in judging whether a response is fair is whether it is in proportion to the seriousness of the wrong or injury.

Example: The response to a cold-blooded murder should be more serious than the response to stealing a bicycle. This is what we mean when we say the punishment should fit the crime.

i. How might a response satisfy the desire for revenge?

Since ancient times, humans have included in their ideas of justice the desire for revenge. In Greek mythology, Nemesis was the goddess of vengeance. Today some people believe revenge should not be a consideration in selecting or evaluating responses. Others, however, believe the desire for revenge is natural and can be considered in allowing society to get even as a part of setting things right.

Example: In 1625, Sir Francis Bacon wrote, "Revenge is a kind of wild justice, which the more man's nature runs to, the more ought law to weed it out."

What do *you* think?

1. How might consideration of values and interests help ensure the fairness with which wrongs and injuries are corrected?

2. What problems might arise if values and interests were not considered in deciding how to respond to wrongs and injuries?

3. How might a response that satisfies the desire for revenge conflict with the values of human dignity or human life? How should this conflict be resolved? Why?

Critical Thinking Exercise

EVALUATING AN ISSUE OF CORRECTIVE JUSTICE BY USING INTELLECTUAL TOOLS

Read the following story based on *Crime and Punishment* by Fyodor Dostoevsky (1821–1881) and work in small groups to complete the intellectual tool chart on pages 191–92. After completing the chart, answer the "What do *you* think?" questions on page 190. Be prepared to share your answers with the class.

The Murder of Aliona Ivanovna

Rodion Raskolnikov left his family's home in the countryside of Russia to move to St. Petersburg to study at the university. His family was poor, but struggled to send him a little money so he could continue his studies. Raskolnikov lived in a tiny, dark room and ate sparingly. He found it increasingly difficult to concentrate on his studies. His own poverty did not disturb him, but he kept thinking about the sacrifices of his family.

What factors should you consider in deciding the seriousness of the wrongs and injuries committed by Roskolnikov?

The young student dreamed of committing the perfect crime. This crime would free his family from poverty and struggle. But it would be more than a crime for money. It would be a crime that would change life for the better, a crime for which Raskolnikov would be thanked.

Raskolnikov resolved to kill Aliona Ivanovna, an elderly pawnbroker who had given many students money in exchange for family heirlooms. The woman had become rich from the poverty of students like Raskolnikov. Yet, she forced her stepsister Lizaveta, a kindly, but slow-witted woman, to work hard to add to the household income. In Raskolnikov's mind, the pawnbroker was a person who did not deserve to live. He believed that Lizaveta and the world would be better off if the pawnbroker died.

Raskolnikov went to the apartment of Aliona Ivanovna and Lizaveta at a time when he knew that Lizaveta would be working in the marketplace. He pretended to the pawnbroker that he had a silver cigarette case to pawn. When she turned her back to him, he struck her with an ax. Once he was sure that she was dead, he began to rob the apartment.

Suddenly, Lizaveta returned home. She was so terrified when she saw the dead body of her stepsister that she could hardly speak or move. Raskolnikov realized that Lizaveta would identify him as the murderer of the pawnbroker. Before Lizaveta could scream or run out of the apartment, he killed her with the ax.

What might be a fair and proper response to the wrongs and injuries in this story? Which goals of corrective justice would the response serve?

He ran out of the apartment and back to his room where he hid the ax. Soon he began to feel guilty about the murders and hinted to friends that he knew who the murderer was. When the police questioned Raskolnikov, he gave them information that led them to identify him as the murderer. Before police could arrest him, however, Raskolnikov confessed to both murders.

What do *you* think?

1. What would be the proper response(s) to the wrongs and injuries described in the story?

2. If Rodion Raskolnikov were to receive separate responses for the two murders, should the response in the killing of Aliona Ivanovna be more severe than the response to the killing of Lizaveta? Why or why not?

3. Are the responses you suggested designed to correct the wrong or injury?

4. Are the responses you suggested designed to prevent further wrongs or injuries?

Using the Lesson

1. Imagine that you live in czarist Russia at the time of the Ivanovna murders. Choose one of the following titles and write a newspaper editorial on the Raskolnikov case and the response you think should have been made to it.

   - Who's the Real Victim?
   - A Travesty of Justice
   - In the Interest of Civil Order
   - An Eye for an Eye
   - True Confessions
   - Violence Against Women

2. Do research to find out how different societies respond to one of the following crimes, and present a report to the class describing what you learn:

   - murder
   - robbery
   - theft of government property

Intellectual Tool Chart for Issues of Corrective Justice

Questions	Answers

1. Identify the wrong or injury:
 	
  a. What was the wrong or injury?
 	
  b. How serious was the wrong or injury? Consider:
 	
     ■ extent
 	
     ■ duration
 	
     ■ impact
 	
     ■ offensiveness	

2. Identify important characteristics of the person or persons causing the wrong or injury:
 	
  a. What was the person's **state of mind** at the time he or she caused the wrong or injury? Consider:
 	
     ■ intent
 	
     ■ recklessness
 	
     ■ carelessness
 	
     ■ knowledge of probable consequences
 	
     ■ control or choice
 	
     ■ duty or obligation
 	
     ■ important values, interests, or responsibilities
 	
  b. What facts about the person's **past history** are relevant in deciding upon a fair response?
 	
  c. What facts about the person's **character** are relevant in deciding upon a fair response?
 	
  d. What **feelings** did the person express after causing the wrong or injury?
 	
  e. What was the person's **role** in causing the wrong or injury?	

3. Identify important characteristics of the person or persons who were wronged or injured:
 	
  a. Did the person or persons **contribute** to causing the wrong or injury he or she suffered?
 	
  b. What is the person's ability to **recover** from the wrong or injury?	

Intellectual Tool Chart for Issues of Corrective Justice

Questions	Answers
4. Examine common responses to wrongs and injuries and their purposes: a. Should we **inform** the person that what he or she did was wrong and injurious? Why? b. Should we **overlook** or **ignore** the wrong or injury? Why? c. Should we **forgive** or **pardon** the person for causing the wrong or injury? Why? d. Should we **punish** the person for causing the wrong or injury? Why? e. Should we require the person to **restore** what was taken or damaged? Why? f. Should we require the person to **compensate** for causing the wrong or injury? Why? g. Should we provide **treatment** or **education** to the wrongdoer? Why?	
5. Consider related values and interests and decide what the proper response would be: a. What responses would **correct** the wrong or injury? b. What responses would **deter** or **prevent** future wrongs or injuries? c. What responses would promote **distributive justice**? d. What responses would preserve **human dignity**? e. What responses would promote the value of **human life**? f. What responses are **practical** given the resources available? g. What responses would protect **freedom**, both of the wrongdoer and of other members of society? h. What responses would be in **proportion** to the seriousness of the wrong or injury? i. What responses might satisfy the desire for **revenge**?	
6. Explain the reasons for your decision.	

LESSON 9

What Would Be Proper Responses to These Wrongs and Injuries?

Purpose of Lesson

In this lesson you use the intellectual tools you have studied in this unit in a final exercise. When you have completed the lesson, you should be able to use these intellectual tools to evaluate, take, and defend positions on issues of corrective justice.

Critical Thinking Exercise

EVALUATING, TAKING, AND DEFENDING A POSITION

Read the fictional "A Scandal in City Government," then do the following:

- Identify the wrongs and injuries caused by some of the officials of the Bay City government.

- Use the intellectual tool chart at the end of this lesson to develop positions on desirable responses.

Your teacher may ask you to report your positions independently or may divide the class into groups to role-play meetings of a mayor's task force. The task force has the responsibility of investigating the scandal and recommending action. Instructions to the mayor's task force follow the fictional newspaper article.

A Scandal in City Government

Widespread Corruption Uncovered In Bay City
A Gazette Exclusive

Bay City—The *Gazette* has learned of widespread corruption on the part of Bay City officials. Dozens of incidents involving bribe-taking and illegal payoffs to city inspectors have been documented. City departments involved include: the Fire Department, the Building Code Office, and the Health Commission. Also implicated are a number of state-licensed building contractors.

In order to investigate the rumors of corruption, the *Gazette* provided funds and authorized reporter Myrta Ramirez to purchase a rundown snack shop. She completed a few repairs, but left many serious building and health code violations. Then, the reporter contacted Robert Manning, a state-licensed building contractor.

Ms. Ramirez asked Mr. Manning if he could arrange the necessary inspections to satisfy the city's building, health, and safety codes. Mr. Manning told her that he would be glad to run things through the city if she first paid him his fee. After Ms. Ramirez paid Mr. Manning a sizable amount in cash, he gave her some of his business cards. He explained that whenever an inspector came to the premises, she should put $100 in an envelope along with his business card and give it to the inspector. If you do that, you won't be hassled, he promised.

The first inspector to come to the shop was from the Fire Department. Ms. Ramirez gave her an envelope and she checked its contents. Then, ignoring a number of serious fire hazards, the inspector filled out a department form stating that the snack shop was safe for occupancy.

Ms. Ramirez followed the same procedure each time an inspector came to the shop. Each supplied the needed verification once he or she was given an envelope. Not one of these city employees conducted a thorough inspection or ordered Ms. Ramirez to make any changes in the conditions of the shop.

After the events described above, the *Gazette* invited the heads of each of the departments involved to meet Ms. Ramirez at the snack shop. Each department head was asked to make a thorough examination of the shop for code violations. They made detailed inspections and noted a total of thirty-eight serious code violations. The department heads who participated in the inspection agreed that the snack shop constituted a serious hazard to public health and safety. ■

Meeting of the Mayor's Task Force

Within a week after publication of the story about corruption in Bay City government, the mayor appointed a task force to examine the problem and make recommendations about what responses the mayor's office or other government agencies should make to the wrongs. If your class is divided into groups for this lesson, each group should act as a task force and complete the following steps:

- Read the witness summaries.

- Fill out the intellectual tool chart on pages 196–97.

- Recommend a response for each of the persons described in the witness summaries.

- Be prepared to explain recommended responses to the entire class.

The witness summaries were taken from transcripts of hearings held by the mayor's task force.

Don R. Duchinsky, Department Head, Building Code Office. Testimony taken February 5, morning session.

Mr. Duchinsky is thirty-seven years old and divorced. He has worked for the city for seventeen years. He has held his present position for the last eight years. His salary is $40,000 per year.

Mr. Duchinsky has a good civil service record and his superior rated him "excellent" in his last personnel evaluation. He has no prior criminal record.

In his testimony, Mr. Duchinsky stated, "I knew nothing about the alleged acts of people in my office. Maybe I should have known, but I didn't."

Then Mr. Duchinsky was reminded that last year the mayor had asked him to look into complaints about bribe-taking by building code inspectors. The department head shrugged his shoulders and said, "I asked a few of my people about it. They said no one was taking bribes. When you've been in city government as long as I have, you learn not to ask too many questions.

Robert Manning, Contractor. Testimony taken February 4, afternoon session.

The witness is fifty-two, married, and the father of four children aged eleven to twenty-six. He has been the possessor of State Contractor's License #15683-A for almost twenty-five years.

Mr. Manning acknowledged that he has personal assets in excess of $1 million, but would not give details as to how he acquired them.

State records indicate that Mr. Manning was suspended from contracting activities in 1980 for six months. The suspension resulted from supplying faulty building materials on a contract. He has no prior criminal or professional violations.

In giving testimony, Mr. Manning admitted that he acted as described in the news article, but seemed surprised at the uproar resulting from the Gazette series. He expressed the belief that his conduct was not in any way unusual. "It's just Bay City," he said. "I've been a contractor here for more than twenty years and that's how things have always been done and always will be."

Jeanine Lepere, Bay City Fire Officer.
Testimony taken February 5, morning session.

Officer Lepere is twenty-three years old and the mother of two children. She has been an inspector with the Fire Department for two years. Her personnel record with the department is very good. She has no prior criminal record, but was once suspended from Bay City High for two weeks for cheating on an exam.

In her testimony, Officer Lepere admitted that she had taken bribes. "Look," she said, "I know it's wrong. When I started with the department, I never took a bribe. Then I saw the other inspectors taking them and nobody seemed to care. I'm alone and I've got two kids to think about, and a Fire Department salary doesn't go very far. So I figured that if I took a few bribes my kids would have decent clothes to wear."

During the February 6 morning session, Officer Lepere delivered a letter to the task force. The letter stated that she would testify about bribe-taking by other inspectors if the task force would recommend that she not be prosecuted.

What do *you* think?

1. What responses did your group recommend for each person described in the witness summaries?

2. Did all the groups agree on the same responses for the wrongs and injuries described in the *Gazette* article?

3. How fair are the suggested responses? Justify.

4. Will the responses suggested correct the wrongs or injuries?

5. Will the responses suggested prevent further such wrongs or injuries?

Using the Lesson

1. Invite a representative of a government "watchdog" agency to class to discuss actual cases similar to the one presented in this lesson. Ask the representative what responses his or her agency looks for in such situations.

2. Do research to find out the responses to one of the following government scandals.

   ■ 1972 Watergate scandal

   ■ Late 1980s Iran-Contra scandal

   Report what you learn to the class.

3. Identify a problem of corrective justice in your school, community, or state. Present a report to your class explaining the problem, how it involves corrective justice, and what other values and interests might be involved. Use the intellectual tool chart from Lesson 8 to develop a position on the issue or explain why you are unable to develop a reasonable position on the basis of the facts available to you.

Intellectual Tool Chart for Issues of Corrective Justice

	Don R. Duchinsky	Robert Manning	Jeanine Lepere
1. Identify the wrong or injury: a. What was the wrong or injury? b. How serious was the wrong or injury? Consider ■ extent ■ duration ■ impact ■ offensiveness			
2. Identify important characteristics of the person or persons causing the wrong or injury: a. What was the person's **state of mind** at the time he or she caused the wrong or injury? Consider: ■ intent ■ recklessness ■ carelessness ■ knowledge of probable consequences ■ control or choice ■ duty or obligation ■ important values, interests, or responsibilities b. What facts about the person's **past history** are relevant in deciding upon a fair response? c. What facts about the person's **character** are relevant in deciding upon a fair response? d. What **feelings** did the person express after causing the wrong or injury? e. What was the person's **role** in causing the wrong or injury?			
3. Identify important characteristics of the person or persons who were wronged or injured: a. Did the person or persons **contribute** to causing the wrong or injury he or she suffered? b. What is the person's ability to **recover** from the wrong or injury?			

Intellectual Tool Chart for Issues of Corrective Justice

		Don R. Duchinsky	Robert Manning	Jeanine Lepere
4.	**Examine common responses to wrongs and injuries and their purposes:**			
a.	Should we **inform** the person that what he or she did was wrong or injurious? Why?			
b.	Should we **overlook** or **ignore** the wrong or injury? Why?			
c.	Should we **forgive** or **pardon** the person for causing the wrong or injury? Why?			
d.	Should we **punish** the person for causing the wrong or injury? Why?			
e.	Should we require the person to **restore** what was taken or damaged? Why?			
f.	Should we require the person to **compensate** for causing the wrong or injury? Why?			
g.	Should we provide **treatment** or **education** to the wrongdoer? Why?			
5.	**Consider related values and interests and decide what the proper response would be:**			
a.	What responses would **correct** the wrong or injury?			
b.	What responses would **deter** or **prevent** future wrongs or injuries?			
c.	What responses would promote **distributive justice**?			
d.	What responses would preserve **human dignity**?			
e.	What responses would promote the value of **human life**?			
f.	What responses are **practical** given the resources available?			
g.	What responses would protect **freedom**, both of the wrongdoer and of other members of society?			
h.	What responses would be in **proportion** to the seriousness of the wrong or injury?			
i.	What responses might satisfy the desire for **revenge**?			
6.	**Explain the reasons for your decision.**			

Unit Four: What Is Procedural Justice?

How do these photographs illustrate issues of procedural justice?

Purpose of Unit

This unit deals with **procedural justice**, that is, with the **fairness** of **procedures** or ways of doing things. You will learn why procedural justice is important and the intellectual tools useful in evaluating, taking, and defending positions on issues of procedural justice.

When you have completed this unit you should be able to define procedural justice and explain its importance. You also should be able to use the intellectual tools presented to make thoughtful decisions about issues of procedural justice.

LESSON 10

Why Is Procedural Justice Important?

Purpose of Lesson

This lesson introduces you to the subject of procedural justice. You learn a definition of procedural justice and why it is important. When you have completed the lesson, you should be able to define procedural justice, explain its importance, and identify issues involving procedural justice from your own experience.

Terms to Know

procedural justice
due process of law

Critical Thinking Exercise

EXAMINING ISSUES OF PROCEDURAL JUSTICE

Work with a study partner. For each of the following situations, answer the "What do *you* think?" questions. Be prepared to share your answers with the class.

- Someone accuses you of having done something wrong and punishes you immediately without giving you an opportunity to tell your side of the story.

- You and several friends have decided to go to the movies. When you arrive at one friend's home to discuss which show the group should see, you are irritated to find that the group has already decided to see a film in which you have no interest, without waiting for your opinion.

- A city council holds a hearing to decide how to spend $5 million of tax money. Notice of the hearing is published so that interested individuals and groups from the community may attend the meeting and express their opinions on the use of the tax funds.

- The authorities tortured a suspected terrorist for five days before she confessed to having participated in several bombings which killed a number of people.

What do *you* think?

1. What procedure was used to gather information or to make a decision?

2. What was fair or unfair about the procedure that was used? Explain your answers.

What are the goals of procedural justice?

Each of the above situations involves an issue of **procedural justice**.

Procedural justice refers to the fairness of how certain things are done. More specifically, procedural justice refers to the following:

- the fairness of how information is gathered

- the fairness of how decisions are made

It **does not** refer to the fairness of the decisions themselves.

The goals of procedural justice are the following:

- to increase the chances that all information necessary for making wise and just decisions is gathered

- to ensure the wise and just use of information in the making of decisions

- to protect the right to privacy, human dignity, freedom, and other important values and interests such as distributive justice and corrective justice; and to promote efficiency

Why is procedural justice considered important?

Scholars and others who have studied procedural justice often claim that it is the keystone of liberty or the heart of the law. Observers of world affairs have sometimes claimed that the degree of procedural justice present in a country is a good indicator of the degree of freedom, respect for human dignity, and other basic human rights in that country. A lack of procedural justice is often considered an indication of an authoritarian or totalitarian political system. Respect for procedural justice is often a key indicator of a democratic political system.

People who are not familiar with the subject often place less importance on procedural justice than on other values or interests. To the average person it is sometimes difficult to believe that how information is gathered and how decisions are made are as important as the outcome. Some might claim, for example, that **how** the Congress or the president or the courts make their decisions is not as important as **what** decisions they make. It is more difficult to be concerned about **how** the police gather evidence or what **procedures** are used in a trial than it is to be concerned about making right decisions and punishing guilty persons.

Although the principal focus in this unit is on the activities of local, state, and federal government agencies, it is important to understand that procedural justice is also important in private matters such as information gathering and decision making in the home, school, community, business, and industry.

What do *you* think?

1. What situations have you observed in your home, school, and community in which issues of procedural justice have arisen?

2. Why might adherence to the goals of procedural justice be important in the private sector?

3. What might be the differences in adherence to the goals of procedural justice among democratic, authoritarian, and totalitarian political systems? What examples can you give from recent or historical events?

Why are law enforcement agencies and the courts responsible for using fair procedures?

Most societies have found it necessary to give certain officials the authority to gather information about suspected crimes and to arrest persons suspected of breaking laws. They also have found it necessary to give authority to certain officials to hold hearings to decide whether or not a person is guilty of a crime or to settle conflicts among people. In the United States, people working in our law enforcement agencies and our courts usually carry out these activities.

Why do we require the police to use fair procedures?

We give great power over human life and property to people working in agencies of government. Therefore, we need a set of rules to limit that power and define how to use it. One set of these rules prohibits the government from taking a person's life, liberty, or property without **due process of law**. In most situations this means that the government cannot act against a person without giving the person a fair hearing. Due process also requires law enforcement agencies to respect important values such as privacy, human dignity, fairness, and freedom when they gather information and arrest people.

Some of the rules of procedural justice that must be followed by law enforcement agencies and courts come from laws and regulations adopted by Congress, state legislatures, and other government agencies.

Other important rules of procedural justice are set forth in the United States Constitution and Bill of Rights. For example, they include the following:

AMENDMENT IV (Bill of Rights, 1791) – The right of the people to be secure in their persons, houses, papers, and effects, against unreasonable searches and seizures, shall not be violated, and no warrants shall issue, but upon probable cause, supported by oath or affirmation, and particularly describing the place to be searched, and the persons or things to be seized.

AMENDMENT V (Bill of Rights, 1791) – No person shall be held to answer for a capital, or otherwise infamous crime, unless on a presentment or indictment of a Grand Jury, except in cases arising in the land or naval forces, or in the militia, when in actual service in time of war or public danger; nor shall any person be subject for the same offense to be twice put in jeopardy of life or limb; nor shall be compelled in any criminal case to be a witness against himself, nor be deprived of life, liberty, or property, without due process of law; nor shall private property be taken for public use, without just compensation.

AMENDMENT VI (Bill of Rights, 1791) – In all criminal prosecutions, the accused shall enjoy the right to a speedy and public trial, by an impartial jury of the state and district wherein the crime shall have been committed, which district shall have been previously ascertained by law, and to be informed of the nature and cause of the accusation; to be confronted with the witnesses against him; to have compulsory process for obtaining witnesses in his favor, and to have the assistance of counsel for his defense.

Why is it important to monitor the executive and legislative branches of government?

We often pay more attention to issues of procedural justice that arise from the activities of law enforcement agencies and the judicial branch than to those that may arise from the activities of other parts of our government. The reason for this attention may be that crimes and trials receive more publicity than the activities of the executive or legislative branches of government.

It is important to watch the activities of the executive and legislative branches of government in our communities, states, and nation. These branches of government also have authority to gather information and make decisions that have a great effect on our everyday lives. For example, they can declare war, control trade, collect taxes, and decide how to spend tax money.

Because the authority granted all government agencies is so great, and because the decisions they make are so important, it is essential that they use proper procedures to gather information and make decisions. The use of proper procedures is necessary not only to increase the chances that decisions will be wise and just, but also to ensure public support of those decisions.

Why is it important for Congress to follow proper procedures when making decisions that affect the well-being of citizens?

What do *you* think?

1. Each constitutional amendment quoted establishes procedures that law enforcement agencies and the courts should use in gathering information about people suspected of crimes, wrongs, or injuries, and in the use of that information in decision making. In what ways does each rule appear to foster the goals of procedural justice?

2. What decisions made by members of legislative or executive branches of local, state, or federal government have had a significant impact on your life, liberty, or property?

3. What situations have you experienced or observed in which the adherence to fair procedures by members of legislative or executive branches of government has led to increased trust in government?

Is procedural justice always important?

An innocent person's conviction through the use of unfair procedures offends virtually everyone's sense of justice. On the other hand, what about situations where the accused person is guilty of serious wrongdoing? Does it really matter what procedures are used in their cases? Or is it more important to prevent them from doing wrong again?

The view that the ends justify the means was championed centuries ago by Niccolo Machiavelli (1469–1527). In *The Prince*, Machiavelli argued that if your goal is a good one, such as the creation of a free republic, it does not matter what you do to achieve it. In his words, "The act accuses, the result excuses."

The Founders of our nation knew from their experience the oppression that can occur without procedural justice. The British government considered our patriots to be traitors. They branded them as criminals and put a price on their heads. British government officials illegally searched the homes of many citizens. They also transported many of them out of the country for secret trial, often by a judge alone without benefit of a trial by jury.

Based on experiences like these, the Founders wanted to limit the power the government exercises over individual citizens. Therefore, when they formed their own nation, they looked for ways to make sure that the government they created would not be able to unfairly search, arrest, question, try, and imprison citizens.

The Founders wanted to create a system or procedure to ensure that, at all times, ordinary citizens would retain control over their government. They wanted to limit the power of government over the individuals the government was created to serve.

NICHOLAS MACHIAVEL.

What problems might arise from Machiavelli's belief that if your goal is a good one, it does not matter what you do to achieve it? What does this have to do with procedural justice?

What do *you* think?

1. Would procedural justice be considered important in a society based on Machiavelli's philosophy? Why or why not?

2. What would be the advantages of a society based on Machiavelli's philosophy? What would be the disadvantages?

3. Which system of government, one based on Machiavelli's philosophy or one based on the Founders' philosophy, would be better able to suppress crime? Which system of government would be better able to suppress political dissent? Which system would be more sure to secure individual liberty and freedom?

Using the Lesson

1. Find examples of issues of procedural justice reported in the press or on television. Describe these issues to your class. Discuss the fairness of the procedures people used to gather information and make decisions in these situations.

2. Read the entire Bill of Rights and the Fourteenth Amendment. Identify the provisions that deal with the procedures the government uses to gather information and make decisions. How do these provisions ensure that people will receive a fair hearing? How do they ensure the protection of important values such as privacy, human dignity, and freedom?

LESSON 11

How Can You Evaluate Procedures to Determine If They Are Fair?

Purpose of Lesson

This lesson reviews the goals of procedural justice and introduces you to three sets of intellectual tools useful in dealing with issues of procedural justice. When you have completed the lesson, you should be able to explain the usefulness of these tools. A fourth set of intellectual tools will be examined in the next lesson.

Terms to Know

comprehensiveness
notice
predictability
flexibility

reliability
impartiality
detection of error

How can you examine issues of procedural justice?

At this point in your study you should be aware that the goals of procedural justice are the following:

■ to increase the chances that all reliable information necessary for making wise and just decisions is gathered

■ to ensure the wise and just use of the information in making decisions

■ to protect important values and interests such as the right to privacy, human dignity, freedom, distributive justice and corrective justice; and to promote efficiency

You can use these basic goals for evaluating procedures to decide if they are fair. The goals are so general, however, they might be difficult to use in specific situations. Therefore, four steps or sets of intellectual tools are provided to determine whether the procedures used by an agency of government or other group are fair.

This lesson provides the first three steps for examining issues of procedural justice. The next lesson presents the fourth step. As you apply these steps to situations presented in this unit, and later to other situations, you will discover that not all the tools are useful in every case.

Critical Thinking Exercise

IDENTIFYING INTELLECTUAL TOOLS TO USE IN INFORMATION GATHERING

You may accomplish this exercise during a class discussion of the steps led by your teacher, or you may examine the steps in small groups and then discuss your responses with the entire class.

Read each step in the procedure. Answer the questions in each step as they apply to the examples provided. Then discuss the usefulness of each step and give examples of how it might apply to situations you have experienced or observed.

STEP 1.

Identify the purposes of the information-gathering procedures.

What information is being sought? Why is this information needed?

Example: A policewoman driving past a bank heard an alarm and saw a person looking frightened leave the bank in a great hurry. She stopped the person and searched him.

Example: A city council held public hearings before deciding what kinds of recreational facilities to build in a public park.

What would be proper procedures for conducting a city council meeting?

STEP 2.

Evaluate the procedures used to gather information.

Do the procedures ensure that all reliable information necessary for making a wise and just decision is gathered?

To answer this question, the procedures should be evaluated in terms of the following considerations:

a. **Comprehensiveness.** Are the procedures comprehensive or complete? That is, do the procedures ensure that **all** information necessary to make a wise and just decision will be gathered from **all** interested persons?

Example: Although Sir Walter Raleigh was granted a trial for conspiring to commit treason, the court did not allow him to present his side of the story.

Example: Often committees of Congress will hold hearings in Washington, D.C. on subjects they think might require new laws, such as medical care or air travel safety. Interested people and groups can participate in these hearings if they travel to Washington, D.C. to make their presentations.

b. **Notice.** Do the procedures provide adequate **notice** or warning of the **time** and the **reason** for the hearing to allow interested persons to prepare adequately?

Example: The authorities did not tell Kelly what the charges against her were or when her trial would occur.

Example: When the city council decided to hold a public hearing on a zoning issue, they advertised the hearing widely in the city during the previous two months.

c. **Effective Presentation.** Do the procedures allow interested persons to **present effectively** the information they wish decision-makers to consider?

Example: Until the Supreme Court's 1963 decision in *Gideon v. Wainwright*, criminal defendants who could not afford an attorney did not receive a lawyer to help them present their side of the story at trial, except in capital cases.

Example: Today, people accused of crimes who do not have enough money to hire lawyers often receive a public defender at taxpayers' expense. Public defenders sometimes have so many people to help

they may have only ten to fifteen minutes to prepare for a hearing.

Clarence Earl Gideon (1910–1972). What do you think are the costs and benefits of the Supreme Court's decision in Gideon v. Wainwright?

d. **Predictability and Flexibility.** Are the procedures sufficiently **predictable**—established in advance—and **flexible**—able to change or adapt to promote justice?

Example: The court made up the procedures used in Alicia's trial as it proceeded.

Example: Although Sarah's name had been placed on the agenda to speak at a meeting of her community group, she was late to the meeting because she had a flat tire. She arrived just before the meeting was about to close. When she explained what had happened, the chairperson allowed her to speak to the group even though she had missed her place on the agenda.

e. **Reliability.** Do the procedures ensure that the information gathered is **reliable** or trustworthy?

Example: The court did not allow Sir Walter Raleigh to cross-examine the person who had accused him of treason.

Example: The court permitted an eyewitness to testify about what he saw when a bridge collapsed. However, he was not permitted to testify about the cause of the collapse because he did not have a college degree in architecture or structural engineering.

STEP 3.

Evaluate the procedures used to make a decision.

Do the procedures ensure that the information gathered will be used wisely and fairly?

To answer this question, the procedures should be evaluated in terms of the following considerations:

a. **Impartiality**. Do the procedures ensure **impartiality**—lack of bias or prejudice—in the making of decisions?

   Examples: One of the judges at Sir Walter Raleigh's trial was Raleigh's sworn enemy.

   In the past, it was common for judges to be paid from fines they imposed on people they had found guilty of breaking laws.

b. **Public Observation**. Do the procedures allow interested members of the **public** to **observe** how information is being used in making decisions?

   Example: The police secretly arrested Maria in the middle of the night and the authorities tried her in the jail without a jury. No one in her village knew what was happening other than the judge, police, and the witness testifying against her.

   Example: The Sixth Amendment to the Constitution of the United States provides all persons accused of crimes the right to a public trial.

c. **Provision for the Detection and Correction of Errors**. Do the procedures allow interested persons to review what was done to **detect**—discover—and **correct errors**?

   Example: Gary was executed immediately after he was convicted. He had no opportunity to appeal the decision in his case.

   Example: No one kept a record of a city council meeting when they decided that the applicant should receive a contract to build a new school.

What do *you* think?

1. Should members of government agencies be allowed to gather information about persons in any way they wish? Why or why not? What values and interests might be endangered?

2. How might the considerations of comprehensiveness, notice, effective presentation, predictability, flexibility, and reliability help you evaluate the fairness of information-gathering procedures?

3. How might the considerations of impartiality, public observation, and provision for the detection and correction of errors help you evaluate the fairness of decision-making procedure?

Using the Lesson

1. Find examples of issues of procedural justice reported in the press or on television. Describe these issues to your class. Discuss the fairness of the procedures people used to gather information and make decisions in these situations.

2. Read the entire Bill of Rights and the Fourteenth Amendment. Identify the provisions that deal with the procedures the government uses to gather information and make decisions. How do these provisions ensure that people will receive a fair hearing? How do they ensure the protection of important values such as privacy, human dignity, and freedom?

LESSON 12

What Values and Interests Should You Consider in Determining Whether Procedures Are Fair?

Purpose of Lesson

In this lesson you examine the fourth set of intellectual tools to be used in dealing with issues of procedural justice. You apply the tools you have studied in this unit to evaluate the procedures used in a fictional case, "The Count of Monte Cristo."

When you have completed this lesson, you should be able to use a chart containing all the tools you have learned to develop and support positions on the fairness of procedures used in various situations.

Why should you consider values and interests?

Steps 1–3 that you have just studied are not enough to enable you to decide an issue of procedural justice. A procedure may be very useful and effective in enabling members of government or others to gather information or evaluate that information, but it may be unfair when it endangers important values and interests. Thus, one also must take into account certain values and interests in deciding whether a procedure is fair. The fourth step, given below, focuses your attention on this subject.

Critical Thinking Exercise

IDENTIFYING INTELLECTUAL TOOLS TO USE IN CONSIDERING VALUES AND INTERESTS

This exercise may be accomplished during a class discussion of the fourth step led by your teacher or you may examine the fourth step in small groups and then discuss your responses with the entire class.

Read each part of the fourth step of the procedure. Answer the questions in each part as they apply to the examples. Then discuss the usefulness of each part and give examples of how it might apply to situations you have experienced or observed. Then answer the "What do *you* think?" questions.

STEP 4.

Consider Related Values and Interests.

Do the procedures protect related values and interests?

To answer this question, consider the following:

a. **Privacy and Freedom.** Do the procedures violate the right to **privacy** or **freedom**?

Example: Today at all air terminals throughout the country, security people screen passengers and x-ray their luggage and may search them if necessary.

Example: Right before the Revolutionary War, British soldiers received the right to search colonists' homes at any time to discover evidence of smuggling or other illegal activities. Today, police officials must persuade a judge that they will likely find evidence in order to get a warrant authorizing the search of someone's home. The warrant does not authorize the search of other homes or places.

Example: During the Civil War, President Lincoln suspended the right to *habeas corpus* in certain areas. As a result, people could be jailed indefinitely without the authorities charging them with a specific crime or trying them.

How did President Lincoln's suspension of habeas corpus conflict with other important values and interests?

b. Human Dignity. Do the procedures violate basic ideas about the right of all persons to be treated with **dignity** no matter what their beliefs or actions may be?

Example: In some countries, authorities torture people suspected of crimes to gain information from them.

Example: In our country, persons involved in certain kinds of cases may request that the court close their trials to the public.

c. Distributive Justice. Do the procedures violate basic principles of **distributive justice**?

Example: At a recent city council meeting on an issue of importance to the community, one group was given thirty minutes to make its presentation, while other groups had only ten minutes each.

Example: Earlier in our nation's history, the government permitted only white males to vote and serve on juries.

d. Practical Considerations. Do the procedures satisfy reasonable **practical considerations**?

Example: After the defendant had interrupted the trial with several outbursts, the judge warned him that he would be removed from the courtroom if he disrupted the trial again.

Example: Martha took her neighbor, Sam, to Small Claims Court to try to get him to pay $35 for damage his dog had done to her lawn. She asked another neighbor to testify on her behalf, but the neighbor refused, saying that although he thought she was right, he did not want to take the time off from work. Martha believed that she would not get a fair hearing unless she could compel the neighbor to testify.

What do *you* think?

1. What is the purpose of considering the values of privacy, freedom, human dignity, and distributive justice in evaluating issues of procedural justice?

2. Why might it be important to take practical considerations into account in evaluating issues of procedural justice?

3. How might an efficient way of gathering information violate important values and interests?

Critical Thinking Exercise
EVALUATING PROCEDURES WITH INTELLECTUAL TOOLS

Read the following adaptation of the *Count of Monte Cristo*, by novelist Alexandre Dumas (1802–1870). Although it is a fictional account, Dumas based his novel on the actual experiences of political prisoners in 19th century France. Work in small groups or with a study partner to complete the intellectual tool chart on p. 211. Be prepared to discuss your answers with the rest of the class.

The Imprisonment of Edmond Dantes

The Captain's Request

It was the winter of 1815. A three-masted ship sailed the Mediterranean Sea, bound for Marseilles. In his cabin below, the captain lay dying of a brain fever. He sent for his first mate, young Edmond Dantes, and made a last request. "My dear Dantes," said he, "swear to do what I am going to tell you, for it is very important."

"I swear," replied Dantes.

"After my death, you will be captain. Stop at the Isle of Elba and give this letter to Napoleon. Perhaps he will give you another letter. If he does, deliver it, as I would have had I lived."

What issues of procedural justice does the story of young Dantes raise?

"I will do it, Captain, but will he see me?"

"Here is my ring," said the captain. "Send it to him, and he will see you." Two hours later the captain was delirious, and the next day he died.

The captain's request bothered Dantes. Napoleon, who had once ruled France, had been defeated and sent into exile on the Isle of Elba, where he was in fact a prisoner. However, there were still many people in France who loved Napoleon and wanted him to come back to rule.

Others thought that these people were traitors to the king of France, and the government imprisoned and executed many of them. To be suspected of liking Napoleon or feeling sorry for him was dangerous in France at that time. Dantes knew this, but he believed that the last request of a dying man should be obeyed, so he did as he had been told. He was only nineteen and had not served under Napoleon. In fact, he had almost no knowledge of politics at all; he felt sure that no one could accuse him of being loyal to Napoleon.

After delivering the letter, Napoleon gave him another one to deliver to a man named Nortier in Paris. Dantes then sailed for Marseilles, where he was to deliver the ship's cargo and marry a beautiful, young girl named Mercedes.

Unknown to Dantes, several men were plotting his downfall. One was jealous that Dantes, a young boy of nineteen, was now captain of the ship. Another was in love with Mercedes and hated Dantes for taking her from him. They sent a letter to the police that said Dantes had seen Napoleon and was carrying a letter to revolutionaries in Paris.

The Arrest of Dantes

Music, laughter, and bright costumes filled the room. The servants had prepared a plentiful feast and set the tables. It was the marriage party of Edmond Dantes and Mercedes. Friends and families of the happy pair filled the room. After the feast all were to go to the church for the marriage ceremony.

"Shall we go?" asked the sweet, silvery voice of Mercedes. "Two o'clock has just struck, and you know we are expected soon."

"To be sure, to be sure!" cried Dantes eagerly. "Let us go right now!"

At this moment they heard the dread sound of marching feet. Nearer and nearer came these sounds of terror. Three loud knocks of a sword hilt against the door increased the fears of the festive party.

"Open the door," said a loud voice, "in the name of the law." An officer and five soldiers entered the room. "Who is Edmond Dantes?"

Dantes stepped forward.

"Edmond Dantes," replied the officer, "I arrest you in the name of the law!"

"Me?" replied Edmond, "For what reason?"

"I cannot tell you, but you will be told at your first examination."

After shaking hands with all of his friends, Dantes surrendered to the officer. He turned to his family and to Mercedes. "Don't worry, there is some little mistake; depend upon it. They shall set me free as soon as they discover it."

"Goodbye, goodbye, Edmond!" cried Mercedes from the balcony.

"Goodbye, sweet Mercedes! We shall soon meet again!"

The Interrogation

At the police station Monsieur de Villefort questioned Dantes. Villefort also was to marry that day, but when he heard of the arrest of this man charged with being a traitor and a friend of Napoleon's, he left the house of his bride. Villefort was in favor with the king, but he knew he had to be very careful to maintain this position. His father had been a supporter of Napoleon and even now was suspected of plotting against the king. Villefort would have nothing to do with his father and had even changed his name to further separate from him. He was a prosecutor for the king, and he knew that if he did not succeed in condemning anyone suspected of being loyal to Napoleon, he himself would be suspected.

His first glance at Dantes softened his heart. He saw that Edmond was intelligent, courageous, and honest. As Dantes told him the story of the dying captain's request and of his ignorance of politics, Villefort could not help but believe him.

"Ah!" said Villefort, "this seems to be the truth. If you are guilty of anything, it is in not acting wisely. And considering that you acted on your captain's orders, I cannot hold you guilty."

"I am free, then, sir?" cried Dantes joyfully.

"Yes, but first give me the letter you were to deliver to Paris."

"You have it already, for it was taken from me by the officers. It was on your desk."

"Stop a minute," said Villefort, as Dantes took his hat and gloves. "To whom is it addressed?"

"To Monsieur Nortier in Paris."

If a thunderbolt had struck the room, Villefort could not have been more shocked. He sank into his chair, drew out the fatal letter, and looked at it with an expression of terror.

"Monsieur Nortier of Paris," he said, growing paler.

"Yes," said Dantes, "do you know him?"

"No!" replied Villefort, "a faithful servant of the King does not know traitors."

"It is a conspiracy then?" asked Dantes. "I knew nothing about it."

"Yes, but you know the name of the person to whom this letter was addressed."

"I had to read the address to know to whom to give it."

"Have you shown this letter to anyone?"

"To no one, on my honor."

Villefort fell back in his chair. "Oh, if the king learns that Nortier is my father, I am ruined," he murmured. "Dantes, I can no longer free you right away. I must talk to the judge. But look how I will help you. The main thing against you is in this letter." Villefort went to the fireplace and cast the letter into the flames. "You see, I destroy it."

"Oh!" exclaimed Dantes, "you have saved me!"

"Do you trust me now?" asked Villefort.

"In every way," replied Dantes.

"Then listen to my advice. Don't tell anyone of the letter, no matter what happens, and all will be well."

"I will swear not to," said Dantes.

Dantes Learns His Fate

Villefort rang a small bell. A policeman appeared. Villefort whispered some words in his ear, and the policeman nodded.

"Follow him," said Villefort.

That night four armed guards took Dantes in a carriage through the streets of the town. The carriage stopped at the port, and twelve more soldiers came out of the darkness.

"Can all this be for me?" Dantes thought.

He was taken to a boat and seated between armed guards. The oarsmen pulled and the boat skimmed over the dark waters of the bay.

"Where are you taking me?" asked Dantes.

"You will know soon enough," answered a guard.

Wild and strange thoughts ran through Dantes' mind. Were they going to leave him on some distant point? There were no ships in the harbor. They had not tied him, and this seemed to mean that they were going to let him go. Besides, Villefort had told him that as long as he did not mention the letter, or the name of Nortier, he would be free. He waited silently, staring through the darkness. He could see a light in the house where Mercedes lived.

If he were to shout she could hear him. He thought how silly the guards would think him if he were to shout like a madman.

He turned to the nearest policeman and said, "Friend, I beg you, as a Christian, to tell me where we are going. I am Captain Dantes, a loyal Frenchman, though accused of treason. Tell me where you are taking me, and I swear upon my honor I won't resist."

"I see no harm in telling you now. You are from Marseilles and a sailor, and you still don't know where we are going?"

"On my honor, I have no idea."

"Look around you then."

Dantes rose to his feet and looked forward. He saw the black and frowning rock on which stands the Chateau d'If. It was a gloomy fortress more than three hundred years old, now used as a prison. To Dantes it looked like a hangman's scaffold.

"Why are we going there?" cried Dantes.

The policeman smiled.

"I am not going to that prison. It is used only for political prisoners. I have not done anything! Are there any judges or courts at the Chateau d'If?"

"No, only a warden, soldiers, and good thick walls."

"You think that I am to be imprisoned there?"

"It looks like it."

"Without a trial?"

"You've had a trial."

Dantes tried to leap overboard but the quick action of the police stopped him. The boat touched shore, and they took him to a cell. Dantes did not fight. He was like a man in a dream. "It is late," said the jailor. "Here is bread, water, and fresh straw, and that is all a prisoner can wish for. Good night."

Dantes was alone in darkness and silence. With the first light of day the jailor returned. He found Dantes in the same position, as if fixed there, his eyes swollen with weeping. He had passed the night standing and without sleep.

The jailor went to Dantes and put a hand on his shoulder.

"Haven't you slept?" he asked.

"I don't know," replied Dantes.

"Are you hungry?" he continued.

"I don't know."

"Do you want anything?"

"I want to see the warden."

"That is impossible."

"Why?"

"It is against the rules. Someday you may see him, if we let you walk around, but he may not listen to you."

"But," asked Dantes, "how long will I have to wait?"

"Ah! A month!six months!a year."

Post script: **Edmond Dantes remained in the Chateau d'If for fourteen years before making his escape.**

Do you think the procedures used to convict young Dantes adequately served the goals of procedural justice? What changes would you make?

Using the Lesson

1. Read the Bill of Rights. Identify the provisions that would have prevented the violations of procedural justice that occurred in the case of Edmond Dantes.

2. Watch television programs involving law-enforcement officers, private detectives, or courts. Evaluate the fairness of the procedures used by applying the intellectual tools you have studied.

Intellectual Tool Chart for Issues of Procedural Justice

Questions	Answers
1. What information is being sought? Why is this information needed?	

2. Do the procedures ensure that all reliable information necessary for making a wise and just decision is gathered? Consider:
 	
  a. comprehensiveness
 	
  b. notice
 	
  c. effective presentation
 	
  d. predictability and flexibility
 	
  e. reliability	

3. Do the procedures ensure that the information gathered will be used wisely and fairly in making a decision? Consider:
 	
  a. impartiality
 	
  b. public observation
 	
  c. detection and correction of errors	

4. Do the procedures protect important values and interests? Consider:
 	
  a. privacy and freedom
 	
  b. human dignity
 	
  c. distributive justice
 	
  d. practical considerations	

5. Do you think the procedures adequately serve the goals of procedural justice? What changes (if any) would you make?	
6. Explain your position.	

Lesson 13

Were the Procedures Used in This Case Fair?

Purpose of Lesson

Now you may apply the intellectual tools you have studied in this unit to a historical case. You evaluate the procedures used to prosecute and uphold the conviction of Sacco and Vanzetti for murder and armed robbery in the 1920s. You role-play a governor's clemency board hearing on whether to recommend that the defendants' death sentences be carried out.

When you have completed this lesson, you should be able to evaluate, take, and defend positions on the fairness of procedures used in this case.

Critical Thinking Exercise

EVALUATING AND TAKING A POSITION ON PROCEDURAL JUSTICE IN A HISTORICAL CASE

Using the intellectual tools you have learned in this unit, tackle the following problem of procedural justice.

Below is an abridged account of the historical facts surrounding the trial of Nicola Sacco and Bartolomeo Vanzetti. This case, which took place in the 1920s, attracted enormous attention around the world. Although the defendants were tried for murder, many suspected they were actually on trial for their political beliefs. The procedures of the trial raised many questions.

After reading about the case, work with a study partner to complete the procedural justice intellectual tool chart on page 211, applying it to the Sacco and Vanzetti situation. What arguments would you make to the governor for or against a stay of execution? Discussion questions follow the story.

The Case of Sacco and Vanzetti

The Crime

On April 15, 1920, the $15,776.51 payroll for the Slater and Morrill shoe factory in South Braintree, Massachusetts was brought to the factory's office. The money was put into pay envelopes and the envelopes were placed in two steel boxes.

At 3 p.m. the paymaster and his guard were carrying the money down the street to the factory when they saw two men leaning on a fence. Suddenly, one of the men stepped forward, pulled a gun, and shot the guard. The guard staggered, fell, and was shot again. The paymaster ran, but was hit in the back by two bullets.

Just then, a dark car drove up with several men inside. The killers threw the money boxes into the car, jumped in, and sped away. As the car drove off, someone in it shot the guard again. The guard died there. The paymaster died the next day.

The Investigation

At the time of the crime, the police were investigating a similar incident in another town. Both cases involved gangs with dark cars. Witnesses to both crimes said they thought the criminals were Italian.

Shortly after the armed robbery, the police found a car being repaired at a garage that seemed to fit the description of the getaway car. The car belonged to an Italian named Mike Boda. On the evening of May 5, 1920, Boda and three other men came to pick up the car. The owner of the garage, who had been alerted by the police, told them that they had not completed the repairs.

What might be fair procedures when arresting persons who neither speak nor understand English very well?

Boda and one of the men then left on a motorcycle. Witnesses saw the other two men get on a streetcar. After they were gone, the garage owner's wife called the police. They arrested the two men who got on the streetcar in the trap set for Boda. However, Boda disappeared and was never seen again.

Neither of the two men arrested had police records. When they were arrested, both were carrying loaded guns. They gave their names as Nicola Sacco and Bartolomeo Vanzetti. Both were Italians, and both were aliens.

When apprehended on the streetcar, police did not tell Sacco and Vanzetti why they were arrested. Neither man spoke English very well, nor did they understand that they had certain constitutional rights.

At the time of the arrest, the police were unaware that the two men were political radicals who were active in anarchist causes. Anarchists generally believe that all forms of political authority are unnecessary and undesirable. When the police chief asked Sacco and Vanzetti questions about their political beliefs, they did not answer honestly. They thought their anarchist associations would get them into trouble.

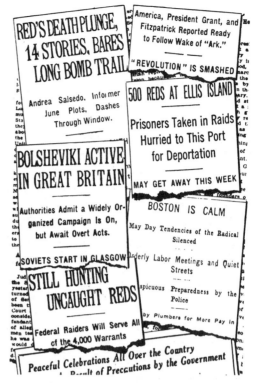

How could attitudes of the general public affect the fairness of a jury trial?

"Red Scare"

In 1920, fear and hysteria over political radicalism were common in the United States and abroad. One reason was that bombings by anarchists killed a number of people.

There also had been a communist revolution in Russia in 1917 when the Bolsheviks, led by Lenin and Trotsky, took over the government. Some people were terrified that anarchists and communists might stir up rebellion in the United States. Because of the widespread public hysteria, law enforcement officers looked everywhere for anyone who might be plotting to overthrow the government. Authorities raided meetings in homes, clubs, and public halls. In 1920 alone, the police arrested almost 4,000 suspected revolutionaries, most of them aliens. Many were eventually deported.

Although they still had not been told why they had been arrested, the district attorney questioned the suspects. When he asked questions about their political beliefs, they lied once again. When the authorities learned that Sacco and Vanzetti were not being truthful, they assumed that the suspects had more to hide than their political convictions.

The Trial

On May 31, 1921, Sacco and Vanzetti were tried for the murders. Their lawyer, Fred Moore, was himself a political radical and made no effort to hide his beliefs. In fact, far from concealing his political views, he let everyone know he thought the case was a clear example of how the capitalist system victimizes downtrodden working people. From the beginning of the trial, there were angry feelings between Judge Webster Thayer and the defendants' lawyer.

During the seven-week trial, the district attorney who had questioned the two suspects when they were first arrested served as prosecutor. The selection of a jury was a long and difficult process; they examined more than 700 people before choosing the twelve jurors.

As the courtroom proceedings began, the quiet little Massachusetts town of Dedham found itself transformed. Crowds gathered. Law enforcement guarded the courthouse and searched everyone who entered. Armed guards marched the defendants, who were always kept in handcuffs, between the jail and the courthouse. No one could escape the impression that these were desperate and dangerous men.

The first witness for the prosecution, Mary Splaine, identified Sacco as the man who had done the shooting from the car. When questioned by Sacco and Vanzetti's lawyer, however, the witness admitted she had seen the car from a distance of seventy feet for no more than three to five seconds, as it was rapidly speeding away.

Cross-examination also uncovered the fact that a year earlier at the police station, Mary had picked a picture of another man as the gunman. However, after seeing Sacco three times alone in the jail—never in a line-up as was the usual procedure—Mary changed her mind.

Other witnesses had also failed to identify Sacco and Vanzetti until they spent some time alone with the two men. Under these conditions, witnesses who had previously said they had not seen the killers clearly enough to identify them altered their statements to identify Sacco and Vanzetti as the men they had seen.

Next, the prosecution showed that Sacco and Vanzetti had lied when questioned at the police station. The district attorney argued that they hid the truth because they were guilty of the murders. The prosecution introduced a cap found at the scene of the crime as evidence. The prosecution claimed it was Sacco's. Sacco, his wife, and his attorney said it was not his and did not even fit him.

The prosecution then produced expert witnesses to show that the gun police took from Vanzetti actually belonged to the guard who had been shot. The prosecution claimed that Vanzetti had stolen the gun at the time of the murder.

Guards outside the prison where Sacco and Vanzetti were held. What issues of procedural justice surface during high-profile cases such as the trial of Sacco and Vanzetti?

The prosecution also tried to prove that the bullet that had killed the guard had been from Sacco's gun. Sacco and Vanzetti's lawyer failed to challenge this testimony, although later they presented their own ballistics experts who said that the bullet had not come from Sacco's gun. In fact, the police who arrested the two men had failed to mark the guns and ammunition properly.

Nicola Sacco   Bartolomeo Vanzetti

Throughout the trial, the prosecutor emphasized the unorthodox political views of the defendants and the fact that they had gone to Mexico during World War I to escape the draft.

After the prosecution presented its case, the defense had its turn. The defense lawyer first called Vanzetti and then Sacco to the witness stand. Both men had trouble proving to the jury's satisfaction where they had been on the day of the murder.

Sacco had not been at work. Vanzetti was self-employed as a fish peddler and could not prove where he had been. When Vanzetti was asked why he carried a gun, he explained that he carried a lot of money when he bought fish for his business and that he needed the gun for self-defense. Vanzetti admitted that he had lied about his political beliefs when questioned by the police, but said it was because he was afraid that he would be sent back to Italy if they knew he was an anarchist.

When Sacco was cross-examined, he admitted that although he had gained many advantages from living in the United States, he had still been quite critical of the government. His defense attorney objected to this line of questioning, saying it had nothing to do with whether Sacco and Vanzetti had committed murder. However, Judge Thayer repeatedly overruled such objections. The defense attorney then produced witnesses that said the defendants had been elsewhere at the time of the murders.

The Verdict

Both sides gave final arguments on July 14, 1921. When the judge gave instructions to the jury, many observers thought his remarks were prejudiced against Sacco and Vanzetti. In his final charge to the jury, Judge Thayer urged jurors to act "as true soldiers... in the spirit of supreme American loyalty."

During the trial, Thayer permitted numerous questions about the defendants' political beliefs. Some people who had attended the trial also claimed that they had overheard the judge outside the courtroom make sneering and hostile remarks about the defendants. However, these claims were never verified.

The jury deliberated for five hours before reaching a verdict. It was the same for both defendants: guilty of murder in the first degree.

The defense attorneys asked for a new trial. Sacco and Vanzetti waited in prison for six years while motions for a new trial moved slowly through the legal system.

The Appeals

The defense presented new evidence to support the request for another trial. A man named Gould said he had been walking behind the guard and pay master when they were shot. He swore that neither Sacco nor Vanzetti had been in the getaway car. However, according to Massachusetts law at that time, requests for a new trial had to be made to the judge who had heard the original trial. Judge Thayer denied the request, ruling that one piece of evidence was not enough to justify a new trial.

Defense attorneys then claimed that the foreman of the jury which had convicted Sacco and Vanzetti had said that radicals should hang whether they were guilty or not. Judge Thayer denied the second request for a new trial as well.

Months passed. They made another appeal. The prosecution's main ballistics expert said if he had been asked directly if the bullet that killed the guard came from Sacco's pistol, he would have said it did not. Judge Thayer again denied the appeal.

Then on November 18, 1925, Celestino Madeiros, a convicted murderer, confessed that he had participated in the shoe factory robbery and murders as part of the notorious Joe Morelli gang. Armed with this new evidence, attorneys appealed to the Supreme Court of Massachusetts.

However, according to the law at that time, the high court could only review the records of the original trial and could not review any new evidence. Thus, the court's decision was to let the verdict stand.

Finally, on April 9, 1927, Sacco and Vanzetti went to court for final sentencing. The judge asked them if they had anything to say. Vanzetti rose and spoke:

"I am suffering because I am a radical and indeed I am a radical. I have suffered because I am an Italian and indeed I am an Italian. I would not wish to a dog or a snake, to the most low and unfortunate creature of this world—I would not wish to any of them what I have had to suffer of things I am not guilty of."

Sacco and Vanzetti were sentenced to die in the electric chair.

A Final Appeal

By this time, public opinion had begun to change and many people, conservatives and liberals alike, began to call for a new trial. Protests grew against the executions. A newspaper editorial summarized people's feelings:

"No man, we submit, should be put to death where so much doubt exists."

Although defense attorneys continued to request a new trial and even tried to appeal the case to the United States Supreme Court, they were unsuccessful. They asked the governor of Massachusetts for a stay of execution.

Judge Webster Thayer

Critical Thinking Exercise

TAKING, AND DEFENDING A POSITION IN A CLEMENCY BOARD HEARING

Now you will role-play a clemency board hearing. To conduct the exercise, a class member should play the role of the governor of Massachusetts. The governor should appoint an advisory board of five to seven class members to advise him on Sacco and Vanzetti's request for a stay of execution. The rest of the class should form two groups. One group should prepare arguments in favor of granting a stay of execution and the other group should prepare arguments against granting a stay.

Each group should select two or three spokespersons to present the arguments to the governor's clemency board. Each group's presentation should be limited to five minutes, followed by a question and answer period of five minutes. While each group is preparing its arguments, the members of the governor's clemency board should prepare questions to ask the spokespersons for each side. After the presentations and question and answer periods are completed, the clemency board should discuss what recommendation to make to the governor, and why. Each member of the board should be able to express his or her views to the governor. After hearing the board's recommendations, the governor should decide whether or not to grant a stay of execution, and should explain the reasons for his or her decision to the class.

What do *you* think?

1. Were the goals of procedural justice met in the Sacco and Vanzetti case? Why or why not?

2. Information made public more than fifty years after the trial ended has been interpreted by some to suggest that Sacco was guilty of murder. He belonged to a Sicilian radical group sworn to secrecy. Recently opened FBI files indicate that the state probably did not have enough evidence to convict Vanzetti of murder, although it suggests he may have been involved with the armed robbery in some way. Other information, however, seems to point to the Morelli gang. Does this information in any way alter your opinion as to whether or not the procedures used in the case were fair?

3. The Governor of Massachusetts denied the request for a stay of execution. Protests grew all over the world. In some countries, crowds marched on American embassies. In France, Italy, and the United States, workers went on strike. Bombs went off in Philadelphia and New York. Meanwhile, Sacco and Vanzetti continued to maintain their innocence. As the hour for the execution approached, several thousand people gathered outside the jail. Hundreds of armed police held back the crowd. At last, on August 23, 1927, after more than seven years in jail,

How does public observation of legal proceedings help achieve the goals of procedural justice?

Sacco and Vanzetti were executed in the electric chair.

After the executions, protest continued. Then in April, 1959, a member of the Massachusetts state legislature proposed that the governor declare a retroactive pardon based on the contention that Sacco and Vanzetti had been denied a fair trial in violation of the due process clause of the Fourteenth Amendment of the U.S. Constitution and protections in the Bill of Rights of the Massachusetts Constitution. If you had been in the legislature, would you have voted for this bill? Why or why not?

4. What, if any, issues of corrective and distributive justice were raised in the Sacco and Vanzetti case?

Glossary

abolitionist. A person who advocated the end of slavery in the United States.

abridge. To reduce in scope; to limit or curtail.

accountable. Obliged to answer for one's actions.

agenda. A list, outline, or plan of things to be considered or done.

Amish. Members of the Mennonite religion that settled in the United States.

appointment. A nonelective office or position.

aristocracy. A governing body or upper class usually made up of an hereditary nobility.

assignment. An appointment to a post or duty.

assistance of counsel. Amendment VI of the Bill of Rights – in all criminal prosecutions, the accused is guaranteed the right to have the help of an attorney for his or her defense.

authority. The rules or the people who govern our lives; the power to influence or command thought, opinion, or behavior.

bailiff. A minor official who guards prisoners and maintains order in a courtroom.

benefits. Things that promote well-being; advantages.

bill. A proposed law presented to a legislature.

bill of attainder. Legislative act that gives notice of termination of a person's civil rights. Bills of attainder are prohibited by the Constitution in Article 1, Section 9.

Bill of Rights. The first ten amendments to the U.S. Constitution, a summary of fundamental rights and privileges guaranteed to a people against violation by the state.

blockade. The closing off of a city or harbor by troops or warships to prevent people and supplies from going in or out.

burden. Something oppressive or worrisome.

capacity. Ability to hold, receive, or contain.

carelessness. Inattentive or negligent behavior.

caucus. A closed meeting of persons belonging to the same political party.

characteristics. Distinguishing traits, qualities, or properties.

civic principles. A rule or code of conduct relating to citizenship.

civil disobedience. Violating a law or protesting a government policy on the grounds that the law or policy is morally unjust.

common-law. Relating to the body of law developed in England primarily from judicial decisions based on custom and precedent, unwritten in statute or code. The basis of the English legal system and of the system in all of the U.S. except Louisiana.

compensate. To make an appropriate payment.

comprehensiveness. Complete or broad coverage of a topic.

compromise. A settlement of differences between opposing sides in which each side gives up some of its claims and agrees to some of the demands of the other.

compulsory process. Amendment VI of the Bill of Rights – in all criminal prosecutions, the accused is guaranteed the right to a speedy and fair trial and the right to have the state follow established procedures for obtaining witnesses in his or her favor.

confidential. Told in secret; entrusted with private matters.

conformity. Action or behavior that is in accord with current rules, customs, or principles.

conscience. Fundamental ideas about right and wrong that come from religion, ethics, and individual morality; the sense or consciousness of the moral goodness or blameworthiness of one's own conduct, intentions, or character together with a feeling of obligation to do right or be good.

conscious choice. A choice marked by thought.

consent. Agreement as to action or opinion.

constituent. One of a group who elects another to represent them in public office

contract. A formal agreement, enforceable by law, between two or more persons or groups.

control or choice. Authority or power to regulate or choose.

correction. An action or instance of bringing into conformity with a standard; an improvement.

corrective justice. Fairness of a response to a wrong or injury to a person or group is an issue of corrective justice; to punish with a view to reforming or improving; to make or set right.

corruption of blood. Barring a person from inheriting, retaining, or transmitting any estate, rank, or title due to the commission of a crime (usually treason) that terminates the person's civil rights.

costs. Losses or penalties incurred in gaining something.

creativity. Originality; inventiveness.

criteria. Characterizing marks or traits; a standard on which a judgment or decision may be based.

custom. Long-established practice considered as unwritten law; the whole body of usages, practices, and conventions that regulate social life.

data bank. A store of information.

desert. Something deserved or merited.

detection of error. Discovery of something incorrect or wrong.

deter. To discourage or hinder.

dilemma. A situation involving a choice between two equally unsatisfactory alternatives.

diligence. Steady, earnest, and energetic effort.

distributive justice. Fairness of dividing something among several people or groups is an issue of distributive justice. That which is distributed or divided can be a benefit, such as pay for work, the right to speak or vote, or it can be a burden, such as taxes, household chores, or homework.

divine right. The belief that God granted to those of royal birth the right to rule their people.

due process of law. Amendment XIV, Section 1 – ...nor shall any State deprive any person of life, liberty, or property, without due process of law. A course of formal proceedings carried out regularly and in accordance with established rules and principles.

duration. Period of time.

duties. Actions required of someone by position, social custom, law, or religion.

economic costs. The expense of supporting institutions or gaining benefits.

effects. Physical belongings.

efficiency. Effective operation as measured by comparing production with cost—as in energy, time, and money.

endangered species. A group of biologically similar animals or plants that are threatened with extinction.

equal protection of the laws. Amendment XIV, Section 1 – ...nor deny to any person within its jurisdiction the equal protection of the laws. All citizens no matter their religion, race, gender, age, or status in society are entitled to the same treatment under the law.

espionage. The practice of spying or use of spies to obtain information about the plans and activities of a foreign government.

establishment of religion. Recognition by law and support by civil authority of a particular religion as the official church of a nation.

ex officio. Originally from Latin. To have privilege or burden by virtue of one's office or position.

ex post facto law. A law passed retroactively.

exclusion. The act of keeping things private; keeping others out.

executive branch. The branch of the government concerned with putting laws into effect.

extent. The size of a particular area; breadth, degree, or magnitude of something.

extinct. No longer existing.

factor. Something that helps bring about a certain result.

flexibility. Capability of adapting to new, different, or changing requirements.

flogging. Beating with a rod or whip.

Fourth Amendment. The right of the people to be secure in their persons, houses, papers and effects, against unreasonable searches and seizures, shall not be violated, and no Warrants shall issue, but upon probable cause, supported by Oath or affirmation, and particularly describing the place to be searched, and the persons or things to be seized.

free exercise of religion. The clause in the First Amendment that states that the government shall make no law forbidding the free practice of religious beliefs.

Freedom of Information Act. A law passed by Congress in 1966 that gives people a legal right to documents from the federal government, unless the documents contain certain types of confidential or classified information.

grand jury. A jury that examines accusations against persons charged with a crime. If the evidence warrants it, the grand jury makes formal charges on which the accused persons are later tried.

habeas corpus. *See writ of habeas corpus.*

hearsay. Information or news heard from another person; rumor.

heredity. The passage of traits from parents to offspring; genetic transmission.

Hippocratic oath. An oath embodying a code of medical ethics usually taken by those about to begin medical practice.

higher law. As used in describing a legal system, refers to the superiority of one set of laws over another. For example, the U.S. Constitution is a higher law than any federal or state law. In the natural rights philosophy, it means that natural law and divine law are superior to laws made by human beings.

humane. Marked by compassion, sympathy, or consideration for human beings or animals.

hypothetical. Presumed; based on supposition.

immunity. Freedom from punishment or restrictions.

impact. The effect of something on the feelings or mind of another.

impartial. Treating or affecting all equally.

inaccessibility. State of being unapproachable.

inalienable rights. Fundamental rights of people that may not be taken away.

incompetent. Lacking adequate ability or qualities.

indictment. A formal written statement framed by a prosecuting authority and found to have merit by a grand jury charging a person with a crime.

injunction. A court order prohibiting or requiring a specific course of action.

injury. Damage, harm, or wound.

institution. An established practice, custom, or pattern of behavior important in the cultural life of a society.

intellectual tools. A set of ideas that are useful in examining various issues; rational practices used for performing operations in a particular vocation or profession.

intellectual stimulation. Increased use of the intellect.

intent. Aim or purpose.

interest. A right to or claim on something.

internment camp. A place where people are detained, especially during wartime.

involuntary servitude. The state of being forced to labor for another against one's will.

isolation. The condition of being separate, alone, or free from external influence.

jeopardy. The danger that an accused person is subjected to when on trial for a criminal offense.

jurisdiction. The limits or territory within which authority may be exercised.

just compensation. Amendment V of the Bill of Rights. Payment made to private citizens by the government in cases of government's confiscation of their property.

justify. To prove or show to be right or reasonable.

kangaroo court. A mock court in which the principles of law and justice are disregarded or perverted.

knowledge of probable consequences. Expectations marked by reason.

legal obligation. A responsibility imposed by law.

legality. The fact of being lawful.

levy (taxes). To impose or collect monies by legal authority.

libel. A written or printed statement that unjustly damages a person's reputation or exposes him or her to ridicule.

limit. Something that restricts or keeps in bounds.

living will. To make one's wishes known in advance in case a life threatening illness or accident should occur that renders one mentally incapacitated.

loitering. To stand around idly; to linger with no apparent purpose.

3. To regulate Commerce with foreign Nations, and among the several States, and with the Indian Tribes;

4. To establish a uniform Rule of Naturalization, and uniform Laws on the subject of Bankruptcies throughout the United States;

5. To coin Money, regulate the Value thereof, and of foreign Coin, and fix the Standard of Weights and Measures;

6. To provide for the Punishment of counterfeiting the Securities and current Coin of the United States;

7. To establish Post Offices and post Roads;

8. To promote the Progress of Science and useful Arts, by securing for limited Times to Authors and Inventors the exclusive Right to their respective Writings and Discoveries;

9. To constitute Tribunals inferior to the Supreme Court;

10. To define and punish Piracies and Felonies committed on the high Seas, and Offenses against the Law of Nations;

11. To declare War, grant Letters of Marque and Reprisal, and make Rules concerning Captures on Land and Water;

12. To raise and support Armies, but no Appropriation of Money to that Use shall be for a longer Term than two Years;

13. To provide and maintain a Navy;

14. To make Rules for the Government and Regulation of the land and naval Forces;

15. To provide for calling forth the Militia to execute the Laws of the Union, suppress Insurrections and repel Invasions;

16. To provide for organizing, arming, and disciplining the Militia, and for governing such Part of them as may be employed in the Service of the United States, reserving to the States respectively, the Appointment of the Officers, and the Authority of training the Militia according to the discipline prescribed by Congress;

17. To exercise exclusive Legislation in all Cases whatsoever, over such District (not exceeding ten Miles square) as may, by Session of particular States, and the Acceptance of Congress, become the Seat of the Government of the United States, and to exercise like Authority over all Places purchased by the Consent of the Legislature of the State in which the Same shall be, for the Erection of Forts, Magazines, Arsenals, dock-Yards and other needful Buildings;—and

18. To make all Laws which shall be necessary and proper for carrying into Execution the foregoing Powers, and all other Powers vested by this Constitution in the Government of the United States, or in any Department or Officer thereof.

Section 9

1. The Migration or Importation of such Persons as any of the States now existing shall think proper to admit, shall not be prohibited by the Congress prior to the Year one thousand eight hundred and eight, but a Tax or duty may be imposed on such Importation, not exceeding ten dollars for each Person.

2. The Privilege of the Writ of Habeas Corpus shall not be suspended, unless when in Cases of Rebellion or Invasion the public Safety may require it.

3. No Bill of Attainder or ex post facto Law shall be passed.

4. [No Capitation, or other direct, Tax shall be laid, unless in Proportion to the Census or Enumeration herein before directed to be taken.]*

5. No Tax or Duty shall be laid on Articles exported from any State.

6. No Preference shall be given by any Regulation of Commerce or Revenue to the Ports of one State over those of another; nor shall Vessels bound to, or from, one State, be obliged to enter, clear, or pay Duties in another.

7. No Money shall be drawn from the Treasury, but in Consequence of Appropriations made by Law; and a regular Statement and Account of the Receipts and Expenditures of all public Money shall be published from time to time.

8. No Title of Nobility shall be granted by the United States: And no Person holding any Office of Profit or Trust under them, shall, without the Consent of the Congress, accept of any present, Emolument, Office, or Title, of any kind whatever, from any King, Prince, or foreign State.

Section 10

1. No State shall enter into any Treaty, Alliance, or Confederation; grant Letters of Marque and Reprisal; coin Money; emit Bills of Credit; make any Thing but gold and silver Coin a Tender in Payment of Debts; pass any Bill of Attainder, ex post facto Law, or Law impairing the Obligation of Contracts, or grant any Title of Nobility.

---

* Changed by the Sixteenth Amendment.

2. No State shall, without the Consent of the Congress, lay any Imposts or Duties on Imports or Exports, except what may be absolutely necessary for executing its inspection Laws: and the net Produce of all Duties and Imposts, laid by any State on Imports or Exports, shall be for the Use of the Treasury of the United States; and all such Laws shall be subject to the Revision and Control of the Congress.

3. No State shall, without the Consent of Congress, lay any Duty of Tonnage, keep Troops, or Ships of War in time of Peace, enter into any Agreement or Compact with another State, or with a foreign Power, or engage in War, unless actually invaded, or in such imminent Danger as will not admit of delay.

ARTICLE II

Section 1

1. The executive Power shall be vested in a President of the United States of America. He shall hold his Office during the term of four Years, and, together with the Vice President, chosen for the same Term, be elected, as follows.

2. Each State shall appoint, in such Manner as the Legislature thereof may direct, a Number of Electors, equal to the whole Number of Senators and Representatives to which the State may be entitled in the Congress: but no Senator or Representative, or Person holding an Office of Trust or Profit under the United States, shall be appointed an Elector.

3. [The Electors shall meet in their respective states, and vote by Ballot for two Persons, of whom one at least shall not be an Inhabitant of the same State with themselves. And they shall make a List of all the Persons voted for, and of the Number of Votes for each; which List they shall sign and certify, and transmit sealed to the Seat of the Government of the United States, directed to the President of the Senate. The President of the Senate shall, in the Presence of the Senate and House of Representatives, open all the Certificates, and the Votes shall then be counted. The Person having the greatest Number of Votes shall be the President, if such Number be a Majority of the whole Number of Electors appointed; and if there be more than one who have such Majority, and have an equal Number of Votes, then the House of Representatives shall immediately choose by Ballot one of them for President; and if no Person have a Majority, then from the five highest on the List the said House shall in like manner choose the President. But in choosing the President, the Votes shall be taken by States, the Representation from each State having one Vote; A quorum for this Purpose shall consist of a Member or Members from two thirds of the States, and a Majority of all the States shall be necessary to a Choice. In every Case, after the Choice of the President, the Person having the greatest Number of Votes of the Electors shall be the Vice President. But if there should remain two or more who have equal Votes, the Senate shall choose from them by Ballot the Vice President.]*

4. The Congress may determine the Time of choosing the Electors, and the day on which they shall give their Votes; which Day shall be the same throughout the United States.

5. No Person except a natural born Citizen, or a Citizen of the United States at the time of the Adoption of this Constitution, shall be eligible to the Office of the President; neither shall any person be eligible to that Office who shall not have attained to the Age of thirty five Years, and been fourteen Years a Resident within the United States.

6. [In Case of the Removal of the President from Office, or of his Death, Resignation, or Inability to discharge the Powers and Duties of the said Office, the Same shall devolve on the Vice President, and the Congress may by Law provide for the Case of Removal, Death, Resignation or Inability, both of the President and Vice President, declaring what Officer shall then act as President, and such Officer shall act accordingly, until the Disability be removed, or a President shall be elected.]**

7. The President shall, at stated Times, receive for his Services, a Compensation, which shall neither be increased nor diminished during the Period for which he shall have been elected, and he shall not receive within that Period any other Emolument from the United States, or any of them.

8. Before he enter the Execution of his Office, he shall take the following Oath or Affirmation:—"I do solemnly swear (or affirm) that I will faithfully execute the Office of President of the United States, and will to the best of my ability, preserve, protect, and defend the Constitution of the United States."

Section 2

1. The President shall be Commander in Chief of the Army and Navy of the United States, and of the Militia of the several States, when called into the actual Service of the United States; he may require the Opinion, in writing, of the principal Officer in each of the executive Departments, upon any Subject relating to the Duties of their respective Offices, and he shall have Power to grant Reprieves and Pardons for Offenses against the United States, except in Cases of Impeachment.

---

* Changed by the Twelfth Amendment.
**Changed by the Twenty-fifth Amendment.

2. He shall have Power, by and with the Advice and Consent of the Senate, to make Treaties, provided two thirds of the Senators present concur; and he shall nominate, and by and with the Advice and Consent of the Senate, shall appoint Ambassadors, other public Ministers and Consuls, Judges of the supreme Court, and all other Officers of the United States, whose Appointments are not herein otherwise provided for, and which shall be established by Law; but the Congress may by Law vest the Appointment of such inferior Officers, as they think proper, in the President alone, in the Courts of Law, or in the Heads of Departments.

3. The President shall have Power to fill up all Vacancies that may happen during the Recess of the Senate, by granting Commissions which shall expire at the End of their next Session.

Section 3

He shall from time to time give to the Congress Information of the State of the Union, and recommend to their Consideration such Measures as he shall judge necessary and expedient; he may, on extraordinary Occasions, convene both Houses, or either of them, and in Case of Disagreement between them, with Respect to the Time of Adjournment, he may adjourn them to such Time as he shall think proper; he shall receive Ambassadors and other public Ministers; he shall take Care that the Laws be faithfully executed, and shall Commission all the Officers of the United States.

Section 4

The President, Vice President and all civil Officers of the United States, shall be removed from Office on Impeachment for, and Conviction of, Treason, Bribery, or other high Crimes and Misdemeanors.

ARTICLE III

Section 1

The judicial Power of the United States, shall be vested in one supreme Court, and in such inferior Courts as the Congress may from time to time ordain and establish. The Judges, both of the supreme and inferior Courts, shall hold their Offices during good Behavior, and shall, at stated Times, receive for their Services a Compensation, which shall not be diminished during their Continuance in Office.

Section 2

1. The judicial Power shall extend to all Cases, in Law and Equity, arising under this Constitution, the Laws of the United States, and Treaties made, or which shall be made, under their Authority;— to all Cases affecting Ambassadors, other public Ministers and Consuls;—to all Cases of admiralty and maritime Jurisdiction;—to Controversies to which the United States shall be a Party;—to Controversies between two or more States; [between a State and Citizens of another State;] between Citizens of different States;—between Citizens of the same State claiming Lands under Grants of different States;—[and between a State, or the Citizens thereof, and foreign States, Citizens or Subjects.]*

2. In all Cases affecting Ambassadors, other public Ministers and Consuls, and those in which a State shall be Party, the supreme Court shall have original Jurisdiction. In all the other Cases before mentioned, the supreme Court shall have appellate Jurisdiction, both as to Law and Fact, with such Exceptions, and under such Regulations as the Congress shall make.

3. The Trial of all Crimes, except in Cases of Impeachment, shall be by Jury; and such Trial shall be held in the State where said Crimes shall have been committed; but when not committed within any State, the Trial shall be at such Place or Places as the Congress may by Law have directed.

Section 3

1. Treason against the United States shall consist only in levying War against them, or in adhering to their Enemies, giving them Aid and Comfort. No Person shall be convicted of Treason unless on the Testimony of two Witnesses to the same overt Act, or on Confession in open Court.

2. The Congress shall have Power to declare the Punishment of Treason, but no Attainder of Treason shall work Corruption of Blood, or Forfeiture except during the Life of the Person attainted.

ARTICLE IV

Section 1

Full Faith and Credit shall be given in each State to the public Acts, Records, and judicial Proceedings of every other State; And the Congress may by general Laws prescribe the manner in which such Acts, Records and Proceedings shall be proved, and the Effect thereof.

Section 2

1. The Citizens of each State shall be entitled to all Privileges and Immunities of Citizens in the several States.

2. A Person charged in any State with Treason, Felony, or other Crime, who shall flee from Justice, and be found

---

* Changed by the Eleventh Amendment.

in another State, shall on Demand of the executive Authority of the State from which he fled, be delivered up, to be removed to the State having Jurisdiction of the Crime.

3. [No person held to Service or Labour in one State, under the Laws thereof, escaping into another, shall, in Consequence of any Law or Regulation therein, be discharged from such Service or Labour, but shall be delivered up on Claim of the Party to whom such Service or Labour may be due.]*

Section 3

1. New States may be admitted by the Congress into this Union; but no new State shall be formed or erected within the Jurisdiction of any other State; nor any State be formed by the Junction of two or more States, or parts of States, without the Consent of the Legislatures of the States concerned as well as of the Congress.

2. The Congress shall have Power to dispose of and make all needful Rules and Regulations respecting the territory or other Property belonging to the United States; and nothing in this Constitution shall be so construed as to Prejudice any Claims of the United States, or of any particular State.

Section 4

The United States shall guarantee to every State in this Union a Republican Form of Government, and shall protect each of them against Invasion; and on Application of the Legislature, or of the Executive (when the Legislature cannot be convened) against domestic Violence.

ARTICLE V

The Congress, whenever two thirds of both Houses shall deem it necessary, shall propose Amendments to this Constitution, or, on the Application of the Legislatures of two thirds of the several States, shall call a Convention for proposing Amendments, which, in either Case, shall be valid to all Intents and Purposes, as Part of this Constitution, when ratified by the Legislatures of three fourths of the several States, or by Conventions in three fourths thereof, as the one or the other Mode of

---

* Changed by the Thirteenth Amendment.

Ratification may be proposed by the Congress; Provided that no Amendment which may be made prior to the Year One thousand eight hundred and eight shall in any Manner affect the first and fourth Clauses in the Ninth Section of the first Article; and that no State, without its Consent, shall be deprived of its equal Suffrage in the Senate.

ARTICLE VI

1. All debts contracted and Engagements entered into, before the Adoption of this Constitution, shall be as valid against the United States under this Constitution, as under the Confederation.

2. This Constitution, and the Laws of the United States which shall be made in Pursuance thereof; and all Treaties made, or which shall be made, under the Authority of the United States, shall be the supreme Law of the Land; and the Judges in every State shall be bound thereby, any Thing in the Constitution or Laws of any State to the Contrary notwithstanding.

3. The Senators and Representatives before mentioned, and the Members of the several State Legislatures, and all executive and judicial Officers, both of the United States and of the several States, shall be bound by Oath or Affirmation, to support this Constitution; but no religious Test shall ever be required as a Qualification to any Office or public Trust under the United States.

ARTICLE VII

The Ratification of the Conventions of nine States, shall be sufficient for the Establishment of this Constitution between the States so ratifying the Same.

Done in Convention by the unanimous consent of the States present the seventeenth day of September in the year of our Lord one thousand seven hundred and eighty seven and of the Independence of the United States of America the Twelfth. In witness whereof we have hereunto subscribed our Names,

George Washington—President
and deputy from Virginia

(This Constitution was adopted on September 17, 1787 by the Constitutional Convention, and was declared ratified on July 2, 1788)

Signers of the Constitution

New-Hampshire
John Langdon
Nicholas Gilman

Massachusetts
Nathaniel Gorham
Rufus King

Connecticut
William Samuel Johnson
Roger Sherman

New York
Alexander Hamilton

New Jersey
William Livingston
David Brearley
William Paterson
Jonathan Dayton

Pennsylvania
Benjamin Franklin
Thomas Mifflin
Robert Morris
George Clymer
Thomas Fitzsimons
Jared Ingersoll
James Wilson
Gouverneur Morris

Delaware
George Read
Gunning Bedford, Jr.
John Dickinson
Richard Bassett
Jacob Broom

Maryland
James McHenry
Daniel of St. Tho. Jenifer
Daniel Carrol

Virginia
John Blair
James Madison, Junior

North Carolina
William Blount
Richard Dobbs Spaight
Hugh Williamson

South Carolina
John Ruthledge
Charles Cotesworth Pinckney
Charles Pinckney
Pierce Butler

Georgia
William Few
Abraham Baldwin

Attest: William Jackson, Secretary

AMENDMENTS TO THE
CONSTITUTION
OF THE
UNITED STATES OF AMERICA

AMENDMENT I

Congress shall make no law respecting an establishment of religion, or prohibiting the free exercise thereof; or abridging the freedom of speech, or of the press, or the right of the people peaceably to assemble, and to petition the Government for a redress of grievances. (Ratified December, 1791.)

AMENDMENT II

A well regulated Militia, being necessary to the security of a free State, the right of the people to keep and bear Arms, shall not be infringed. (Ratified December, 1791.)

AMENDMENT III

No Soldier shall, in time of peace be quartered in any house, without the consent of the Owner, nor in time of war, but in a manner to be prescribed by law. (Ratified December, 1791.)

AMENDMENT IV

The right of the people to be secure in their persons, houses, papers, and effects, against unreasonable searches and seizures, shall not be violated, and no Warrants shall issue, but upon probable cause, supported by Oath or affirmation, and particularly describing the place to be searched, and the persons or things to be seized. (Ratified December, 1791.)

AMENDMENT V

No person shall be held to answer for a capital, or otherwise infamous crime, unless on a presentment or indictment of a Grand Jury, except in cases arising in the land or naval forces, or in the Militia, when in actual service in time of War or public danger; nor shall any person be subject for the same offence to be twice put in jeopardy of life or limb, nor shall be compelled in any criminal case to be a witness against himself, nor be deprived of life, liberty, or property, without due process of law; nor shall private property be taken for public use without just compensation. (Ratified December, 1791.)

AMENDMENT VI

In all criminal prosecutions, the accused shall enjoy the right to a speedy and public trial, by an impartial jury of the State and district wherein the crime shall have been committed; which district shall have been previously ascertained by law, and to be informed of the nature and cause of the accusation; to be confronted with the witnesses against him; to have compulsory process for obtaining witnesses in his favor, and to have the assistance of counsel for his defence. (Ratified December, 1791.)

AMENDMENT VII

In Suits at common law, where the value in controversy shall exceed twenty dollars, the right of trial by jury shall be preserved, and no fact tried by a jury shall be otherwise re-examined in any Court of the United States, than according to the rules of the common law. (Ratified December, 1791.)

AMENDMENT VIII

Excessive bail shall not be required, nor excessive fines imposed, nor cruel and unusual punishments inflicted. (Ratified December, 1791.)

AMENDMENT IX

The enumeration in the Constitution of certain rights shall not be construed to deny or disparage others retained by the people. (Ratified December, 1791.)

AMENDMENT X

The powers not delegated to the United States by the Constitution, nor prohibited by it to the States, are reserved to the States respectively, or to the people. (Ratified December, 1791.)

AMENDMENT XI

The Judicial power of the United States shall not be construed to extend to any suit in law or equity, commenced or prosecuted against one of the United States by Citizens of another State, or by Citizens or Subjects of any Foreign State. (Ratified February, 1795.)

AMENDMENT XII

The Electors shall meet in their respective states, and vote by ballot for President and Vice President, one of whom, at least, shall not be an inhabitant of the same state with themselves; they shall name in their ballots the person voted for as President, and in distinct ballots the person voted for as Vice-President, and they shall make distinct lists of all persons voted for as President, and of all persons voted for as Vice-President, and of the number of votes for each, which lists they shall sign and certify, and transmit sealed to the seat of the government of the

United States, directed to the President of the Senate;—The President of the Senate shall, in the presence of the Senate and House of Representatives, open all the certificates and the votes shall then be counted;—The person having the greatest number of votes for President, shall be the President, if such number be a majority of the whole number of Electors appointed; and if no person have such majority, then from the persons having the highest numbers not exceeding three on the list of those voted for as President, the House of Representatives shall choose immediately, by ballot, the President. But in choosing the President, the votes shall be taken by states, the representation from each state having one vote; a quorum for this purpose shall consist of a member or members from two-thirds of the states, and a majority of all the states shall be necessary to a choice. [And if the House of Representatives shall not choose a President whenever the right of choice shall devolve upon them, before the fourth day of March next following, then the Vice-President shall act as President, as in the case of the death or other constitutional disability of the President—]* The person having the greatest number of votes as Vice-President, shall be the Vice-President, if such number be a majority of the whole number of Electors appointed, and if no person have a majority, then from the two highest numbers on the list, the Senate shall choose the Vice-President; a quorum for the purpose shall consist of two-thirds of the whole number of Senators, and a majority of the whole number shall be necessary to a choice. But no person constitutionally ineligible to the office of President shall be eligible to that of Vice-President of the United States. (Ratified June, 1804.)

AMENDMENT XIII

Section 1

Neither slavery nor involuntary servitude, except as a punishment for crime whereof the party shall have been duly convicted, shall exist within the United States, or any place subject to their jurisdiction.

Section 2

Congress shall have power to enforce this article by appropriate legislation. (Ratified December, 1865.)

AMENDMENT XIV

Section 1

All persons born or naturalized in the United States and subject to the jurisdiction thereof, are citizens of the United States and of the State wherein they reside. No State shall make or enforce any law which shall abridge the privileges or immunities of citizens of the United States; nor shall any State deprive any person of life, liberty, or property, without due process of law; nor deny to any person within its jurisdiction the equal protection of the laws.

Section 2

Representatives shall be apportioned among the several States according to their respective numbers, counting the whole number of persons in each State, excluding Indians not taxed. But when the right to vote at any election for the choice of electors for President and Vice President of the United States, Representatives in Congress, the Executive and Judicial officers of a State, or the members of the Legislature thereof, is denied to any of the male inhabitants of such State, being twenty-one years of age, and citizens of the United States, or in any way abridged, except for participation in rebellion, or other crime, the basis of representation therein shall be reduced in the proportion which the number of such male citizens shall bear to the whole number of male citizens twenty-one years of age in such State.

Section 3

No person shall be a Senator or a Representative in Congress, or elector of President and Vice President, or hold any office, civil or military, under the United States, or under any State, who, having previously taken an oath, as a member of Congress, or as an officer of the United States, or as a member of any State legislature, or as an executive or judicial officer of any State, to support the Constitution of the United States, shall have engaged in insurrection or rebellion against the same, or given aid or comfort to the enemies thereof. But Congress may by a vote of two-thirds of each House, remove such disability.

Section 4

The validity of the public debt of the United States, authorized by law, including debts incurred for payment of pensions and bounties for services in suppressing insurrection or rebellion, shall not be questioned. But neither the United States nor any State shall assume or pay any debt or obligation incurred in aid of insurrection or rebellion against the United States, or any claim for the loss or emancipation of any slave; but all such debts, obligations and claims shall be held illegal and void.

Section 5

The Congress shall have power to enforce, by appropriate legislation, the provisions of this article. (Ratified July, 1868.)

* Superseded by Section 3 of the Twentieth Amendment.

AMENDMENT XV

Section 1

The right of citizens of the United States to vote shall not be denied or abridged by the United States or by any State on account of race, color, or previous condition of servitude.

Section 2

The Congress shall have power to enforce this article by appropriate legislation. (Ratified February, 1870.)

AMENDMENT XVI

The Congress shall have power to lay and collect taxes on incomes, from whatever source derived, without apportionment among the several States, and without regard to any census or enumeration. (Ratified February, 1913.)

AMENDMENT XVII

The Senate of the United States shall be composed of two Senators from each State, elected by the people thereof, for six years; and each Senator shall have one vote. The electors in each State shall have the qualifications requisite for electors of the most numerous branch of the State legislatures.

When vacancies happen in the representation of any State in the Senate, the executive authority of such State shall issue writs of election to fill such vacancies: Provided, That the legislature of any State may empower the executive thereof to make temporary appointments until the people fill the vacancies by election as the legislature may direct.

This amendment shall not be so construed as to affect the election or term of any Senator chosen before it becomes valid as part of the Constitution. (Ratified April, 1913.)

AMENDMENT XVIII

Section 1

After one year from the ratification of this article the manufacture, sale, or transportation of intoxicating liquors within, the importation thereof into, or the exportation thereof from the United States and all territory subject to the jurisdiction thereof for beverage purposes is hereby prohibited.

Section 2

The Congress and the several States shall have concurrent power to enforce this article by appropriate legislation.

Section 3

This article shall be inoperative unless it shall have been ratified as an amendment to the Constitution by the legislatures of the several States, as provided in the Constitution, within seven years from the date of the submission hereof to the States by the Congress.]* (Ratified January, 1919.)

AMENDMENT XIX

The right of citizens of the United States to vote shall not be denied or abridged by the United States or by any State on account of sex.

Congress shall have power to enforce this article by appropriate legislation.(Ratified August, 1920.)

AMENDMENT XX

Section 1

The terms of the President and Vice President shall end at noon on the 20th day of January, and the terms of Senators and Representatives at noon on the 3d day of January, of the years in which such terms would have ended if this article had not been ratified; and the terms of their successors shall then begin.

Section 2

The Congress shall assemble at least once in every year, and such meeting shall begin at noon on the 3d day of January, unless they shall by law appoint a different day.

Section 3

If, at the time fixed for the beginning of the term of the President, the President elect shall have died, the Vice President elect shall become President. If a President shall not have been chosen before the time fixed for the beginning of his term, or if the President elect shall have failed to qualify, then the Vice President elect shall act as President until a President shall have qualified; and the Congress may by law provide for the case wherein neither a President elect nor a Vice President elect shall have qualified, declaring who shall then act as President, or the manner in which one who is to act shall be selected, and such person shall act accordingly until a President or Vice President shall have qualified.

Section 4

The Congress may by law provide for the case of the death of any of the persons from whom the House of Representatives may choose a President whenever the

---

* Repealed by the Twenty-first Amendment.

right of choice shall have devolved upon them, and for the case of the death of any of the persons from whom the Senate may choose a Vice President whenever the right of choice shall have devolved upon them.

Section 5

Sections 1 and 2 shall take effect on the 15th day of October following the ratification of this article.

Section 6

This article shall be inoperative unless it shall have been ratified as an amendment to the Constitution by the legislatures of three-fourths of the several States within seven years from the date of its submission. (Ratified January, 1933.)

AMENDMENT XXI

Section 1

The eighteenth article of amendment to the Constitution of the United States is hereby repealed.

Section 2

The transportation or importation into any State, Territory, or possession of the United States for delivery or use therein of intoxicating liquors, in violation of the laws thereof, is hereby prohibited.

Section 3

This article shall be inoperative unless it shall have been ratified as an amendment to the Constitution by conventions in the several States, as provided in the Constitution, within seven years from the date of the submission hereof to the States by the Congress. (Ratified December, 1933.)

AMENDMENT XXII

Section 1

No person shall be elected to the office of the President more than twice, and no person who has held the office of President, or acted as President, for more than two years of a term to which some other person was elected President shall be elected to the office of the President more than once. But this Article shall not apply to any person holding the office of President when this Article was proposed by the Congress, and shall not prevent any

person who may be holding the office of President, or acting as President, during the term within which this Article becomes operative from holding the office of President or acting as President during the remainder of such term.

Section 2

This article shall be inoperative unless it shall have been ratified as an amendment to the Constitution by the legislatures of three-fourths of the several States within seven years from the date of its submission to the States by the Congress. (Ratified February, 1951.)

AMENDMENT XXIII

Section 1

The District constituting the seat of Government of the United States shall appoint in such manner as the Congress may direct:

A number of electors of President and Vice President equal to the whole number of Senators and Representatives in Congress to which the District would be entitled if it were a State, but in no event more than the least populous State; they shall be in addition to those appointed by the States, but they shall be considered, for the purposes of the election of President and Vice President, to be electors appointed by a State; and they shall meet in the District and perform such duties as provided by the twelfth article of amendment.

Section 2

The Congress shall have power to enforce this article by appropriate legislation. (Ratified March, 1961.)

AMENDMENT XXIV

Section 1

The right of citizens of the United States to vote in any primary or other election for President or Vice President, for electors for President or Vice President, or for Senator or Representative in Congress, shall not be denied or abridged by the United States or any State by reason of failure to pay any poll tax or other tax.

Section 2

The Congress shall have power to enforce this article by appropriate legislation. (Ratified January, 1964.)

AMENDMENT XXV

Section 1

In case of the removal of the President from office or of his death or resignation, the Vice President shall become President.

Section 2

Whenever there is a vacancy in the office of the Vice President, the President shall nominate a Vice President who shall take office upon confirmation by a majority vote of both Houses of Congress.

Section 3

Whenever the President transmits to the President pro tempore of the Senate and the Speaker of the House of Representatives his written declaration that he is unable to discharge the powers and duties of his office, and until he transmits to them a written declaration to the contrary, such powers and duties shall be discharged by the Vice President as Acting President.

Section 4

Whenever the Vice President and a majority of either the principal officers of the executive departments or of such other body as Congress may by law provide, transmit to the President pro tempore of the Senate and the Speaker of the House of Representatives their written declaration that the President is unable to discharge the powers and duties of his office, the Vice President shall immediately assume the powers and duties of the office as Acting President.

Thereafter, when the President transmits to the President pro tempore of the Senate and the Speaker of the House of Representatives his written declaration that no inability exists, he shall resume the powers and duties of his office unless the Vice President and a majority of either the principal officers of the executive department or of such other body as Congress may by law provide, transmit within four days to the President pro tempore of the Senate and the Speaker of the House of Representatives their written declaration that the President is unable to discharge the powers and duties of his office. Thereupon Congress shall decide the issue, assembling within forty-eight hours for that purpose if not in session. If the Congress, within twenty-one days after receipt of the latter written declaration, or, if Congress is not in session, within twenty-one days after Congress is required to assemble, determines by two-thirds vote of both Houses that the President is unable to discharge the powers and duties of his office, the Vice President shall continue to discharge the same as Acting President; otherwise, the President shall resume the powers and duties of his office. (Ratified February, 1967.)

AMENDMENT XXVI

Section 1

The right of citizens of the United States, who are eighteen years of age or older, to vote shall not be denied or abridged by the United States or by any State on account of age.

Section 2

The Congress shall have power to enforce this article by appropriate legislation. (Ratified July, 1971.)

AMENDMENT XXVII

No law varying the compensation for the services of the Senators or Representatives, shall take effect, until an election of Representatives shall have intervened. (Ratified May, 1992.)

Descriptive headings have been added by editors. Passages in brackets marked by an asterisk indicate that they were changed by amendment.

Photo Credits

Pages 3, 20, 23, 24, 43, 105, 121, 125, 129, 130, 141, 194, 195, 203 —American Stock Photography Inc.; Page 157 — American Telephone and Telegraph Archives, Paul Conklin; Cover, pages iii, 6, 8, 12, 14, 15, 18, 22, 26, 30, 31, 33, 35, 49, 54, 55, 63, 70, 72, 76, 77, 79, 91, 94, 95, 98, 103, 114, 115, 117, 118, 119, 121, 124, 131, 139, 144, 145, 146, 148, 149, 151, 152, 153, 158, 160, 162, 163, 166, 174, 180, 183, 186, 198, 200, 201 — AP/Wide World Photo; Page 15 — Christian Science Monitor, Peter Morton; Pages 189, 190 — Fritz Eichenberg/ The Heritage Reprints; Pages 72, 81, 10, 170, 172, 176, 198, 202 — FPG International; Pages 13, 63, 81, 112 — Eric Frutram Photography; Pages 3, 7 — with kind permission, Ralph D. Jones; Page 143 — Jim Leatherman; Page 111 — Harlee Little Photography; Pages 2, 9, 158, 204 — Library of Congress; Pages 4, 10, 5, 35, 40, 48, 152, 155, 206 — National Archives and Records Administration, Washington, D.C.; Pages 5, 62 — Supreme Court Historical Society; Page 67 — United States Holocaust Museum, Helen Ungemach Benedite; Pages 135, 156, 175, 214, 215 — UPI/Bettman.